Center of the Universe

Center of the Universe

*Transforming the 27 Types
of Narcissism from the Inside Out*

Sterlin L. Mosley

BLOOMSBURY ACADEMIC
NEW YORK • LONDON • OXFORD • NEW DELHI • SYDNEY

BLOOMSBURY ACADEMIC

Bloomsbury Publishing Inc, 1385 Broadway, New York, NY 10018, USA
Bloomsbury Publishing Plc, 50 Bedford Square, London, WC1B 3DP, UK
Bloomsbury Publishing Ireland, 29 Earlsfort Terrace, Dublin 2, D02 AY28, Ireland

BLOOMSBURY, BLOOMSBURY ACADEMIC
and the Diana logo are trademarks of Bloomsbury Publishing Plc

First published in the United States of America 2025

Copyright © Sterlin L. Mosley, 2025

Cover image © Thapana Onphalai / iStock / Getty Images

All rights reserved. No part of this publication may be: i) reproduced or transmitted in any form, electronic or mechanical, including photocopying, recording or by means of any information storage or retrieval system without prior permission in writing from the publishers; or ii) used or reproduced in any way for the training, development or operation of artificial intelligence (AI) technologies, including generative AI technologies. The rights holders expressly reserve this publication from the text and data mining exception as per Article 4(3) of the Digital Single Market Directive (EU) 2019/790.

Bloomsbury Publishing Inc does not have any control over, or responsibility for, any third-party websites referred to or in this book. All internet addresses given in this book were correct at the time of going to press. The author and publisher regret any inconvenience caused if addresses have changed or sites have ceased to exist, but can accept no responsibility for any such changes.

A catalog record for this book is available from the Library of Congress.

ISBN: HB: 978-1-5381-8643-5
ePDF: 979-8-7651-5429-8
eBook: 978-1-5381-8644-2

Typeset by Susan Ramundo
Printed and bound in the United States of America

For product safety related questions contact productsafety@bloomsbury.com.

To find out more about our authors and books
visit www.bloomsbury.com and sign up for our newsletters.

This book is dedicated to my father,
my dearest friend Aaron, my Aunt Joy,
and anyone wishing to heal from their
pasts and live more fully in their present.

CONTENTS

Introduction ix

Chapter 1 Narcissism: Then, Now, and Forever? 1
Chapter 2 Narcissism Rising: Cultural and Generational Shifts . . . 25
Chapter 3 It Starts with I: Narcissism Begins 45
Chapter 4 When "We" Becomes "Me" 83
Chapter 5 Oh, What Toxic Webs We Weave: Broadening
           the Scope 129
Chapter 6 The Center Cannot Hold: Narcissistic Ideologies in
           Organizational, Political, and Familial Systems 181
Chapter 7 Out of Darkness: Breaking Free of Narcissistic
           Dysfunction 201

Notes 213
Glossary 219
Bibliography 225
Index 229
About the Author 237

INTRODUCTION

I sat at my favorite coffee shop, enjoying my daily infusion of nitro cold brew coffee. Quite commonly, as a distraction from the work I should be doing, I stop to tune in (some might say eavesdrop) on the conversations around me. I can't help it. My social eavesdropping tendencies were nurtured during my graduate education as a mental health clinician and qualitative research scholar. I still hear the voice of my qualitative research methods professor, "If you stop and listen to the world around you, you find research questions everywhere." Most conversations I hear are snippets of business negotiations; casual chitchat between friends; and, occasionally, spirited political, religious, or philosophical discussions. Due to the shop's proximity to a neighborhood with many school-aged kids, I also like to take the proverbial pulse of Gen Z. Despite the memeworthy debates between the millennials (my generation) and Gen Z about whether skinny jeans are still cool or the proper way to take a selfie, I find my generational successors fascinating (even if they do enjoy roasting millennials a little too much). Typically, their conversations are relatively benign and involve a slew of names, slang terms, interpersonal dramas, and circumstances that are meaningless to me.

However, on an unseasonably warm December afternoon, I had the opportunity to observe the machinations of youth culture in the wild more carefully. There were four kids, two young women and two young men, urgently and emotionally trading opinions. The apparent leader of the small group was a young man, about 16 years old (we'll

INTRODUCTION

name him "Zack"), who instructed his compadres like a battlefield general on how to manage a "publicity nightmare" that had come about due to a text made on a Discord server about their friend group. Zack's friends listened intently as he laid out the battle plan for how to combat their slanderers' "effed up lies."

Zack rallied his troops. "Alright, guys, I just read the Discord thread, and I think we need to figure out how we're going to get in front of this story they posted."

"What are we going to do about it, though?! This could totally ruin our TikTok reputation!," one girl exclaimed, distressed, looking around her because she felt Zack had surely been speaking too loudly.

"No, it won't. I'll be damned if my future is screwed 'cause of some jealous haters. Colton told me they plan to do a series of videos to expose us as frauds."

Zack paused to grab his vanilla latte with two extra espresso shots from the counter. After taking a sip of his caffeinated elixir, he continued talking to the other boy with the authority of a parent.

"I've spent too long building my reputation to have it ruined by these clowns. So here's what we're going to do. I think we should say they're attacking us for being neurodivergent. I saw a YouTube video about how *empaths* do this because they're jealous of our power. Just because we're narcissists doesn't mean we're not people!" The disdain with which Zack sneered the word *empath* was startling. An older woman sitting near me looked up from her book, glancing at me and back at Zack with the same disbelief. The other three kids nod in vehement agreement. It seemed to me that Zack felt like he was, at that moment, the only person in the room.

"They don't know our struggles, having to pretend like we have feelings like everyone else, and I'm tired of being discriminated against," Zack continued.

"Yeah, I think narcissistic awareness needs to be way more of a thing," the other young woman proclaimed passionately, cutting Zack off.

"Right, so we turn it on them and make the empaths look like the assholes." Zack went on, seemingly annoyed at being interrupted.

"We know we'll ultimately win because we always do, but I'm not going to be made to look like a monster because I'm not all obsessed with pretending like I give a shit about people's feelings when I don't." He took another sip of his latte, glancing around the room as though he just realized other people were there.

"Okay, so after I eat dinner tonight, you all can come over, and we'll edit our video together and make them feel bad for making *us* feel bad for not having empathy," the other young woman said resolutely.

The other boy, a seemingly innocuous redheaded kid with an endearing smile wearing a soccer T-shirt, spoke excitedly, "Dude, this is so screwed up. I'm proud of being a narc, and eff them for trying to guilt trip me like my parents."

And just like that, the surreal cast of teenagers, who seemed to step straight out of a dystopian teen drama, made their way out of the coffee shop. My brief window into a pro-narcissistic advocacy group gave me a glimpse into a phenomenon I had hitherto only observed on YouTube and the recesses of seedy online forums and chat rooms dedicated to the support of narcissists, sociopaths, and psychopaths that I had observed due to the nature of my academic interest in the topics of narcissism and psychopathy. I didn't expect to unofficially corroborate a meta-data longitudinal study I recently read, which demonstrated a marked increase in narcissistic traits (e.g., selfishness; grandiosity; lack of empathy; and preoccupation with fame, power, and success) among young adults (i.e., ages 15–24) (Bushman et al., 2021).

Maybe you read the story of Zack and his "narc-positive" friends and thought, so what? This sounds like a bunch of kids trying to be cool and relevant or simply finding their footing in the treacherous jungles of high school. Cut them some slack, Sterlin. You were a teenager once! In that case, I raise you one Zack and present you with a more bewildering example of narcissistic grandiosity playing out on a much larger scale.

George Santos became a household name in only a few months due to the sensational and often unbelievable made-for-true-crime documentary drama unfolding around the newly minted congressman. During the 2022 midterm elections, Santos flipped a Democratic seat in the third district of New York primarily due to his impressive biography and a laundry list of "accomplishments," leading voters to believe he would be a highly qualified and effective representative of their political interests. However, the bizarre tale of *The Talented Mr. Santos* took a befuddling (and dark) turn as it became clear that Santos's stellar accomplishments (and other banal details of his life) are primarily (allegedly) fabricated. Santos's mistruths include claims about attending an elite preparatory school, being Jewish (a central selling point for voters in the second district of New York), earning an MBA at New York University, and playing volleyball at Baruch College (where he also claims to have earned a degree in finance, although no such record exists). Santos has also seemingly lied about his mother's death during the attacks on the Twin Towers on 9/11 as well as being accused of having multiple aliases, starting and maintaining a false charity, Brazilian check fraud allegations, numerous evictions, even questionable claims about being mugged in New York City, and who knows what else. In my estimation, Santos matches the profile of the *Disingenuous Opportunist*,[1] someone who believes cultivating a winning and successful image is more important than reality, which I wrote about in *The Narcissist in You and Everyone Else*.

Santos makes an excellent case study of a career con man. What I found most disturbing, however, is that his presence on our newsfeeds and in the American political process was met with a mixture of amusing and halfhearted derision from fellow congressional colleagues and news media outlets. The general blasé acceptance of one of the most flagrant manifestations of sociopathy gracing the political stage is partly due to the dulling of our outrage barometers. However, our outrage desensitization has a traceable origin and is deeply rooted in our relationship with media and the internet. The fast-paced kaleidoscope of horrifying news flashing across our collective screens paints a grotesque mosaic of exploitation, greed, cynical power grabs, and suffering that renders many numb. This inability to

INTRODUCTION

care due to an overload of negative, shocking, or humanity-defying news causes many people to temporarily shut down their empathetic capabilities, a phenomenon that psychologists call "compassion fatigue," which I like to call "empathy burnout." One of the unsettling residual effects of compassion fatigue is a lessening of outrage or shock over flagrantly self-interested, amoral, unethical, or unsavory behavior.

Nonetheless, while debriefing the insanity of the Santos saga with my aunt, she, unimpressed by the three-ring circus that had become commonplace in stories about the entertainment, political, and business world, said, "This is the new normal, I guess." How did flagrant displays of malignant narcissistic dysfunction within the ranks of every layer of the human ecosystem become "the new normal"? And, more importantly, why have we become so comfortable with that reality?

Political trends aside, the 2024 election and the undeniable "Trump effect" in America help us understand how classically narcissistic traits have been embraced by over half of the American electorate. Exit polls in 2024 indicated that for many voters, Donald Trump's authenticity, brashness, and unapologetic speaking style resonated, indicating a decisive move away from traits such as compassion, empathy, and thoughtfulness for a more brazen, bullish, and confrontational approach.

I have already presented my view (based on my research) of narcissism on the individual psyche in my first book, *The Narcissist in You and Everyone Else*. Thus, I already understood the effects of narcissism on human psychology and the immediate effect of that psychology on narcissists and those in relationship with them. From their mouths and those of their loved ones, coworkers, and friends, I knew that their frequent lack of empathy; pathological self-focus; grandiosity; propensity toward antagonistic behavior; and obsession with image, prestige, and entitlement had wide-reaching effects on the world around them. By their accounts, they were the center of their universes and wouldn't have it any other way. However, in *The Narcissist in You and Everyone Else*, I had little time to explore the multifaceted effects of narcissism on the greater world. Therefore, this book will do just that.

So, as we think back to our cast of teenage "narcs," I pose a few rhetorical questions. What happens when these kids grow up and get jobs, start families, run businesses, run for political office, or make egregiously self-interested decisions that affect the world around them? At best, they become your toxic boss, selfish partner, or arrogant and sneaky coworker and, at worst, George Santos, Benito Mussolini, Jim Jones, or Harvey Weinstein. And if this is any indication of the future of American culture, we are, to quote a wise man, "screwed." What becomes of a world and its people who mold themselves around the predominant values of selfishness, egotism, power, greed, deception, or ruthless self-satisfaction?

I didn't have to look far for the answer to that question because we already live in a world revolving around these narcissistic values. It may not surprise you that those with a high propensity for narcissistic traits have already found themselves in the highest and most potent institutions worldwide. It will also not surprise you to find out that the increase in flagrant displays of narcissistic traits in individuals, social structures, and institutions is historically linked to a rapid decline in democratic civilizations as power, greed, competition, and unbridled exploitation begin to crush the idealism of cooperation, charity, and goodwill. We need only recall the atrocities of the Holocaust, slavery, apartheid, or any ideological war to see its detrimental effects on humanity.

However, it is not my goal to merely illustrate how narcissistic values have become an accepted way of life for many of us living in industrialized, individualistic cultures. I want to move us toward a practical methodology of shifting these erosive narcissistic ideals. Through a holistic exploration of narcissism, I hope we can find our way out of the erosive damage of these structures to something more inclusive, compassionate, and sustainable, lest we continue our free fall down the rabbit hole of narcissistic delusion. Narcissism is our inherited collective shadow. In Jungian psychological terms, the shadow comprises aspects of selfhood that remain out of our conscious awareness due to that material's uncomfortable or undesirable nature. Typically, shadow material reveals our least desirable traits, but the shadow has the dubious power to blot out the light of our higher natures if left unilluminated and unexamined.

This book aims to illuminate the dark recesses of narcissism, from its psychological origins to its relational, social, institutional, and ideological effects in those around you and perhaps even within yourself. In the process, I will illustrate how narcissism changes the molecular structure of all it touches. This book also demonstrates how empathy, compassion, and radical self-awareness achieve the same alchemical transformation as narcissism, selfishness, and ignorance, with less collateral damage than their erosive counterparts.

You may have picked up this book because you or your partner, child, mother, father, boss, elected leader, or spiritual guide exhibit narcissistic tendencies.[2] This book will teach you about the 27 types of narcissism and how they mold relational, social, and cultural dynamics and thus shape our inner realities as well as the outer world.

You may have picked up this book because words such as *gaslighting*, *love bombing*, *DARVO*, *triangulation*, or *breadcrumbing* have made their way into your lexicon due to an increase in public awareness of the narcissist's toolbox. Narcissism is undeniably a hot topic. For every person who believes it needs to be understood to reverse its damaging effects, there are others, like Zack or his friends, who feel that their natural narcissistic tendencies are under attack from an increasingly "intolerant" and persecutory empathic cabal, or still others who find the antics of Zack and George Santos entertaining. For those of you who sympathize with Zack and his friends, I assure you that I'm not on a witch hunt against narcissists but, rather, I intend to help them find ways of interacting with those around them with less conflict, trauma, and resistance.

That said, I *am* admittedly hard on narcissists. Their antagonistic behaviors undeniably damage their lives and those in relationship with them. But I would be a hypocrite if I couldn't extend the narcissist empathy because I have seen how they, too, often get in their own way and experience the universal pangs of rejection and abandonment due to their frequent lack of awareness or concern for their effect on others. For many, their inability or lack of desire to understand the mechanisms behind their behavior creates repeated frustration, anger, and often avoidable grief.

For those of you touched by the effects of narcissistic abuse and trauma, I am intimately acquainted with your struggles. I hope to provide you with a holistic understanding and practical tools for healing or removing yourself from narcissists or narcissistic systems and ideologies and their subsequent effects.

This book begins by discussing the characteristics of narcissism and how twenty-first-century culture helps to encourage narcissistic traits. We will begin by exploring narcissism as a concept and situate our conceptual understanding of narcissism and its beginnings from the cautionary tale of Narcissus, as told by the ancient Greeks, to "insta" fame, influencer culture, selfies, and other modern iterations of narcissistic culture.

Chapter 1 reviews the concepts from *The Narcissist in You and Everyone Else*. You'll need to understand what narcissism is and isn't. Additionally, as narcissistic traits become increasingly prevalent, answering some of the most pervasive and controversial questions around the topic is necessary. Such questions include the following: Is narcissism a psychological disorder or a personality type? How can we distinguish between a narcissist and a run-of-the-mill "jerk"? Is the word *narcissist* reserved for only mental health clinicians, or can anybody use the term? Is calling out narcissism ableist? Does being spoiled, privileged, and overly indulged as a child create narcissism, or is it something inborn and predetermined in the psyche? And, finally, can narcissists change, and even if they can, should we expect them to?

Chapter 2 takes a cross-generational approach to understanding narcissism, looking at research that suggests that views on selfishness, egotism, and narcissism have shifted dramatically, particularly for millennials and Gen Z due to the influences of social media and technology and an increasing obsession with fame, power, and popularity.

INTRODUCTION

We will then dive into how narcissism manifests in the various levels of human life through various fictionalized case studies inspired by my research interviews, case studies, and famous narcissist exemplars to illustrate how narcissism manifests from the individual level to a broader, systemic world perspective. In Chapters 3 and 4, we'll follow the development of narcissism and its effects from its earliest stirrings in a young child and its effect on the family system to subsequent other personal and familial relationships. We will also see how some of the various narcissistic types I presented in *The Narcissist in You and Everyone Else* deploy tools such as gaslighting, the DARVO method, goalpost moving, love bombing, breadcrumbing, obfuscation, victimization, minimization, triangulation, guilt-tripping, blaming, and projection.

In Chapter 5, we'll delve more deeply into how narcissism affects intimate, platonic, and familial relationships through a bird's-eye view of our three anti-heroes' relationships. Through their stories, you will learn how to recognize the effects of narcissism in a family system (including the inherited trauma inflicted by narcissistic caregivers), intimate partner abuse, and the broad strokes of trying to function within the distorted values of narcissistic friendships and coworker relationships.

Chapter 6 critically examines how the effects of our anti-heroes' narcissistic or antagonistic interpersonal strategies translate to the social world at large. We will explore how even narcissists often begin with inspired or partially well-meaning intentions as they enter group dynamics. Still, their desire for control, admiration, power, wealth, and attention predictably corrodes everything from friend groups and neighborhood associations to church or spiritual groups, political parties, or anywhere people gather.

Chapter 7 explores how our anti-heroes' narcissistic ideologies penetrate group dynamics and give way to structural narcissism affecting the ideologies that underlie human life through analyzing how political, religious, and economic structures can become infected with virulent narcissistic ideals.

INTRODUCTION

In Chapter 8, we'll tie it all together, and suggestions for implementing lasting change for narcissistic relationship survivors and narcissists alike will be offered as a means of providing hope as we struggle collectively with the overgrowth of selfishness and lack of compassion in an increasingly disconnected world.

The task before us is simultaneously massive and incredibly simple. By the end of this book, your awareness of the effects of narcissism on the psychological, cultural, ideological, and spiritual lives of you and your fellow human beings will be clear. More than that, I sincerely hope that as you read about antagonistic egoism on these various levels of your life, you will become an advocate for increasing compassion everywhere. Maya Angelou said, "I believe we all have empathy; we may not have the courage to display it." I hope this book gives you the courage and tools to deal with narcissistic people in your lives. I hope this book also helps shine the light of empathy and understanding on your unacknowledged narcissistic shadows. In psychological and self-help circles, people often talk about "shadow work," that often tricky but fruitful illumination of the recesses of human motivation, behaviors, or desires that when left unexamined, threaten our emotional, spiritual, or even physical survival. Allow this book to serve as a lamppost as you work through the shadowlands of the ego first in yourself and, as a result, in the world.

CHAPTER ONE
NARCISSISM
Then, Now, and Forever?

When I tell people I research and write about narcissism and empathy, their responses tend to fall into two categories. One group often says something like "Oh well, you should interview me about my mother/father/boss/ex-partner/child; you'll have plenty of data." Alternatively, the other group often says something like "It seems like everybody is talking about that now, but I don't know if I've ever met a narcissist in real life." The first group, having had firsthand experience of narcissism in action, are often "survivors" to some extent and want to share their frustrations with dealing with the narcissistic person in their lives and may or may not have a full, crystalized definition of narcissism in their minds.

In contrast, the second group tends to feel uncomfortable using the word *narcissism*, believing themselves unqualified to "diagnose" people because they're not psychologists. The second group also often has a very grandiose vision of narcissism that would encompass only the most apparent historical examples, such as Napoleon or Bernie Madoff. For these people, I always assure them that they have indeed met a narcissist before and that person is probably closer to them than they realize. As I outlined in *The Narcissist in You and Everyone Else*, at its most basic definition, narcissism is a set of personality strategies that include an increased sense of one's importance, talents, significance, or difficulty or an inability to empathize with others (mainly, if doing so would challenge their interests) and a tendency toward antagonistic or challenging relational strategies that minimize or diminish others' needs, emotions, or interests and centralize their own. I am, along with a growing number of mental health clinicians and psychiatrists, increasingly unconvinced that narcissism should be classified as a clinical personality disorder despite its often disordered relational strategies. We should unpack this a little more fully and you can decide for yourself.

Is Narcissism a Psychological Disorder?

This is a loaded and fraught question in the mental health world at the time of this writing. As awareness of narcissism has grown, the discourse around what constitutes disease or disorder has also been hotly debated. As defined by the DSM-5,[1] narcissistic personality disorder (NPD) constellates around two categories dealing with self-image and relationship dynamics.

1. Impairment in self-functioning, with two sub-categories of impairment
   a. Exaggerated self-importance (either positive or negative)
   b. A tendency to seek excessive external approval and praise from others stemming from a belief in their own relative superiority to others
2. Interpersonal impairment
   a. An impaired ability to empathize with others (unless doing so would benefit them in some way)
   b. An inability to form intimate connections (including a lack of interest in others or inability to be vulnerable or emotionally revealing)
   c. Another sub-category within this second subset of criteria is defined by pathological and antagonistic interpersonal strategies in two different areas: grandiosity and attention seeking.

The DSM-5 also states that these criteria must be relatively consistent across an adult lifespan (i.e., you can't diagnose NPD in children). These traits are also not explained by some other cultural or social convention through which the person is functioning, nor can these traits arise from other external factors, such as substance abuse or some other physiological trauma (e.g., head trauma, dementia, or Alzheimer's).

So, to answer whether narcissism is a psychological disorder, we must first acknowledge that within the medical model of mental health, anything that is divergent from consensual human functioning within a particular culture is considered disordered. However, hundreds, maybe even thousands, of variations in thinking, feeling, and acting can present in human behavior, representing a neurodivergent or atypical method of functioning that may not be considered disordered.

The word *disorder*, from the Latin roots *dis*, meaning *not*, and *ordinare*, meaning *ordinary*, could apply to all of us at some point in our lives. Not all disordered thinking, behavior, or feeling states are disruptive to either the person experiencing those states or those affected by those states. There are two primary categories of disorder.

1. **Beneficial.** Some disordered states can benefit others, such as the insights gleaned from the unusual mental, emotional, and physical states of spiritually minded mystics, seers, teachers, and philosophers throughout history. In contrast, other disordered states can disrupt the one experiencing those states as well as others.
2. **Negative.** The second category of disorder is associated with disruption, impairment, or some subjectively experienced negative consequence. In the case of personality disorders, very often, the one experiencing the disordered psychological functioning remains unaffected or unbothered by their state. This is particularly true in the case of antagonistic personality disorders, namely, NPD and antisocial personality disorder (ASPD).

CHAPTER ONE

This brings us back to the original notion of disorder: if the person does not have a subjective experience of impairment or negative consequences, which is the cornerstone of mental health diagnosis, should we honestly think of it as a clinical diagnosis? I must give a resoundingly unsatisfying response: yes and no. The antagonistic personality disorders have apparent adverse effects on the person experiencing these personality traits and even more so on those affected by the person's behavior. Still, the antagonistic person often does not interpret these experiences as problematic. In fact, in most cases, these people think it's everyone else's problem and not theirs to fix. As Chris, a 2021 study respondent, summarized:

> Other people think I'm an asshole, but I couldn't care less. That sounds like a personal problem to me, and what other people think of me isn't my business. If you're stupid enough to get in my way when I want something, you deserve what you get. (Chris, 46, accountant)

To complicate matters, research suggests that only 0.5% to 5% of the population suffers from NPD, which is an incredibly conservative number given that in my research, I identified 13% to 18% of my study participants self-reporting clinically significant narcissistic personality traits. However, only three had been formally diagnosed with NPD by a licensed mental health professional. Most research participants were quite satisfied with themselves and, not surprisingly, identified most of their problems as originating from others' responses to their behavior and choices and not a problem they felt they should have to correct. In other words, other people's issues with them sounded like a "personal problem," to quote Chris from the previous excerpt. Even those who were consciously aware of existing somewhere along the narcissistic spectrum didn't perceive their traits as disordered, problematic, or particularly troubling and, in many cases, found their orientation to relationships and life overall superior. Remember Zack's diatribe from the introduction? This is a common refrain from people who see their personality characteristics as assets rather than deficits.

I hate this shaming of so-called narcissism that's so popular. No offense to your research, but I think it's a load of crap. We're demonizing people who are ambitious, driven, and sure of themselves because people who are insecure, lazy, and weak don't understand us. If I walked around empathizing with everyone all day, I wouldn't have gotten to where I am in my career. It's not a disorder; it's just my personality. (Brent, 45, attorney)

Shockingly, I agree with Brent, at least partially. Narcissism is a personality style, or more accurately, a personality overlay. I outlined the 27 variations narcissism can take, synthesizing the traits of narcissism with the 27 instinctual subtypes of the Enneagram personality system to elucidate the nuances narcissism can take within the human ego structure. In my initial study, I found that the incidence of high narcissism rarely interfered with most participants' subjective experience of their lives or, at least, not so much that they thought *they* could be the problem. Not surprisingly, many participants experienced the everyday stressors of daily life (e.g., work or school problems, financial stress, and health issues) and the experiences of depression, anxiety, relationship issues, and so on that are common among many of us.

Narcissism often serves as a buffer against any actual estimation of their shortcomings and an increased perception of others' misunderstanding or lack of appreciation for their specialness. Subsequently, because narcissists prioritize their goals, needs, wishes, emotions, and desires over others around them, they feel justified in some of the more exploitative or manipulative strategies they employ. By now, you may be wondering how or why one person ends up being narcissistic while others don't. The answer is complex, but let's discuss some significant factors that influence the formation of narcissistic traits.

Born This Way?

Nurture plays a considerable role in shaping how an individual performs various personality traits. Still, the traits seem to be a mixture of inherent or inherited tendencies. Narcissism is no exception because research has shown that early developmental factors, such as early trauma, parental style, and the prevalence of narcissism in one or both parents, tend to exacerbate narcissistic traits in children.[2] In *The Narcissist in You and Everyone Else*, I discussed the various aspects of human existence that play a pivotal role in shaping our personalities. However, we can review them here for quick reference.

The first and most foundational factor is biology (including hormones, neurology, and other genetic factors). Some studies with narcissistic individuals have shown decreased gray matter volume in the brain in areas that relate to empathy and increased activity in areas of the brain related to self-interest and social dominance.[3] Additionally, some research suggests that some narcissistic individuals have higher oxidative stress and hypersensitivity to shame and embarrassment, both of which potentially correlate to habitual empathy shutdown over time.[4]

Early childhood development and developmental traumas and delays have also been shown to influence the formation of narcissistic traits. Early experiences of rejection by a primary caregiver in combination with a propensity toward a more sensitive or "fragile ego" structure have been shown to increase the incidence of narcissism in some cases.[5] The idea that how we experience the world and other people shapes our psychology and relational strategies is nothing new in developmental psychology. Narcissists often report ambivalence or even antagonism toward an early caregiver for not having given them something fundamentally necessary for their egoic functioning; thus, they develop an increased need for external validation and a decreased patience when their psychological or physical needs are not met. Narcissists aren't alone in this phenomenon because nearly all humans develop less-than-ideal conditions to some degree. So it could be that their genetic predisposition toward narcissism or the environment played an increased role in helping their narcissism defenses to bud.

The environment, in a broader sense, includes everything from our mother's womb to the home, city, state, country, and planet. While there may be some correlation between in utero conditions and the development of narcissism, it's difficult to get conclusive data on those effects. However, our immediate families and broader communities of origin are easier to measure. We know these larger environmental constructs significantly shape our psychological defenses and experiences of others and the world around us. My research with both narcissistic people and those who have or had been in a relationship with a narcissist provided circumstantial evidence of a narcissist present in the family of origin (e.g., a parent, sibling, or grandparent who may have been narcissistic), resulting in reinforcement of narcissistic relational strategies as desirable or "normal." In addition, my research showed that the presence of a narcissistic caregiver made many non-narcissistic participants subconsciously seek familiarity in subsequent adult narcissistic relationships.

I prefer a holistic approach to understanding people and conclude that all these factors play a significant role in shaping our personalities, as well as how healthy or compromised our personalities are within a given environment, and narcissists are no exception to this rule.

Empathy and Vulnerability

We can't fully understand narcissism without understanding the role of empathy and emotional vulnerability. Empathy is a multifaceted and complex mechanism, and without giving you a 3,000-page essay, I'll review some of the necessary foundational aspects of empathy.

At its most basic level, empathy is the ability to feel or understand what another person is experiencing. Empathy is as nuanced as the nature versus nurture question and seems to form (or not) based on similar factors (e.g., biology, environment, and development). It's important to understand that empathy exists on a continuum; like almost all human traits, I outlined seven levels ranging from 0 (no empathy) to 7 (maximum empathy) in my 2021 study. Based on that study, most people fall within the average range of empathy (level 4 or 5). In contrast, those we would consider narcissistic tend to fall into the lower ranges of empathy from 0 to 3. Additionally, empathy is a dynamic process, and we all have moments of higher levels of empathetic resonance with others around us. Conversely, we may exhibit temporary signs of reduced empathic functioning in times of stress, trauma, or upheaval.

There is a multitude of ways in which empathy can manifest itself in human beings. One of the most rudimentary forms of empathy is somatic empathy, where one may physically or emotionally feel what another is feeling in a very tangible way. This likely developed in human beings to stay connected to others in our community and to sense and navigate situations that could endanger the community. However, human beings also exhibit other empathic pathways, such as cognitive empathy (i.e., the ability to understand another's thoughts, ideologies, or mental processes) and spiritual or what I call "quantum" empathy (i.e., encompassing the more elusive intuitive faculties, like when a mother just knows their child is in distress).

Another critical feature of narcissism is an aversion to vulnerability, particularly in interpersonal relationships. Vulnerability has become a buzzword in recent years, but at its root is the ability to be transparent about one's shortcomings, weaknesses, or fears. For many narcissistic people, vulnerability is unacceptable because it betrays their sense of strength and subsequent superiority. Sharing vulnerability in relationships helps to increase intimacy and fosters greater closeness in relationships because it helps both parties to feel like they have invested equally by revealing potentially unflattering or weak points in each other's life or psyche.

While it is difficult for narcissists to be vulnerable with themselves because admitting weakness or shortcomings shatters their typical grandiose sense of themselves, some narcissistic individuals may use selective vulnerability to their advantage. Those more vulnerable narcissists who utilize selective vulnerability tend to focus their dialogue on what others did to them to make them feel a certain way rather than revealing their weaknesses. This can be confusing and sometimes makes the vulnerable narcissist seem more self-aware or sensitive than grandiose narcissists who refuse to acknowledge or discuss their faults.

For the vulnerable narcissistic variants, their faults become excuses for why they cannot or should not be treated like everyone else and, as such, deserve special treatment. They may leverage genuine challenges (e.g., depression, ADHD, and anxiety) to justify their ill-treatment of others, whereby their proclaimed weaknesses are leveraged to manipulate others in their lives. Furthermore, some narcissistic individuals utilize selective revelation of vulnerabilities to trauma bond[6] with those with whom they are trying to get close.

Narcissist, Psychopath, or Sociopath

In *The Narcissist in You and Everyone Else*, I spend considerable time parsing the differences between narcissistic people, sociopaths, and psychopathic people. It's unnecessary to revisit all the nuances between these three delineations here. However, some review of the overarching differences between them is helpful. Psychopathy in and of itself is not a diagnosis. However, the DSM-5 has diagnostic criteria for people who exhibit antisocial personality disorder, typically including some degree of psychopathy.

Psychopathy is a set of personality traits characterized by lowered empathy and pain sensitivity; increased aggression; and a propensity toward sadism, manipulation, and increased presence of exploitative inclinations. Not all psychopaths exhibit physically violent tendencies; for example, the "corporate psychopath" may never have to resort to physical violence. However, almost all psychopaths exhibit an interpersonal orientation whereby others are seen as objects (a trait they share with narcissists), believing in their strength and superiority and thus their right to control, dominate, or subjugate those they've positioned as inferior. Psychopaths invariably experience little to no empathy, compared to narcissists, who may have moments or periods of increased empathy. Psychopathy, by definition, implies the presence of narcissism but with an added element of rage that often makes them more potentially dangerous in interpersonal dynamics.

Virtually all the world's most well-known serial killers, rapists, or other predatory individuals display some degree of psychopathy.

CHAPTER ONE

Psychopaths have been shown to exhibit unusually low fear arousal and decreased ability to experience pain, sadness, or other vulnerable emotions. Subsequently, they report a colder or emotionally flat interior world paired with diminished impulse control or concern for others' emotions, well-being, or needs. Comparatively, narcissistic people tend to have more access to fear and sadness, even if they hide or conceal such emotions.

Individuals who exhibit sociopathy, which has no official clinical diagnosis, may or may not exhibit violent tendencies. Sociopaths share similarities with narcissistic people, who tend to be more emotionally labile and may experience momentary shame or guilt. However, like psychopathic people, they feel that they must manipulate and control others to ensure that their desires and needs are met. Sociopaths may, for example, run an elaborate scheme to steal others' money to satisfy their desire to be rich, disregarding the pain or anguish they caused and feeling justified in doing what they feel they need to do. Sociopaths may or may not act violently, but they tend to have less control over their emotional reactions compared to psychopaths, who often make conscious choices to hurt or harm others for their satisfaction. Incidentally, sociopaths have a higher incidence of trauma, and some can trace the development of sociopath-like behaviors as a defense mechanism in difficult, dangerous, or abusive environments whereby vulnerability and empathy had to be heavily mitigated to survive.

Sociopaths, psychopaths, and other malignant or aggressive narcissistic subtypes exhibit "dark triad" traits. The *dark triad* is a term first coined by Paulhus and Williams;[7] it outlines three overarching personality trait clusters that include narcissism, Machiavellism, and psychopathy. Since we've already covered psychopathy and narcissism, let's discuss Machiavellism. Machiavellism is named after the infamous Italian historian, diplomat, and author Niccolò Machiavelli (1469–1527), whose seminal work, *Il Principe* (The Prince), rationalizes and justifies violence, manipulation, and deception to gain power and increase self-interested aspirations through the subjugation of other less ruthless subordinates.[8] The combination of these three trait structures creates a personality structure that many consider to be potentially dangerous due to their propensity toward harming others through interpersonal, physical, financial, mental, or spiritual forms of abuse.

Narcissist versus "Jerk"

Now that we know what narcissism is from a clinical perspective, you may be wondering what the difference is between someone who is a narcissist and someone who is simply a "jerk" or "full of themselves." We can look at this through two separate lenses. Most people, except perhaps those affected by narcissism or familiar with clinical terminology, rarely use the term *narcissism* as colloquially as those in the mental health space (although this is rapidly changing). My aunt won't even use the word *narcissism* because she "doesn't speak like that in [her] everyday life." She, and many like her, prefers to use less clinically loaded terminology, such as *jerk*, *asshole*, *arrogant*, or some other less formalized word. I see this as a curious linguistic convention with which people seek to avoid pathologizing the person yet feel perfectly comfortable using a more derogatory word in place of *narcissist*. Because of this, if someone prefers less formal verbiage to explain narcissistic or antagonistic behavior, it's difficult to assess whether the person is talking about someone who is genuinely narcissistic or perhaps just a jerk. This brings me to the second way to view this linguistic hairsplitting.

Some people may be arrogant, selfish, and full of themselves and not be narcissists. The primary difference is whether the person can correct their problematic behavior and, more importantly, whether they demonstrate empathy, compassion, and conscientiousness more often than not. Jerkiness can arise due to various personality traits and life factors. It may not rise to the level of narcissism because their jerk-like behavior may be generously interspersed with behaviors and feelings demonstrating their ability to care about others and their needs above their own. That said, even the most deeply entrenched narcissists have moments of empathic resonance, altruism, and compassion. I know what you must be thinking. This is getting fuzzier and fuzzier the deeper we go. And, again, my answer is frustrating but resounding: tell me about it!

If you are describing someone who has a history of being antagonistic, selfish, self-centered, grandiose, non-empathetic, superficial, or manipulative, by all means, use the word *narcissist*. You don't have to be a therapist, psychologist, or psychiatrist to identify narcissism. You must, however, have the qualifications and clinical experience to proclaim that someone has NPD. However, if you feel more comfortable with the less loaded terminology of *jerk* or some other derivative, use that term.

Be mindful, however, that for some who have been on the receiving end of narcissistic abuse, the refusal to utter the word may feel invalidating. We would all benefit from greater awareness about when the term *narcissist* is appropriate. I have seen all behaviors, from taking a selfie to caring about one's appearance, labeled as narcissistic, which is a gross misunderstanding of what constitutes narcissism. A quick Google search engine trend revealed that since 2004, the terms *narcissist* and *narcissism* have risen over 20% in online search engines, peaking in February 2017 and remaining steadily above the 50% mark. In Chapter 2, we'll delve more deeply into the differences between confidence and narcissism, and in Chapter 3, we'll parse these distinctions further by looking at the effects of social media and generational changes in self-conception.

Is Calling Someone a Narcissist Ableist?

Another delicate but worthwhile discussion around using the word *narcissist* to describe someone's personality is whether doing so is diminishing, ableist, or psychologically elitist. Undoubtedly, lumping all characteristics we don't like about a person into the narcissistic basket is ethically problematic and dehumanizing. Grouping any characteristics and using those labels to position the person as "other" or "bad" due to their differences is an unfortunate and pervasively problematic tendency for human beings, particularly in the Western world. The

Western obsession with grouping and labeling has wrought some positive and useful distinctions, such as our modern understanding of the mineral, plant, and animal kingdoms. However, in the context of human behavior, it has quickly devolved into reductionistic and biased stereotyping of ethnic, racial, religious, and cultural communities, resulting in the justification of all manner of indignities, from systemic oppression to genocide. In almost all circumstances, discrimination against or singling out anyone for a perceived difference is a slippery slope toward alienation. It can quickly breed a lack of compassion at best and justification for abuse at worst. In psychology, mainly when dealing with unseen differences (e.g., depression, anxiety, bipolar disorder, ADD, and learning disabilities), separating the person from their diagnosis is paramount to maintaining their humanity.

It wasn't so long ago that people with emotional or psychological differences that are quite prevalent were immediately institutionalized for conditions that are now seen as commonplace, such as depression and anxiety and the shameful history of labeling many women as hysterical simply for being emotionally expressive, tired, or unsatisfied with their lives. However, with antagonistic personality types, things become a bit more complex because these elements aren't necessarily unseen but manifest in relationship to others, and the very nature of those traits typically makes copacetic relating more difficult. This doesn't justify the ill-treatment or discrimination of those with significant relational challenges. In truth, dealing with antagonistic personality traits often requires more awareness, patience, and empathy.

So the question remains whether calling out narcissism is ableist. I think this is the wrong question because, quite often, hurling the word toward a narcissistic person in question does nothing but amplify relational problems and create an increasingly adversarial relationship with the person. Additionally, calling someone narcissistic, while helpful in understanding their behavior, has almost no effect on the narcissistic traits themselves and, in many instances, amplifies the behavior or results in its being turned around on the labeler.

CHAPTER ONE

It would be ableist to expect someone who exhibits low empathy, high attention seeking, grandiosity, and selfishness to be a different person than they are. On the other hand, calling out narcissism for those who have been victims of narcissistic abuse can be healing and affirming, particularly when the person has likely been gaslighted to believe they're the problem.

Understanding that narcissism is a character armor, not unlike any other psychological defense, can help release both the narcissist and those in a relationship with them from the pressure of trying to change them. By all clinical accounts, narcissism is notoriously difficult to treat, albeit the narcissist can learn behavioral and interpersonal strategies to increase relational ease if they genuinely want to change. This doesn't mean that people who find themselves in relationship with a narcissist should excuse, enable, or endure their bad behavior but rather recognize that underneath that behavior lies a wound that has manifested itself as an antagonistic style. That said, I believe holding those with narcissistic traits to basic standards of decency and kindness is necessary to reduce the effect of their damage on others.

Ableism implies discrimination and prevents the person discriminated against from rising to the occasion of any particular task, relationship, job, and so on. Discrimination inherently lacks compassion and stereotypes and underestimates people without discernment. Compassion is understanding someone's differences and adjusting (within reasonable limits) as necessary so they can succeed in each arena. This was the intention behind the standards of "reasonable accommodation." I think holding the reality of the difficulty of permanently breaking through narcissistic psychological defenses, particularly in an adult person, allows us to foster an energy of reasonable accommodation, whereby those in relationship with the narcissist recognize their limitations and function within those limits in a way that is respectful of the others' autonomy to be themselves while maintaining a semblance of mental health and emotional safety. This looks different for each dynamic, and for some, the only way to maintain an equitable relationship means cutting the narcissist out completely; for others, this is impossible or undesirable.

There is power in naming things, and that power can be positive or destructive. In the case of narcissism, calling it what it is can help organize what is often experienced as chaos (particularly for those in relationship with the narcissist). There is power in understanding one's narcissistic tendencies because doing so can often be the impetus to uncover and heal the conditions that helped create the narcissism in the first place. One participant articulately expressed the value of understanding her narcissism:

> I knew something was "wrong" with me when I was very little because I just didn't care about others how I thought I was supposed to. I thought I was perhaps autistic or had some other neurological issues. Finally, I had myself tested for all those things, and it wasn't that. I knew I thought highly of myself, needed lots of attention, and had trouble thinking about others in a way that made people feel valued (unless I needed something from them). It wasn't until I worked with a very honest therapist while complaining about my almost daily fights with my husband and kids that the word narcissism was used to describe me. I'd heard "selfish," "attention whore," "superficial," and "ambitious," but it didn't land the same way. Initially, it kind of hurt to hear it, and I rejected it. But when I read more, I had to be honest that I saw myself in it. That was the only thing that allowed me to get real and start working on the behaviors that create conflict and very slowly doing the work I needed to do to figure out why I couldn't be vulnerable. (Joan, 54, attorney)

Twenty-Seven Flavors of Narcissism

All narcissists, regardless of where they fall on the spectrum of narcissism, share some degree of the traits we've discussed in this chapter, namely, deficits in empathy; a propensity toward a grandiose self-image; inability to be vulnerable; and increased manipulative, exploitative, or other transgressive relational strategies. However, the flavor of narcissism differs depending on the fixation of the individual's ego and instinctual drives.

CHAPTER ONE

According to my research, there are 27 distinct subtypes of narcissism. These subtypes are developed from the cross-section of the 27 Enneagram personality instinctual subtypes and how these distinct personality profiles manifest narcissism. Some of these personality types encompass the more recognizable forms of narcissism (e.g., Madoff or Napoleon), while others may fly under the radar and seem, to many people, to be relatively benign. They all share the overall umbrella of narcissistic qualities outlined above. Still, the motivations for their behavior, the relational strategies, and the performance of those behaviors differ considerably depending on their personality type. Because of my original academic love, personality typology, I was already intimately aware of the varying flavors of personality motivation and behavior and many systems used to describe these variations. The Enneagram, which has risen in popularity in waves over the past 50 years, is the most comprehensive and holistic model. Therefore, I can't entirely agree with some narcissism experts and researchers on the idea that narcissism is in and of itself a personality type. Instead, I see narcissism as an overlay or additional armor different personality types have intertwined with their primary psychological ego motivations.

Let's review the 27 narcissistic subtypes I discovered as outlined in *The Narcissist in You and Everyone Else*, with the addition of some overarching categories to help organize the subtypes for quick reference. Each narcissistic subtype in the following categories is either primarily focused on self-preservation concerns (e.g., money, security, food, and resources), social inclusion or exclusion (e.g., group dynamics, politics, hierarchies, trends, and social relationships), or intimate/sexual pair bonds (e.g., attraction/repulsion, allure, intimacy, desirability and influence, and sexual competition with chosen intimates). For quick referencing, the self-preservation subtypes are indicated by "SP"; the social subtypes, by "SO"; and the intimate or sexual subtypes, by "SX."

The 27 Narcissistic Subtypes

The Rigid-Moralistic Types

The Puritanical Fussbudget (SP): Judgmental, patrician, and stern, this subtype derives their sense of superiority by making others adhere to their strict moral and ethical standards and punishing or diminishing others they see as frivolous, unprincipled, or selfish. They can be highly self-serving, hypocritical, and unkind in their behavior and demanding, cold, and prone to extreme rigidity.

The Moralistic Inquisitor (SO): Injudicious, rigid, and punitive, this subtype believes themselves to be morally superior and thus positions themselves as judge and administrator of punishment. They hold rigid ideals, standards, and morals and may demonstrate their moral superiority. They may be spectacularly hypocritical and surprisingly snobbish and can be demeaning, punishing, and self-righteous.

The Zealous Crusader (SX): Fiery, audacious, and zealous, this subtype feels entitled to enact their moral and ethical principles upon their environment. Often inappropriate or bombastic, they believe they're morally and ethically perfect and push intimates to strive to meet their impossible standards. They can be incredibly jealous and possessive of their intimates and uncharacteristically emotional and explosive with close relations. They can also be sanctimonious, arrogant, and rageful.

The Prideful-Flattering Types

The Entitled Caregiver (SP): Demanding, histrionic and manipulative, this subtype believes themselves to be more valuable, supportive, and helpful than others and thus deserving of special treatment and the satiation of their desires. They alternate between giving others what they believe they need and demanding (often covertly) that they receive the best money can buy. They can be dramatic, ingratiating, and prideful.

CHAPTER ONE

The Flattering Networker (SO): Seductive, flattering, and manipulative, this subtype strives to gain power and influence among those they deem important by ingratiating themselves. Highly ambitious and often charming, they believe they are integral to others' lives and thus deserve to be recognized and rewarded for their support and attention. They can be falsely humble, cutthroat, and envious of those receiving the attention or praise they desire.

The Manipulative Seducer (SX): Aggressive, seductive, and demanding, this subtype is the most aggressively manipulative type and uses their considerable charm, love-bombing techniques, and adaptability to enchant others. They believe they shouldn't be denied anyone or anything they want and will temporarily use their adaptability skills to become the other's ideal partner. They can be conniving, emotionally careless, and disingenuous.

The Ambitious-Deceptive Types

The Ruthless Workaholic (SP): Cutthroat, pragmatic, and materialistic, this subtype ensures they amass enough wealth and status to engender others' respect and admiration. Highly acquisitive, they believe they work harder and more efficiently than most others and value money and efficiency over relationships. They can be greedy and deceptive and are often highly competitive and equally successful.

Disingenuous Opportunist (SO): Charming, superficial, and duplicitous, this subtype strives to gain success and influence through appearances and associations with those who mirror their grand self-image. Being the most status conscious of all 27 subtypes, they need fame and popularity to feel worthy. They can be disingenuous and opportunistic and are focused on style over substance.

The Untouchable Star (SX): Seductive, polished, and competitive, this subtype strives to be the image of sexual perfection and professional power to attract a partner who mirrors their focus on outward beauty and success. They often find indulgence in sexual conquest and enjoy grooming partners to be their perfect companions. They can be controlling, rigid, and extremely vain.

The Moody-Entitled Types

The Fussy Masochist (SP): Dissatisfied, entitled, and exempt, this subtype feels entitled to excuse themselves from day-to-day details or responsibilities due to feeling extraordinary in their abilities and emotionally overwhelmed. Convinced that they suffer more acutely, they implicitly or explicitly demand that others tend to their emotional and material whims to counteract their discomfort. They can be complaining, demanding, and emotionally manipulative.

The Entitled Outcast (SO): Snobbish, aloof, and critical, this subtype believes themselves intellectually, artistically, or otherwise exempt from "normal society." Exaggerating their perceived specialness and defectiveness, they can be highly rejecting, judgmental, and dismissive of anything or anyone they believe is below their aesthetic or intellectual standards.

The Tempestuous Diva (SX): Temperamental, audacious, and domineering, this subtype derives their sense of specialness by manipulating and demanding that their intimates mirror their specialness. Highly insecure, they emotionally manipulate others through false displays of empathy or performative insightfulness to gain control over others' emotions and psyches. They can be emotionally volatile, hateful, and deeply envious of others' gifts, talents, and successes.

The Remote-Intellectual Types

The Miserly Misanthrope (SP): Stingy, unemotional, and cantankerous, this subtype is the most misanthropic and overtly withholding of the 27 subtypes. Concerned with ensuring their inner and outer resources are not drained, they become unapologetically resentful of any demands on their time, money, energy, or resources. Above all else, they want to ensure their material survival through hoarding resources. They can be cold and insensitive or Scrooge-like.

CHAPTER ONE

The Intellectual Elitist (SO): Status conscious, snobbish, and competitive, this subtype wants to be regarded as learned, intelligent, or intellectually powerful. They can seem like Enneagram Type Threes in their attempts to gain power and influence. Concerned more with being the "knowledge holder" than popular or attractive, they can be incredibly unlikable, glib, and arrogant in pursuing intellectual status and power.

The Dark Voyeur (SX): Secretive, remote, and dark minded, this subtype strives to find an intimate with whom they can share and potentially realize their taboo sexual or emotional desires and fantasies. Preferring to keep their distance from chosen intimates, they may draw others in with intellectual or emotional insight and then desire to control them without becoming too emotionally invested.

The Anxious-Skeptical Types

The Defensive Pessimist (SP): Negativistic; temperamental; ambivalent; and demanding that others walk on eggshells around their sensitivities, fears, and phobias, this subtype can alternate between being emotionally erratic, blaming, and unsure or bold, demanding, and uncompromising. They disdain others' self-assuredness, confidence, and ease and thus antagonize or diminish those they see as threats to their security or self-image. They can be suspicious, argumentative, and reactive.

The Ambivalent Underminer (SO): Obsequious, undermining, and provocative, this subtype aligns itself for (or against) a chosen group, cause, or institution and alternates between allegiance and rebellion. They desire to control and influence others out of a belief in their superiority but fear responsibility or blame. They quickly become envious of others' power, popularity, or influence in a group and strive to undermine or sow doubt to amass power. They can be dutiful, scheming, and cagey.

NARCISSISM

The Overreactive Rebel (SX): Reactive, posturing, and insecure, this subtype focuses on appearing beautiful, strong, fearless, and intelligent to attract a desirable mate. They may be entirely unaware of their anxiety and expect intimates to cater to their demands and insecurities and thus look more confident than they feel internally. They alternate between vulnerability and extreme power plays of control or love testing. They can be aggressive, adrenaline seeking, and emotionally erratic.

The Hedonistic-Exuberant Types

The Selfish Hedonist (SP): Materialistic, gluttonous, and mischievous, this subtype is focused primarily on personal pleasure and enjoyment. They prioritize their needs, wishes, plans, and wants over most other people's and can become highly aggressive or dismissive if people get in the way of their plans. They may enjoy debauchery in the guise of "fun" at the expense of others' safety or comfort, particularly if they become bored. They can be hedonistic, impulsive, and insensitive.

The Gleeful Charlatan (SO): Slick, exaggerating, and charismatic, this subtype staves off fears of boredom or stagnation by enrolling others in their grandiose visions for the future. Often convincing and likable, they easily lie to support their ideas, plans, or schemes. They are skilled charlatans and may garner trust from others only to later evade or relinquish responsibility for details if their plans go awry. They can be fraudulent, overconfident, and irresponsible.

The Flippant Rake (SX): Captivating, noncommittal, and careless, this subtype seeks to relieve their constant boredom and inner scarcity through engendering intimate relationships and devotion from others without their corresponding commitment. Often highly suggestive, charismatic, and persuasive, they are blown about by their whims and are emotionally irresponsible. They can be flaky, erratic, and unethical.

CHAPTER ONE

The Powerful-Aggressive Types

The Cynical Tyrant (SP): Controlling, materialistic, and aggressive, this subtype focuses on their fear of vulnerability and weakness in the physical realm and ensures they maintain complete control over all aspects of life. They are highly aggressive, typically grandiose, and unconcerned with others' feelings or sensitivity (particularly if they contradict their immediate needs). They demand loyalty and obedience from others. They can be blunt, materialistic, and callous.

The Mafia Don (SO): Intimidating, influential, and overbearing, above all else, this subtype desires power and control over their chosen social group. They consolidate and amass power by offering their protection in return for unyielding loyalty and devotion. Alternatingly persuasive, protective, and threatening, they make bold shows of their influence, status, power, or wealth. They can be power hungry, flashy, and domineering.

The Charismatic Bully (SX): Charismatic, bold, and uncompromising, this subtype wants to wholly possess the object(s) of their affection. They offer protection and power in exchange for others' total submission and surrender to their dictates, whims, and demands. They are more emotionally aware than other Powerful-Aggressive subtypes and use their charisma and audaciousness to engender admiration. They can be unreasonable, unscrupulous, and demanding.

The Ambivalent-Neglectful Types

The Neglectful Grouch (SP): Neglectful, passive-aggressive, and grouchy, this subtype strives above all else to ensure and maintain comfort and ease. While less antagonistic than other narcissistic subtypes, they can become quite aggressive when others threaten their routines, pleasure seeking, comfort, or security. They can be callous and dismissive of others' legitimate practical or emotional needs while superficially appearing easygoing, relaxed, or laid-back. They can be irresponsible, selfish, and unexpectedly rageful.

The Ambivalent Avoider (SO): Placating, wishy-washy, and spiteful, this subtype appears amicable, kind, and easygoing, but they spend considerable energy trying to gain and maintain power, status, or influence with minimal effort. Often quite duplicitous, they use their good-natured personality to present themselves as unassuming or harmless while constantly undermining or thwarting those who oppose their aspirations. They may seem like everyone's friend but occasionally show snobbishness or uncharacteristic showboating. They can be backbiting, arrogant, and secretly ambitious.

The Unassuming Manipulator (SX): Alluring, unassuming, and manipulative, this subtype allays their fears of being disconnected from others by becoming a blank slate for others on which to project their desires. All the while, they aim to gain control and influence over others who they fear may leave them. They are deftly manipulative and seductive in ensuring they're never abandoned, while they may be hypocritical, deceptive, and noncommittal. They can be possessive, disingenuous, and dishonest.

CHAPTER TWO
NARCISSISM RISING
Cultural and Generational Shifts

Narcissist Rising

Since 2004, the term *narcissism* in Google searches has steadily risen anywhere from 15% to 25%, peaking in 2015 to 2016 (particularly around the 2016 presidential election). The term *gaslighting* has seen an 85% increase from November 2015 to November 2021. Documentaries on all manner of swindlers, con people, sociopaths, psychopaths, and grifters have become standard fare and assured ratings generators on television and streaming apps. Terms such as *love bombing* and *trauma bonding* (refer to the Glossary for a definition of these terms) have become clickbait keywords on social media apps, such as TikTok and Instagram. So why have narcissism and the various interpersonal strategies used by narcissists captured the attention of people around the world? I suppose many of these questions can be boiled down to one fundamental question: is narcissism more prevalent than it used to be, or are we just more aware of it than before? You guessed it. The answer is yes.

Narcissism is a uniquely Western problem. That is not to say that people in non-Western cultures don't have narcissistic people; undoubtedly, they do. However, many non-Western cultures lean toward a more collectivist orientation. Therefore, the unmitigated growth of the individual ego is thwarted by cultural expectations that make narcissistic psychological defenses challenging to maintain (at least, out

CHAPTER TWO

in the open). However, in the Western world, by the very nature of our cultural development standards, narcissism is a by-product of our expectations about self-actualization.

In the United States, we expect healthy, functioning members of society to develop a strong sense of individual identity. We expect children aged eight or nine to proclaim what they want to be when they grow up. We stress the importance of confidence, goal setting, perseverance, and simultaneously suppressing weakness or vulnerability so as not to appear insecure. On the surface, these values are healthy and promote a positive self-image and a sense of productivity and resilience.

The theoretical foundations of our idea of healthy development even include a distinct stage of "individuation" and suppose that all people should develop an identity as a separate entity from those around them. Although shifting (albeit slowly) to a more quantum and thus holistic perspective, our scientific worldview is built on the suppositions of dualism, materialism, and separation. Arguably, some dignities have been born out of the dualistic worldview. Some of the triumphs include the development of many branches of science; economic growth; and the subsequent benefits on people's health, well-being, and safety and a widespread belief in the power of the individual to make an impact on the world at large.

The pitfalls of the dualistic, separatist universe arguably outweigh many of its benefits and have contributed to the growth of environmental destruction (why save the planet and its natural resources if you don't see yourself as a part of the planet), war, oppression, and genocide (the rationalization of an "us vs. them" mentality justifying various forms of violence), and growing economic disparity (a systemic separation of the "haves" from the "have-nots").

The West's value and veneration of the individual "I" over the collective "we" have many tantalizing benefits, such as fame, wealth, and power. The conception of being rich and famous, particularly compared to those who are poor and unknown, has become the gold standard of self-actualization in the modern world. Ask four average teenagers what they want to be when they grow up, and invariably, two will proclaim their desire to be an "influencer" or, quite simply, "famous." However, their desire to imprint themselves on the world isn't entirely their fault because they've been told that without the demonstration and public validation of their worth, they are destined to live an unremarkable and thus forgettable existence. Leaving behind a legacy, whether in the form of families, intellectual or artistic contributions, wealth, or other tangible impressions on the world, has become synonymous with living a "purpose-driven life." And who doesn't want to live a life of purpose? Unfortunately, the definition of *purpose* has steadily shifted from an intrinsic to an extrinsic focus.

Achieving one's purpose in the Western world requires hard work, determination, and an unflinching confidence and belief in one's value. Psychologist Dean Radin, when discussing the impediments to the average Westerner's openness to expanded states of consciousness, aptly theorizes that "the ideal Western ego is an isolated, ruggedly independently separate entity, all alone in a dead universe devoid of meaning or consciousness. The leather-faced cowboy pondering empty thoughts. Social psychologists have found that buying into that gloomy worldview leads to a reduction in beneficial behaviors such as helpfulness and empathy."[1]

While we often cursorily champion teamwork, kindness to others, and a willingness to help those less fortunate than us due to the influence of Judeo-Christian religious ideologies, we also learn that to be valuable, we must be exceptional. For the lucky, exceptionalism can come from some innate talent or aptitude, but for most others, being or becoming exceptional requires cultivating a skill set (preferably one that has the potential to be economically viable).

The necessity to be exceptional lies at the heart of narcissistic wounding. When a fragile ego (and let's face it, all egos are fragile) is cultivated in a culture obsessed with being exceptional meets the inevitable reality of others who are more exceptional, psychological (over)compensation is inescapable. Compensation takes many forms: self-inflation, deception, overestimating one's talents, opportunism, undermining, and outright aggression toward anyone threatening one's sense of specialness.

CHAPTER TWO

I'm not suggesting that narcissism is merely a by-product of cultural ideologies that support self-aggrandizement. We know that many factors contribute to the creation and development of narcissism. However, Western culture undoubtedly rewards narcissistic strategies, and increasingly, twenty-first-century life even encourages exceptionalism unlike any other time in our history.

Influencer Mania

Despite cultural pressure to be ashamed of my millennial status, I am an unabashed child of the late eighties and nineties. Millennials have been blamed for everything from the decline in births to the housing market decline (I can't quite figure out the math on this one), and much of the criticism of my generation is based on displaced scapegoating and overgeneralizations. This aside, there is one thing my generation popularized that cannot be undone: social media. We are the first generation to straddle the divide between the analog and digital ages. I grew up learning how to use computers and, in rudimentary forms, the internet. While you may hear a pod of aging millennials sit around reminiscing about the glacial connection speed of their modem dialup connection to AOL or CompuServe, you will just as likely hear us complaining about how kids today don't know how to play outside anymore or otherwise entertain themselves without the use of technology.

I have fond memories of carefully rearranging my Myspace "top friends" list and remember when Facebook was rolled out to college campuses and the now defunct (and some may say creepy) "poking" function. That said, our slow indoctrination into the digital world of social media image started innocently enough when people shared quaint observations about how they were feeling that day or, by the time Instagram exploded onto the scene, a blissfully unpretentious photo of the pizza they just ordered. While Myspace and Facebook began as novel ways to keep track of friends, particularly nonlocal friends, Instagram ushered in a new way of viewing our worlds that slowly required increasing attention to social presentation.

Corresponding to the rise in social media was the increased production of reality television, which, for the first time in the entertainment industry's history, allowed "regular" people to become famous by presenting their "everyday" lives to the public. As the television industry capitalized on the new cultural zeitgeist of voyeurism, previously distant aspirations of fame and fortune became more tenable for the average person. Some early reality television shows, such as *American Idol, The Amazing Race, Fear Factor, Survivor, America's Next Top Model*, and *Big Brother*, were a hybrid of familiar competition-based game shows and soap operas. These television shows capitalized on placing contestants in extreme conditions with a heavy dose of interpersonal drama to increase watchability. The result was addictive.

A new crop of reality shows soon appeared, which showcased people with no discernible purpose or talent other than to show people living their everyday lives. However, the entertainment industry, being wise to the fact that watching your average person live their life would lose its value quickly, thus began to create shows that injected copious amounts of fabricated storylines, producer-fueled interpersonal drama, and the encouragement of extreme personalities and behaviors to feed the public's hunger for spectacle.

Shows such as *The Real World* (which pioneered the reality TV format), which maintained a somewhat authentic depiction of its cast members' experiences living with strangers, gave way to shows that showcased people who became famous for simply being famous. *The Simple Life*, the quirky and retrospectively problematic reality show starring millionaire "it girls" Paris Hilton and Nicole Richie, and *Keeping Up with the Kardashians* introduced people to "being yourself" (or at least, a glamorized version of oneself) on television as a career. The idea of becoming known or exceptional became much more accessible to the average person. Many of these early reality shows also captured the public's attention due to their rare glimpse into the lives of the rich and famous juxtaposed, showing the relatability of some celebrities with the surreality of extreme wealth or fame. *The Osbournes, Newlyweds: Nick* [Lachey] *and Jessica* [Simpson], and *The Simple Life* made these often larger-than-life characters seem more like everyone else. As celebrities recognized the benefits of allowing the public a glimpse into their lives, they increased their viewers' voyeuristic curiosity while stoking their desire for the same kind of attention. Many people began to feel, however unconsciously, that their lives, with their predictable ups and downs and relational challenges, were suitable for reality television.

As reality television tropes shifted, so did the way we used technology. Increasingly advanced camera cell phones and the social media apps intended for these smart devices were now in the hands of average Americans, connecting them to a constant stream of information about . . . well, anything.

By the mid-2000s, the smartphone compelled people to share themselves and their lives for increasingly public consumption. If you let Paris Hilton tell it, she introduced the world to the "selfie,"[2] a now culturally ingrained manner of taking a photo of oneself often to display on a social media platform. Thus, the subtle shift in self-focused social media also shifted our brains toward seeking validation for displaying ourselves in a particular way. Simple photos of our yummy spaghetti dinner or blurry flip-phone photos of the ocean gave way to curated "food porn" or intricate photo shoots in exotic locales. Image manipulation is nothing new. We need only look at highly stylized 19th-century photos of families and friends to see that image matters, particularly in U.S. culture. What changed with the growth of self-focused social media engagement was that more and more people began to increasingly live for public consumption in much the same way as celebrities and contestants on our favorite reality television shows.

With more and more people desirous of the attention of their peers for a well-styled photo of their vacation to Cabo or pictures showing just how many friends joined us on said trip, our brains began to interpret "likes" with feel-good emotions. In other words, for many, whether they wanted it or not, the sense of personal value and affirmation of their lives became tied to the approval of others. Many studies have now shown the effect of social media interaction on the dopamine signals in the brain, illustrating that those likes serve much the same neurological purpose as a swig of alcohol or a hit of cocaine.[3]

Staging one's photos for optimum likes on Instagram not only became a necessity to ensure that the images we were crafting reflected our desired outcomes. It also became an art form and eventually (as with anything else in a capitalist society) a financial opportunity.

With the increase in the use of social media platforms, namely, Facebook, Instagram, and X (formerly known as Twitter), came the rise in a burgeoning digital economy eager to capitalize on the millions of eyes glued to the screens of their cell phones and computers. Initially, many of these apps were proudly advertising free because Gen X and young millennial-skewed Silicon Valley start-ups valued the innovation of social media connection more than the financial promises it could provide. However, as Facebook, Instagram, and X began to recognize their web spaces' untapped advertising gold mine, it was clear that billions of dollars could be made with the users as the primary marketers. The shift to user-generated marketing spurred the now highly lucrative influencer industry, which is expected to grow to a $199.6 billion industry by 2032.[4]

Cultural influencing isn't a new phenomenon. However, this role was previously occupied by the glamorous elite (e.g., movie stars, athletes, politicians, musicians, and rock stars). The ability to influence cultural trends has traditionally been a marriage between the famous and the marketers and advertisers who capitalized on celebrity fame to sell more products. It wasn't until the mid-20th century that celebrity was used to sell to consumers. For example, if Michael Jackson drank Coca-Cola, the world craved Coca-Cola. By the 2000s, celebrity endorsement of fashion, music, and products was so baked into the cultural landscape that it's easy to forget it wasn't always this way.

Social media, in combination with the narrowing of the fame accessibility gap due to the proliferation of reality television, forced consumer-based industries to shift their idea of credibility and influence to include those outside of the uber-famous elite. By the 2010s, the growth of the internet-influencer economy was in full swing. By

CHAPTER TWO

2016, being a "social media influencer" was considered a legitimate career option for graduating high school seniors. Influencer economics allowed social media–savvy teenagers to leverage their personalities' power for profit without already being famous.

By now, you're probably wondering why we needed to take such an extended detour down the rabbit hole of social media, marketing, and reality television. However, I think the connections between the cultural shift to universal access to media promotion and the rise in typical narcissistic traits, such as feelings of self-importance, grandiosity, superficiality, and external validation seeking, are vital. Even the current Zoomer slang *main character syndrome* refers to people who, because of their sometimes overinflated self-importance, believe themselves to be the stars of their mini reality show. An enlightening conversation with one of my research participants strikingly illustrated this phenomenon:

> I feel like I could totally have my own reality show. I have big main character energy. So, I'm trying to build a big enough audience on TikTok to be the next Addison Rae or Charli D'Amelio. If they can do it, so can I. I'm funny and cute, and people care what I say about stuff; honestly, that's all that matters in the Influencer world. I make anywhere from $500-$800 a post now, which is still "mid," but I'm gaining clout. Anyway, I'm taking a year off from college to prove to my parents that I can be the next big thing. I already have 300 thousand followers on Instagram and 80 thousand on TikTok. I'm manifesting my reality. (Brooklyn, 20, influencer)

I admired Brooklyn's self-confidence; quite honestly, she's earning 100% more than I ever have on any of my social media posts. However, when I asked her to discuss her relationship to self-image and what success means to her, the egocentric focus of her worldview struck me. There's nothing qualitatively wrong with wanting to be an influencer, but having adopted the "main character" role in her life and viewing others in her life as "supporting characters" echoed the objectifying and dissociative language I've heard from other narcissistic clients, rendering fame and notoriety more important than relational depth, authenticity, or quality.

Indeed, to some extent, we're all main characters in the sagas of our lives. However, viewing one's life and relationships as a reality television show primarily for the consumption of others' gaze reinforces one's self-importance and bolsters a superficiality that ostensibly undermines the value of meaningful connection with others outside of their value in increasing one's clout. More disturbingly, Brooklyn's aspirations and influencer-tinged reality world–centric perception isn't unusual, particularly among millennials and Gen Zs in the Western world. That is not to say that everyone who aspires to be an influencer, or even everyone aspiring to fame or notoriety, is a narcissist. However, the increasing social acceptability and celebration of flagrant self-interest and attention-seeking behaviors and motivations are markedly different.

Social Media and Empathy

A student emailed me, anxious to meet about her slipping grades and many missed deadlines. While these frantic emails from students aren't uncommon (particularly around essay due dates or exams), she insisted that she needed help navigating an issue she was sure I could help her with. Upon meeting with her, she popped up on my computer screen for our virtual meeting, visibly tired and anxious:

"Thanks for meeting with me, Dr. Mosley. I'm just really struggling right now in this class because I recently lost like 800 followers on TikTok due to something one of my friends posted on her account about me that portrayed me as racist."

"Well, can you tell me more about the racist portrayal?" I said quizzically.

"It's not the racism part that bothers me. Basically, she recorded me mouthing the 'N' word in an Ice Spice song during a video we were making, and I knew that was wrong, but I was just feeling the lyrics and forgot to edit that out. I'm not worried about people who know me thinking I'm racist because they (and I) know I'm not. I'm more depressed about losing the followers and what it's done to my reputation because I was really building good engagement, and it's all ruined now."

"I see. So it's more what the perception did to your reputation on social media than the perception itself?"

"Exactly! The loss of followers really hit me where it hurts. My followers and engagement are something I'm most proud of in my life. I'll probably get demonetized," she said, almost tearfully.

There is a picture emerging about the role of social media on mental health, and the prognosis is not great, particularly for children and teens. As social media use becomes ubiquitous in the modern world, so, too, do its effects on everything from our self-image to our ability to form and maintain relationships. Before we delve into the adverse effects of social media on mental health, we would be remiss if we didn't acknowledge the positive aspects of social media use.

Social media has increased feelings of social support and connectivity, helping people feel more closely connected to friends, loved ones, and like-minded people worldwide without having to navigate physical distance.[5] Additionally, social media has strengthened awareness of social issues and even played a positive role in assisting in relieving injustices (e.g., police brutality, awareness of the effects of war and genocide, and political transparency). News now travels faster than ever, and as such, events worldwide make it into our awareness in near real time, allowing for more proactivity in situations that require intervention.

That said, a sobering picture of the adverse effects of social media, particularly on young people, is becoming more evident. Bullying, an unfortunate but age-old social effect designed to isolate, humiliate, or shame a perceived outcast or enemy, used to be something that primarily occurred in the presence of the bully and the victim. Social media has allowed bullying to live in the suspended time of the internet and created novel methods for bullies to terrorize victims.

Revenge porn, doxing, digital impersonation to exploit the victim, and much more are only a few of the techniques now available to would-be bullies.

I am thankful (and amused) for my irrational and now retrospectively quaint fear that on my first day of middle school, I would be scooped up by a huge upperclassman named Biff and deposited into the nearest trashcan in front of my peers. Fears of being demonetized, canceled, or doxed on YouTube or TikTok because a friend captured an embarrassing misstep are thus alien to me. Whatever the case, these are the coming-of-age realities that many young people are forced to navigate in addition to the baked-in complexities of adolescence and young adulthood.

Besides cyberbullying, one of the most prominent adverse mental health effects of social media is its degradation of body image and self-esteem, which has become so problematic (particularly for young women and increasingly young men) that many schools have developed task forces to help parents and teachers recognize the signs of body dysmorphia and the subsequent anxiety and depression. Watching near-perfect "normal" people, who in many cases have altered their appearance using now widely available photoshopping apps, apply makeup, do innocuous dances, or talk about an issue triggers an inevitable self-comparison, particularly for young people. Popularity can now reach well beyond one's immediate circle or school, potentially encompassing a much broader audience than what was originally intended. The pressure to keep up with our favorite YouTube, Instagram, or TikTok influencers increases anxiety over deviation from social media beauty, financial, or lifestyle standards, which are often entirely fabricated to perpetuate a myth of perfection and generate clicks and, thus, more revenue.

For those generations who have never known a world without YouTube, Instagram, or Facebook, there is an intuitive ease in navigating online spaces that often makes the heads of anyone born before 1970 spin. Still, the intrinsic technological prowess of younger people comes at a high cost to their mental health. According to the Pew Research Center, as of 2018, 59% of teens have experienced cyberbullying.[6] Additionally, there has been a significant increase in depression and anxiety diagnoses in teens correlated to screen time, which has been charted from 2009 to 2017, and a substantial increase in negative body image in young people due to social media use.[7]

Narcissism as a Collective Shadow

By now, you have probably noticed similar trends I have observed with the rise in social media, celebrity veneration, and the increasingly dissociated world mitigated by technology as the lines between humanity and technology become increasingly blurred by the rise of AI and the increasing effort involved in differentiating what makes us human (i.e., emotional vulnerability, empathy, compassion, and fallibility).

Keeping a close eye on our peers is a "normal" part of human behavior. We like to know that we're on the right track, so to speak, and as such, social comparison arguably aids in progressing ideas and trends and helps to establish norms and mores. The barometer for success has become increasingly unattainable, resulting in increased feelings of comparative inferiority. Post–World War II, success was often measured by embodying the American Dream (e.g., marriage, a modest home, 2.5 children, and a full-time job). While models of the American Dream needed to evolve to be more inclusive to a broader range of identities (and it has), the dream has also become wrought with many problematic expectations exacerbated by social media, fame, wealth veneration, and increasingly complicated sociopolitical limitations.

While we are theoretically more connected to each other than ever, rates of depression, anxiety, loneliness, and stress-related illness have risen steadily because of the internet. For tech-native generations (i.e., millennials, Gen Z, and the emerging Gen Alpha and beyond), an economic and political world full of uncertainty and turmoil inherited from baby boomers and the Silent Generation has created an anxious urgency and given birth to often unrealistic expectations of notoriety, wealth, social acceptance, and admiration.

The game has shifted from keeping up with the Joneses to *Keeping Up with the Kardashians*. Models of success are increasingly predicated on figures who perform their lives demonstrating egocentrism, exhibitionism, and wealth fetishization, and the economy has followed suit. Social media has only strengthened the old American adage of "fake it till you make it" and birthed a new and arguably more toxic fantasy that maybe one day, you, too, will be as valuable as Jay Z and Beyonce, Taylor Swift, Kim Kardashian, or Jeff Bezos. No fantasizing would be problematic if achieving "the good life" didn't mean adopting a value system based on competition, appearance, and a crushing expectation to maintain an aspirational and positive outlook.

Toxic positivity, as it has been aptly named, is ingrained in the American psyche (and increasingly in other cultures). Denial of our vulnerabilities is a cultural value that has made a relatively young America one of the world's primary superpowers. Denial of our collective historical demons has created a predictable cycle of reliving indignities and traumas that threatens the very fiber of our collective psyches and creates a compensatory (and erosive) focus on wealth, power, and success by any means necessary that lays over the nation like a dark blanket. "Good vibes only" means that we deny our sensitivities while simultaneously becoming increasingly more sensitive and insecure in ways that exacerbate toxic relational strategies.

Canceling the Shadow

"Canceling" anyone we deem problematic, initially reserved for egregious offenders of moral decency, has become commonplace. Many discussions around the proliferation of "cancel culture" are frequently peppered with thinly veiled ideological biases and a way for toxic individuals to maintain their toxicity. However, the emphasis on canceling, rather than redemption, teaching, or compassionate reintegration, reflects a growing refusal to acknowledge the cultural and psychological shadows that cancelable behaviors evoke. That is not to say that some ideologies and violent behaviors don't deserve to be canceled (e.g., sexism, homophobia, transphobia, racism, and religious intolerance), but canceling the people who commit the offense has been shown only to strengthen their position. In many cases, public shaming only produces more shame and dysfunction. The inability of a culture to discern nuance reflects the growth of a collective refusal to acknowledge the human tendency to fail. This also demonstrates a rejection of forgiveness, imperfection, and as such, the ability to acknowledge vulnerabilities (which are decisively narcissistic traits).

As we become theoretically more tolerant of differing identities, lifestyles, and expressions of humanity, we have become increasingly opposed to acknowledging our shadows by stuffing them into a proverbial closet bathed in a toxic neon light. Instead, we hustle and grind to the top, documenting our successes (real or imagined) on Instagram, Facebook, or TikTok. At the same time, we strive to overcome our snarling demons in a shiny veneer of American ingenuity and image management.

Narcissism, Violence, and Dissociation

Egocentrism, dissociation, and an abject terror of inadequacy or inferiority breed a particularly toxic set of behaviors in the human psyche. The more disconnected we become from ourselves and, subsequently, each other, the easier it becomes to justify various forms of violence. Once the empathy circuitry is interrupted by trauma, acting in compassionate or regenerative ways to ourselves and others becomes increasingly more difficult. Feelings of inferiority and the need to be something or someone in the eyes of ourselves or others are relatively normal consequences of having an ego.

The ego needs others to exist and would prefer to be seen by others as valuable or worthy. However, the ego is notorious for distorting perceived disapproval, rejection, abandonment, or insult and thus quickly becomes fixated on ensuring its survival through various forms of posturing designed to prove to itself and other fixated egos that it matters. In some cases, chronic stressors test the ego's ability to balance and begin to create a schism that sees itself as fundamentally separate from everything else and, in some cases, a subsequent desire to harm or eliminate those who threaten its perceived survival. Violence inflicted on another due to perceived "otherness" (compared to literal survival-based violence) is arguably the result of an inability to sense one's shared humanity.

Narcissism is often considered an interpersonal relational style because the narcissists see themselves as exempt, exceptional, or unique compared to others around them. Their sense of importance creates an identity divide so vast that many implicitly believe that their needs, desires, emotions, and problems are more important than others' and that others should behave accordingly. In many cases, narcissists (depending on their personality style) will employ various forms of manipulation and covert and overt forms of interpersonal violence to ensure that their needs and desires are met. Their intolerance of feelings of vulnerability, negative emotion, or compensation for a real or imagined sense of inferiority (or superiority) can sometimes erupt, causing them to lash out at those they believe are creating these emotional states.

Heartbreakingly, we see this playing out in an obviously gendered and increasingly dangerous drama on the cultural stage, starring men as the aggrieved yet historically "superior" arbiters of corrective justice. An excellent *Atlantic* article by Tom Nichols, *The Narcissism of the Angry Young Men*, aptly noted that the collective feelings of inferiority in young men, exacerbated by a toxic masculine animus that tells them women and sexual minorities are phasing them out, are radicalized by extreme ideological positions built on the perception of their decreased cultural value.[8] Nichols writes:

> The Lost Boys are mostly young and male, largely middle- or working-class. Frustrated by their own social awkwardness, they are so often described as "loners" that the trope has been around from as early as the 1980s. But these young males, no matter how "quiet," are filled with an astonishing level of enraged resentment and entitlement about their roles as men, and they seek rationalizations for inflicting violence on a society they think has both

ignored and injured them. They become what the German writer Hans Magnus Enzensberger called "radical losers," unsuccessful men who feel that they have been denied their dominant role in society and who then channel their blunted male social impulses toward destruction.[9]

And they are, above all, staggeringly narcissistic. Almost all of the recent mass killers, for example, thought they had a special mission in the world. We know this because they felt compelled to tell us so.

When thousands of years of assumed gender superiority meet increasingly equitable professional spaces, growing educational disparities (women are now overall more educated than men), rampant loneliness, dissociation, and easily accessible unmoderated virtual spaces filled with hateful rhetoric meet a young, disenchanted male ego, violence (either self- or other-inflicted) becomes inevitable. In fact, the 2024 US presidential election result was deemed by many political scientists to be the inevitable by-product of the bruised, aggrieved collective masculine seeking to regain its perceived lost power and influence in a rapidly changing social and political hierarchy.

Violence isn't always physical, and we can see this evidenced in the uptick in hate crimes; extreme ideological rhetoric; and a noticeable increase in adult and adolescent anxiety, pessimism about the future, and cynicism about the nature of human goodness. Empathy has all but exited the political world, and our fascination with exaggerated egotism, unapologetic and often brash expressions, and power have given rise to increasingly more flagrant narcissistic political figures worldwide. The rejection of vulnerability and the subsequent fear of "the other" has helped redefine political discourse. Those with authoritarian leanings have gained favor with increasingly larger swathes of people in the West. The desire for a "strong man" represents more of the rejection of our collective weakness and a sign that people would rather consolidate power in a blustery influential leader with egregiously simple solutions to complex problems than do the challenging social, cultural, and emotional work of creating lasting equitable change. When a public figure, particularly a public servant and their public or constituents, view apologizing for a transgression (even a flagrantly unethical or illegal one) as a sign of weakness, you know we're in trouble.

Okay, So Now What?

So how do we fix this mess? The remainder of this book will provide some clues as to how to both recognize and understand narcissism from the eyes of narcissists themselves and, as such, find solutions for undoing or, at least, loosening the vice of narcissistic armoring strategies. Much of this book will be an exercise in radical empathy as we view the world through the narcissist's eyes; I will provide psychological or psychosocial context and potential explanations for their behavior because understanding breeds compassion.

Throughout this chapter, I have provided a glimpse into how narcissism has influenced different aspects of human behavior. While we've focused primarily on the growth of narcissism in the larger social world, we must view the issue from a completely holistic perspective. Much of *The Narcissist in You and Everyone Else* was focused on the psychological or subjective expression of narcissism through the lens of the various personality types. However, we are going to expand our perspective to see how narcissism at the individual level has a knock-on effect on everything and virtually everyone who encounters narcissistic energy.

For a moment, let's consider human behavior from the point of view of quantum entanglement (which exemplifies an emerging field called quantum social behavior). The quantum scientific worldview increasingly recognizes the interrelatedness of the universe. An article on the space news and blog site space.com quite eloquently defined quantum entanglement as "a bizarre, counterintuitive phenomenon that explains how two subatomic particles can be intimately linked to each other even if separated by billions of light-years of space."[10] Put even more simply, this theory assumes that the universe is intrinsically (and often mysteriously) interconnected whereby each action, event, feeling, and thought affects something else, even across vast distances. From this premise, we can assume that the social world, which is just a collection of human subatomic particles, is subject to the laws of quantum entanglement. And, therefore, narcissism at any level (i.e., individual, familial, social, or institutional) has far-reaching and often indiscernible effects on the world at large.

Many know that our behavior can affect those around us, and some know that our emotions can have similar (albeit more subtle) effects. Narcissism is not only a set of behaviors influenced by a psychological perspective predicated on protecting one's vulnerability. It is also an emotional energy and ideological viewpoint that constructs the world in polarized dichotomies (e.g., winning/losing, right/wrong, weak/strong, and good/bad) that contribute to a degradation of nuance to both the narcissist and those with whom they interact.

So, while many are focused on the genuine and prescient psychological and interpersonal consequences (and, at times, benefits) of narcissism, to find a more effective means of healing its damage means also addressing the cultural, societal, and institutional systems that are simultaneously created and influenced by narcissistic attitudes.

Quantum Narcissistic Trauma

Let's explore an analogy to illustrate the principle of quantum narcissistic trauma and its far-reaching effects. Consider for a moment that your father, growing up, exhibited behaviors and attitudes that demonstrated a lack of emotional vulnerability, self-inflation, denial of weakness, selfishness, a focus on competition and winning, entitlement, and an often braggadocious or boastful manner of speaking. You never quite knew how to classify his behavior, and when your partner suggested the term *narcissism*, you felt it was too harsh, unwarranted, or mean. You prefer to describe your father as "difficult" yet as an adult, decide to limit your interactions with him to decrease your stress and prevent conflict. Having become inoculated early to a set of narcissistic relational strategies, you then become accustomed to viewing romantic partners, friends, or coworkers who exhibit these characteristics as familiar at best and comforting at worst.

You continue to work at a job where your boss, although a woman, displays the same cold detachment and invulnerability as your father because she's a "good boss" despite her flagrant mistreatment of other colleagues who are less adept at managing her massive ego. Despite your better judgment and the similar feelings of invalidation, anger, and sadness these types of people sometimes evoke, you view their behaviors as "quirks" of the personality, thus strengthening your tolerance to narcissistic behaviors. Subsequently, you, too, have internalized some of your dad's denial of weakness and refusal to back down as a show of strength and begin to suppress your sensitivities and vulnerabilities (maybe not to the extent of your father). Still, nobody likes a crybaby, and everyone loves a winner, right? You often hear yourself repeating the refrains to "toughen up" to your children, particularly your more sensitive child who seems disinterested in competition and cries a little too much for your comfort (particularly since your father openly expressed his disdain for the weak one).

You then find that when choosing a candidate in your local governor's race, you choose one who exhibits qualities similar to your dad's. You're more likely to excuse the growing public displays of unethical, unkind, flagrantly boastful, and harsh treatment of others because you want to believe that underneath the blustery bravado lies someone who really cares because you know and must believe that your father loves you (even though he rarely, if ever, said it). Luckily, for various reasons, some similar to yours, others shared your belief in the candidate's rough and tough cowboy-esque exterior, believing he would be your state's most effective leader if elected.

Your guy is elected due to the collective endorsement of his "difficult" qualities as solid leadership, and many (like you) feel safer under the protection of someone who "won't back down." In his first few months as governor, he enacts increasingly unkind, controversial, and outrageous policies that highlight his disdain for others and high opinion of himself. Your newly minted governor quickly finds himself embroiled in various financial scandals, public feuds with other leaders and citizens, and an unabashed refusal to apologize. You look the other way, publicly steadfast in your choice (although privately regretful), because to deny him becomes subconsciously anathema to denying your father.

Through a series of unconscious or semiconscious choices harkening back to your childhood, you have now unwittingly participated in helping to reproduce the trauma you experienced from your father's narcissism. Your choices are exacerbated by the fact that you have yet to name and identify that your dad's behavior and attitudes reflect underlying narcissism. Of course, this says nothing about how much you love or respect your father's positive contributions to your life and your development as a person, but denying the shadow that has now followed you throughout most of your relationships, from the interpersonal to the institutional, has contributed to the strengthening and unconscious endorsement of his more objectionable traits as acceptable. Your choices and psychological resonance with toxic behavior like this affected not just you but potentially hundreds to thousands of people whom you will never meet.

As we move forward, we're going to delve into the four primary spheres that influence our world, not only what narcissism looks like in the subjective, social, cultural, and institutional spheres of human life, but also explore some potential remedies for challenging or reshaping or healing narcissistic attitudes to move toward greater compassion and empathy in humanity.

CHAPTER THREE
IT STARTS WITH I
Narcissism Begins

In this chapter, we'll explore three cases that will serve as our access point for the remainder of the book as we explore the far-reaching effects of narcissism. To understand the holistic effect of narcissism, which we'll discuss further in Chapter 6, we need to understand the formative psychological and subjective experiences of encapsulated narcissists.

The following case studies are composites of various clients' narratives, with generous modifications and fictionalizations for privacy and effect. Additionally, we will focus on three distinct subtypes of narcissism (*The Gleeful Charlatan*, *The Entitled Caregiver*, and *The Charismatic Bully*), with supporting characters of the other six overall narcissistic categories to provide color and intertextual richness. That said, many of the behaviors, childhood experiences, emotional orientations, and intra- and interpersonal strategies are shared among all 27 narcissistic subtypes, even if the focus and rules of engagement change from subtype to subtype. This is because narcissism, as previously discussed, is an armoring or overlay that influences the personality type's focus and interpersonal strategies depending on the ego's specific fixation. As we'll see in Chapter 4, the interpersonal strategies (breadcrumbing, gaslighting, goalpost moving, blame deflection) are shared (to a greater or lesser degree) among almost all narcissists regardless of subtype.

CHAPTER THREE

The case studies are written from an omniscient perspective. They provide a bird's-eye view of the subject and a glimpse into how their histories affect their internal processes, psychological defense strategies, and interpersonal strategies. These are certainly not exhaustive psychological profiles because they would be beyond the scope of this book. However, this chapter will provide the foundation for holistically understanding the effect of their behaviors and thought processes.

Luke

The Gleeful Charlatan (SO): *Slick, exaggerating, and charismatic, this subtype staves off fears of boredom or stagnation by engaging others in their grandiose visions for the future. Often convincing and likable, they easily lie to support their ideas, plans, or schemes. They are skilled charlatans and may garner trust from others only to later evade or relinquish responsibility for details if their plans go awry. They can be fraudulent, overconfident, and irresponsible.*

Jocelyn was an unassuming but devoted elementary school teacher. Her husband, Julio, worked as an insurance salesman. They built a comfortable, average, middle-class life quickly after being married. They thoroughly enjoyed creating their life together but were even more thrilled that they would welcome a baby boy into the world a few years into their marriage. Generally, Jocelyn had a passive and anxious personality, but she found that as her pregnancy progressed, she was increasingly more nervous and had a low threshold for stress.

Julio, raised in a traditional Mexican household, had integrated his fair share of traits from his father, who frowned on too much emotional expression or demonstrations of weakness or vulnerability. He deeply loved his wife but struggled to empathize with her fretting. He dealt with it the best way he knew how, telling her, "Don't worry; everything's going to be fine." Some of Jocelyn's anxiety centered around how they were going to parent their child, knowing that while she wanted to raise a child with more emotional intelligence than Julio had, she worried he would undermine her efforts, fearing that "coddling" the child would result in having a weak son. For the most part, Jocelyn was thrilled to embark on this new adventure as a parent, but her trepidation couldn't quiet her concerns about the future.

As Jocelyn neared her due date, she and Julio increasingly fought because he was unable to understand her emotionality. Rather than learning how to comfort his wife, he grew more distant, afraid to engage with her lest he upset her even further. Julio's emotional withdrawal felt like a slap in the face from a man who already suffered from low emotional intelligence. She gave birth to a healthy, smiling baby boy, Lucas (Luke), and despite the everyday chaos associated with caring for a newborn, the two found themselves in a state of new-baby bliss.

It wasn't long before disagreements began about sleep training and how and when to console Luke. Predictably, Julio felt that unless Luke needed a diaper change or was ill or hungry, his "fussing" could be ignored, because he was looking for attention. To compensate for Julio's more detached approach, Jocelyn paid excessive attention to her son, often missing opportunities for adult time with her husband to focus on Luke. Julio grew increasingly jealous of Luke, and because Jocelyn was more attached to Luke, he felt a simmering resentment toward both his son and wife, which he processed by pouring himself more into his professional life. He believed that his primary role was to be a provider for his family and thus left the bulk of the parenting to Jocelyn, outside of disciplinary endeavors, which Jocelyn found challenging to execute.

By the time Luke was 4, he had learned that Mommy provided him with the praise and attention he craved and Daddy was only interested when he excelled at something. Luke was thrilled when he came home from school and showed his father that he had won Star Kid at day care. His father's wanting him to grow up and follow in his footsteps to become an athlete and be the first man in his family to go to college began to encourage Luke to be a winner at any cost. Luke realized early that he had to be exceptional to gain his

CHAPTER THREE

father's attention, while his mother seemed to indulge and encourage his every wish.

By first grade, Luke had developed an outgoing and gregarious personality. He quickly made friends at school and found that he could gain the approval and attention of his teachers by being helpful, innovative, and funny. He loved attention, particularly toward women, but developed an intensely competitive attitude toward his male classmates. Because Luke established himself as a Star Kid in his short academic career, Jocelyn and Julio were surprised to receive a call to attend a one-on-one meeting with Luke's teacher to discuss Luke's "concerning behavior."

Luke's teacher, Mrs. Lancaster, shared with Jocelyn and Julio that Luke displayed aggressive tendencies toward his classmates, particularly during competitions, such as mini spelling bees held in the classroom and especially field day activities where trophies or awards were given. Upon winning, Luke would exhibit a pattern of gloating endlessly to his peers that he had won (albeit in a joking way) and, upon losing, would become enraged and threatening to his classmates, teachers, and coaches. Julio brushed off Mrs. Lancaster's concerns, stating, "He's a competitive boy, and that's what's going to make him succeed." Similarly, Jocelyn was offended by the suggestion that her sweet boy was criticized since his grades and academic performance were among the best in the class. Julio was proud of his son for exhibiting the same kind of competitive spirit he had, and concerns about his wife's "coddling" proved to be unfounded since he seemed "on the right track."

Jocelyn privately worried that he was developing the less desirable characteristics of her husband because Luke often avoided sharing anything that he didn't feel was positive or wouldn't garner praise or attention. Jocelyn also noticed that Luke struggled to understand the value of sharing with classmates and cousins. He frequently took opportunities to grab his favorite position as the center of attention, often inappropriately launching into comedy routines of knock-knock jokes and magic tricks meant to capture adults' attention while also stealing the spotlight from his cousin or other children.

Over time, Luke grew increasingly adept at managing his aggression and displayed greater self-control. By high school, Luke had gained a reputation for being well liked, popular, and funny. He frequently found himself in positions of power as he pursued soccer to demonstrate his athletic prowess. Luke was also a staple on student councils throughout middle and high school and had garnered a reputation for being the class clown. While he typically dodged disciplinary action, he became infamous for his pranks (often at other students' and teachers' expense).

From as early as Luke can remember, he felt his mother loved him more than his dad. However, he was strangely annoyed with his mother's emotional gushing and naivety to his manipulation strategies. He knew that his mother would always do whatever she could to ensure his happiness, and at times, he would push the limits to see how much he could get away with before she reprimanded him. From his perspective, her lack of boundaries was a major character flaw; although his father often came across as disapproving, he admired Luke's grit. Luke hated showing emotion because it reminded him of his mom, and he never wanted anyone to be able to manipulate him the way he was able to manipulate her. He attributed this to her softheartedness and accommodating demeanor. While he found those qualities admirable in specific contexts (particularly as they related to him), he often felt like this allowed his father to "walk all over her."

Luke learned to approach his mother when he wanted sympathy or to do something his father would generally object to. As early as five years old, Luke remembered that all he had to do was whine a little, compliment her, and show her affection, and without fail, she would acquiesce. In those times, he felt like he loved her more because he admittedly hated when people told him no, in any capacity. To avoid being denied, Luke convinced others that what he wanted was what others wanted. Of course, people rarely said no to him

CHAPTER THREE

because of his undeniable charisma, persuasive skills, and slightly threatening demeanor.

On occasions when charm wasn't effective, Luke would resort to intimidation or lying and doing what he wanted to do anyway. Luke generally avoided conflict but wasn't averse if it meant missing out on something he wanted or believed he deserved. He thought people would want to give him what he wanted because he was funny, charming, and interesting. He also interpreted no as a lack of love and unconsciously felt his father's disapproval, filling him with shame and embarrassment.

Underneath Luke's confident, charismatic, and gregarious persona lurked a persistent feeling of not being enough. He could almost hear his father's critical, unemotional voice whispering constantly in his mind. When he gained the attention of a group, won a game, made someone laugh, or got what he wanted, he felt like a winner. Unfortunately, those moments weren't as plentiful as he would like, so he frequently felt, embarrassingly, like a loser. Most of the time, he could shake the feeling of inferiority, and by high school, he found that having a girlfriend and a large clique of popular friends helped boost his self-esteem.

Luke was an average-looking kid, but his personality and charisma helped him immensely in the dating world. He found it easy to approach women and won them over quickly with his sense of humor and tendency toward flattery, compliments, and feigned attention to others, a tactic he perfected early with his mother.

What Luke liked most about having a girlfriend was that he seemed to have a more constant stream of attention and admiration. He would gladly perform grand gestures; give gifts to his girlfriends; and shower friends and partners with encouraging, positive affirmation. However, he became moody, anxious, and petulant if they didn't reciprocate. He found the easiest way to regain control of the relationship was to pull away, remembering that when he would do this with his mother, she often sought him out more aggressively. Luke fancied himself a bit of a martyr for his loved ones and friends because he felt almost everyone was more boring than he, constantly suppressing his energy for the group overall.

From his friends' and partners' perspectives, Luke was hot and cold, alternating between being generous, funny, and complimentary to withholding, cold, and selfish. He would become distant and punitive if others weren't available or responsive to his constant need to be positive and happy.

His friends cycled depending on the school year, their popularity, and his constant need for change and variation. They found Luke's need to be the center of attention exhausting. Nonetheless, they also enjoyed the social capital his popularity afforded them. Luke repeatedly declared himself the pack leader, deciding who was in or out depending on how cool or relevant he felt they were. His best friend, Jack, whom he'd met in second grade, was a staple, but he figured out that remaining "in" with Luke required a dedication to unequivocally allowing Luke to be the star of the show. Jack frequently cleaned up Luke's interpersonal messes, apologizing for distasteful jokes; disrespectful or dismissive behavior; or in some cases, flat-out bullying behavior. Having intuited the vulnerability behind Luke's boastful nature, Jack empathized with him, realizing he needed far more validation than most.

Luke developed a keen interest in politics in college and had prominent student government roles throughout his school career. He was a natural politician and passionately felt the world needed strong, decisive leaders who were also entertaining and likable. By his senior year, Luke had begun dating his future wife, Kerri. Luke and Kerri felt an immediate attraction to one another, and because Luke had dated plenty of women in college, he decided it was time to settle down and find "wife material." Kerri was (not unlike his best friend, Jack) accepting and passive and, in many ways, mimicked the characteristics of his mother. On some level, Luke knew he needed people close to him who wouldn't try to upstage him. Kerri saw his gifts, strengths, and talents and could more easily forgive the parts of him others criticized.

Since middle school, Luke had heard what he believed to be unfair assessments and criticisms of his character. Adjectives such as *selfish*, *annoying*, *smug*, and *manipulative* were peppered between the more frequent praises he preferred to internalize. Thus, he developed a method of completely dismissing criticisms and mentally adopted the phrase "losers are always haters" to avoid reflecting on his faults and shortcomings. Criticism evoked intolerable shame and made him feel like a punished child. After a particularly intense fight when an ex-girlfriend suggested that he consider going to therapy to uncover "the roots of his aggression," he was particularly offended. Luke found introspection (particularly emotionally charged pursuits such as therapy) to be activities entertained only by friendless losers. Since then, his disdain for mental health or any topic related to psychological health has been rage inducing and triggering. Similarly, he resented the emerging emphasis on mental health and emotional exploration in the cultural zeitgeist and integrated this into his political ideologies and leadership style, believing, like his father often repeated, that people need to toughen up.

By the time Luke graduated college, the foundations of his personality were well set. He had adequately positioned himself for entry into a prestigious law school and, if he had his way (which he usually did), a successful career in politics.

Understanding Luke

Luke had a relatively "normal" childhood. Like most parents, his didn't get everything right either, but they were consistent overall, providing a stable ground for Luke to thrive and succeed. Julio's lack of emotional intelligence likely hindered Luke's emotional development and played a role in Luke's avoidance and unconscious shame around vulnerable emotional displays. Conversely, while adoring, Jocelyn missed opportunities to help Luke understand the value of no and the necessity of limits and consequences. Because Jocelyn overcompensated for Julio's emotional avoidance by doting and enabling, Luke received mixed messages about genuine love and affection. Luke viewed his mother's tendency to capitulate to his whims and demands for attention as a representation of love. He also viewed her seeming fear of criticism or rebuke, even of his transgressive behavior, as weak, diminishing his trust in his mother and the world to hold him accountable.

Like all children, Luke needed boundaries and limitations. Instead, he learned that manipulation and deception pushed his mother (and later the broader social world) to bend to his desires. For those with a propensity toward narcissism, boundaries are essential to developing healthy communication. The earlier boundaries and respect for others' needs and wants are reinforced, the more likely a person will be able to demonstrate empathy or at least respect for others.

Julio's engaging with Luke depending on whether Luke demonstrated traits Julio deemed masculine and aspirational also significantly shaped Luke's self-worth and value. While Luke appears to exhibit high self-esteem and self-worth, this is an overcompensation for deep feelings of inferiority and valuelessness. Luke received the most attention when he was entertaining, funny, and a winner. While his mother freely gave him the attention he craved, he seems to be living life unconsciously, seeking attention and praise from a withholding father. Also, ironically, Luke expects others to be adoring (like his mother).

On the other hand, he appears to project his disapproval and thwarted desires onto the world at large, creating the characteristic narcissistic rage.[1] Luke's "thwarted wanting" ignites his entitlement and anger. Luke fundamentally wants others to like him, and he has learned that his value lies in his ability to charm, entertain, and dazzle others, which also positions him as superior.

Attention seeking and wanting to entertain others do not constitute narcissism. Similarly, being charismatic, funny, and wanting to be successful are not endemic to narcissism. However, ego armor is reinforced when these desires consistently override our ability to empathize with others or create interpersonal strategies that rely on manipulation, intimidation, or callousness, making it difficult to make real connections with others.

Luke seems unable to allow for exploration of his interior world, creating a relationship with life and others that relies on surface emotions and the promise of praise, attention, and admiration, which make him the star of the show and others secondary.

As *The Gleeful Charlatan*, Luke prioritizes pleasure and fun, creating an environment that allows him to bypass his negative emotions. His need for approval and acceptance by the larger social group affords him more self-control than some of the other hedonistic, narcissistic subtypes because he is more aware of his image and thus strives to maintain a level of social acceptability.

> Some people of this subtype are not overtly malignant but may enjoy deceiving or rabble-rousing others. They can have a solid mischievous or antisocial streak and trouble following rules or regulations. They may also be proponents of chaos as a philosophy and embrace anarchy as a way of life. However, unlike the antisocial, narcissistic [Powerful Aggressive] subtypes, the Gleeful Charlatan is typically upbeat, which helps them get away with far more than they possibly should. They utilize their spritely and gregarious interpersonal skills to circumvent consequences if possible.[2]

It is precisely Luke's social focus that has led him to consider a political career. His career choice is an ideal fit in many ways given his high need for attention and charismatic and socially conscious personality. While he will undoubtedly provide his constituents with a dazzling show and plenty of entertainment, we will see that his frivolity; superficiality; and disdain for interiority, restriction, and vulnerable emotionality color his leadership style in a way that can devastate others.

Possible Interventions for Change

Luke has many redeemable qualities. His humor, charisma, and general positivity are excellent assets. While Luke may not be amenable to therapy because of its negative connotation, he may be more open to something like life coaching, which could help him explore introspection and self-reflection on his behavior with others without the negative stigma. Luke's narcissism functions at a mild to moderate level, and it's likely that in his younger years, it had yet to cause significant impairments that would cause him to seek intervention. Luke's emotional literacy is low, and he hasn't been equipped with many tools from either of his parents on how to identify or name emotions. This is difficult for many people, not just narcissists, so helping Luke gain a deeper understanding of the underlying emotions surrounding his flare-ups of bullying or denial of vulnerability might help him garner more profound insights into why he occasionally finds himself in conflict when he seemingly seeks fun and positivity.

A clinician or coach working with Luke might give him simple, tangible ways to manage his inner world, name emotions, and express them more appropriately, which would go a long way. For example, showing Luke the feelings wheel, which indicates the five basic emotions—anger, sadness, happiness, disgust, and fear and their sub-emotional states—might help him identify what's happening internally without seeming too daunting or overly introspective. That said, like most narcissists, most of Luke's emotional world would be relegated to happiness, disgust, or anger because he would vehemently deny the presence of sadness or fear.

People of Luke's narcissistic subtype tend to deny anything negative, although it could be argued that many narcissists deny negativity for fear of looking weak. The denial of vulnerability becomes the very obstacle that prevents narcissistic people from forming deep relationships and often leaves them with feelings of emptiness and pointlessness, particularly as they age. While it would be unlikely that Luke would appear in a therapeutic setting, people around him who did have an awareness of his narcissistic tendencies could help foster a sense of personal responsibility by developing healthy boundaries. As we'll see in the following two chapters, his narcissistic traits become most problematic in relational and social dynamics, and his propensity toward manipulation and bullying becomes more prescient the more power and influence he garners in the outside world.

While it's often exceedingly difficult to extend narcissistic people empathy, particularly when on the receiving end of their mistreatment, meeting someone like Luke with hostility or attempting to

CHAPTER THREE

compete with him, or worse yet, shame him, will only strengthen his resolve not to be seen as inferior and increase his feelings of intense shame. Extending him grace without sacrificing boundaries or allowing him to manipulate or wash away problems is thus a more sustainable and realistic approach.

Sue

The Entitled Caregiver (SP): Demanding, histrionic, and manipulative, this subtype believes they are more valuable, supportive, and helpful than others and thus deserving of special treatment and the satiation of their desires. They alternate between giving others what they believe they need and demanding (often covertly) that they receive the best money can buy. They can be dramatic, ingratiating, and prideful.

When Li and her husband, Zhou, first arrived in the United States from China to pursue their bachelor's degrees in economics and physics, respectively, they were unsure if they could make a life for themselves in the United States after years of struggling financially. Li and Zhou were extraordinarily hard working and focused much of their attention on academic success and building a solid economic foundation. When they decided to start trying to conceive a child, Li was unsure if they would have success due to an underlying medical condition that she was told would make getting pregnant and, particularly, carrying a child more difficult. However, after only a few months of trying, Zhou and Li were expecting their first child, whom they decided they would name Sue after Li's grandmother. Both were thrilled to welcome a new life into the world but held persistent anxieties over succeeding in the United States. Zhou had been accepted into a prestigious physics graduate program, while Li received a graduate fellowship in economics upon graduation.

Li was always emotionally reticent, authoritative, stern, and results oriented. Meanwhile, Zhou was more emotionally sensitive yet gentle and passive. Zhou often deferred to Li for major decisions and detested conflict. They both decided they would raise their daughter with the values that would instill a sense of drive, determination, and success so that she, too, could bring honor to her family. Like many other Chinese parents, Li believed that while they wanted Sue to enjoy being a child, she must also have a strong sense of discipline and must learn very early not to inflict shame upon her family, culture, or herself. The first few years of Sue's childhood were relatively carefree, and she was instilled with a strong sense of appropriateness and manners while still being allowed to make mistakes as any toddler might.

By the time Sue was three years old, Li had begun searching for preschools to help build the foundations of a high academic achiever. Although outside of their budget, she found a prestigious Montessori school that would help ensure Sue's future academic success. While Zhou and Li's financial situation was steadily improving, they were not yet where they wanted to be, and the stress of trying to achieve as immigrants created an atmosphere whereby their home life left little room for fun or levity. Sue was enrolled in ballet classes, piano lessons, and preschool by four years old. She also worked with a language tutor to help her learn English more fluently to switch seamlessly between Mandarin and English.

When Sue was five years old, a school speech pathologist diagnosed her with dyslexia and dyscalculia. Li (insulted by the diagnosis) refused to place Sue in a special education class to help her develop the skills necessary to manage and improve her reading, writing, and arithmetic neurodivergence. By first grade, Sue realized she struggled more than the other children with reading, writing, and math. She excelled in music, dance, and art and preferred her father's passive approach to her mother's stern, critical parenting style. Her teachers always commented on Sue's willingness to assist other students and teachers. They also noted that Sue seemed to become very emotional, with a propensity toward temper tantrums, if she didn't get special treatment. She loved being chosen first for games and, if possible, would position herself as the group leader so she could "be in charge." She was particularly infuriated during snack time because she always felt she deserved more snacks than the other children because she was helpful to her peers and the teachers.

CHAPTER THREE

Sue's entitled behavior wasn't unfamiliar to Li and Zhou, who were used to her offering to help around the house, drawing a picture, or being exceptionally affectionate and then pouting over being denied her whims or desires. Zhou was likelier to acquiesce to Sue's tantrums, secretly buying her toys, cookies, and other gifts despite her mother's insistence that he was "spoiling her rotten." Li cared less about Sue's helpfulness and more about her academic performance. She was openly disdainful of Sue's propensity toward art and her effusive, emotional, and often cloying manner of endearing herself to others to get what she wanted.

Sue's ability to charm others afforded her some friends and equally as many enemies because she often cycled through best friends weekly. Not liking to be told no, Sue could easily fall out with a current best friend because they failed to follow her orders or for seemingly no discernible reason. Despite her willful and bossy demeanor in social situations, she was noticeably well behaved and more disciplined in ballet classes and the once-a-week art class she begged her father to enroll her in, provided she improved her schoolwork. Sue was simultaneously very independent and needed copious amounts of attention from others.

By nine years old, Sue developed a dynamic with her parents where she aligned herself almost entirely with her father and opposed her mother's strictness. However, because out-and-out rebellion is highly discouraged in Chinese culture, she began to experience shame and anger at not being able to do the same things as her white peers. In fact, Li was constantly reminding Sue that to succeed as a Chinese American, she had to try harder and achieve more than her white counterparts. Sue was an enigma to her mother, confused by her alternatingly loving, generous, and dutiful nature and the self-involved, dramatic, and flagrantly selfish outbursts that lay below the surface of her sweetness.

By the time Sue was in high school, she had a small group of stable friends and had begun seeing the benefits of the dyslexia counseling she secretly sought at school to avoid her mother's judgment. She dropped out of ballet in her freshman year to pursue becoming a cheerleader and seemed to enjoy the popularity and social capital it afforded her. Being a cheerleader wasn't her mother's vision of success; she knew, though, that extracurricular activities would help Sue's college prospects, so she allowed it. While generally well liked, Sue had gotten a reputation for being a "princess" since she often flaunted designer labels and other status symbols purchased mainly by her father. Despite her princess-like persona, she also enjoyed being the special friend to whom others divulged their secrets, although she was also widely known as a gossip.

From Sue's perspective, she's always been a relatively sensitive person when it comes to her feelings, emotions, and concerns. She always felt like her mother "didn't get her," and thus, she was more bonded with her father, who understood that she was worthy of what she needed and wanted. Since the age of five, she had loved receiving gifts, and she made her birthday a weeklong affair during which she insisted on being adored and catered. She felt she wasn't honored or appreciated enough because she had earned the right to be cared for and pampered. She saw her mother as cold and unfeeling and, thus, from an early age, strove to do everything the opposite of her mother. She also profoundly resented her mother for not agreeing to put her in the special education classes she needed to excel in school, thus experiencing incredible shame and embarrassment from having fallen behind the other students in reading and math.

Sue took great pride in her artistic abilities, particularly painting and dance, and her keen people skills, allowing her to easily win friends. She learned very early on that by flattering her father, she could increase the likelihood of getting what she wanted, a skill she adopted seamlessly into her other relationships.

Because Sue's father adored her, she, in turn, became a "Daddy's girl" and was uncharacteristically compliant and deferred to her father most of the time. She would often fix him breakfast on Saturday mornings before her mother awakened and took an interest in all his

CHAPTER THREE

favorite television shows and sports teams. She knew her closeness with her father angered her mother, making her even more determined to demonstrate their bond. By contrast, her mother seemed constantly annoyed by Sue, notably when she showed emotion, which Sue recalls would only make her cry, scream, or pout more aggressively. Additionally, Li's constant reminder of Sue's Chinese identity made her feel inadequate and, at times, shameful since she wanted to be accepted and liked by the white girls at school.

Sue reshaped her image in high school as a stylish, gregarious, and vibrant personality. She gained a reputation for being a diva, which she liked because she often sought to set herself apart in ways that made her seem superior. She wanted to have designer clothes or other markers of success, letting her friends and peers know that her dad would buy her whatever she wanted. And, indeed, Zhou spared no expense for his little girl. She, however, loved to help support people, including teachers and coaches, and would frequently position herself close to others because, in her mind, it was always good to have "friends in high places." Sue took great pride in influencing people to get what she wanted. She was also an effective leader and was elected in her senior year to chair the homecoming dance committee due to her discerning eye and uncompromising and militant approach to getting things done.

Sue always felt like the other girls in her school viewed her as inferior and thus always made an extra effort to ensure she was always well dressed and groomed and communicated some level of glamor or prestige. Her best friend, Jenny, a reserved, bookish, and unassuming first-generation Asian American student, had become her "right hand" since they met in fifth grade. Sue felt like Jenny needed her and thus often viewed Jenny like a project, dispensing advice about virtually every aspect of Jenny's life. In turn, Jenny was agreeable and always eager to please Sue. On the rare occasion that Jenny would push back on one of Sue's demands or suggestions, Sue would become cold and dismissive. In fact, after a particularly heated fight in their sophomore year over Jenny's inability to attend Sue's birthday celebration because she had to go to her grandfather's funeral, Sue made it a point to befriend one of Jenny's enemies. Sue refused to speak to Jenny for a whole semester, believing her to be ungrateful and uncaring about Sue's most special day. From Sue's perspective, Jenny should do whatever it took to make it to her party because Sue had been such a good friend throughout the years. Jenny's pleading that she had no control over going to her grandfather's funeral out of town that weekend was no excuse in Sue's mind, to which she replied, "You didn't even like your grandpa; just skip it and come to my party!"

In truth, Sue felt insecure and worthless without Jenny's friendship because Jenny was the only other person besides her father who she felt cared enough about her to give her what she wanted. Sue, however, loathed apologizing for anything, even if she knew objectively that she may be wrong. Thus, she decided to start talking to Jenny again one day, never mentioning the three-and-a-half-month stint of ignoring her.

Sue also liked that Jenny would, no matter what, always be less attractive and gregarious than Sue, which thus made her feel safe. Even though she would never admit it, her cheerleader friends always made her feel inferior since most of them were white and blonde. She felt she was the most authentic with Jenny and that Jenny valued Sue's advice and direction more than anyone else, which made Sue feel valuable.

Sue felt like she had the luxury of being quite selective when it came to boys and thus decided early on to make any man she dated work hard for her attention and considerable affection. Although she wasn't allowed to date until she was 17, she would tell young men who expressed interest in her that they would have to prove that they liked her. Often, this translated as their buying her small gifts or other gestures of affection. Sue equated gifts and being allowed to do whatever she wanted with love. She secretly felt like the only way she could secure her independence would be to serve others in some way. She then felt like she earned the right to be cared for. At times, Sue would trade sexual favors for attention, particularly from the most popular or wealthiest boys, garnering her a reputation for being "easy." Sue liked being flirtatious and, at times, downright aggressive

CHAPTER THREE

when she liked a boy and found any attention to be good. Hence, the rumors about her sexual behavior rarely fazed her.

By Sue's senior year, she had amassed enough social capital to feel popular and superior to many other students. She particularly enjoyed her senior superlative, "most likely to become a queen," because she always thought she should be treated like a queen her whole life. Sue felt entitled to all the love and affection she could get from anyone else because of her mother's emotional flatness and sternness. However, like her mother, she had extreme difficulty expressing her love or care for others and preferred doing things for them to show her value and worth. Sue always felt "one down" when she told someone she appreciated or cared for them and secretly feared others using it to their advantage, possibly because when others admitted their feelings for her, she sometimes exploited their feelings to get her needs met. She justified her behavior, believing that "everyone does it," and saw herself as loving, kind, generous, and selfless. Sue enjoyed helping or supporting others because she liked taking credit for others' happiness or success, knowing that each time she made herself useful in the eyes of others, it earned her the right to be pampered and cared for.

Sue preferred to be happy and generally disliked conflict if she could avoid it. However, Sue could quickly show a more vicious side if anyone dared to refuse her requests or demands. Sue was cold and vindictive when people crossed her. The few times in her life when her father denied her, she went days or even weeks without acknowledging his existence. In her estimation, when people refused or denied her "reasonable" requests, they deserved to be ignored because she believed she was always there for everyone else and rarely asked for anything "unreasonable."

Sue entered college as a marketing and public relations major since she felt it would best suit her natural people-oriented skill set. She liked helping other people gain popularity or notoriety. A bonus to her major was that her mother found it frivolous, silly, and unlikely to yield a reliable job. Truthfully, Sue's primary college objective was to live a full social life and, hopefully, find a husband who could support the lifestyle she wanted. She joined a sorority primarily for social life and access to affluent and attractive boys.

She was immediately enamored when she met Mark her junior year at her sorority's annual ball. She had known about Mark for a while because he was from a wealthy and prominent family. However, she knew he dated only blonde, white women. She positioned herself as confident and aloof to combat her feelings of inferiority, and her calculation paid off. Eventually, Mark approached her at the ball and asked if she wanted a drink. She turned him down once because she didn't want to seem too eager, and she tried to position herself as unconcerned when, internally, she was thrilled that one of the most popular men on campus was showing interest in her.

Sue was determined to show her mother that she didn't have to become a successful businesswoman or go to law school or medical school to make it in the world, and quite honestly, Sue wanted the path of least resistance to a life of optimal luxury. It certainly helped that Mark was attractive and ambitious and seemed eager to please. She had always been aware that she preferred men who were solid yet passive because she wanted to "wear the pants" and because she had a pervasive fear of being dominated or controlled. On their first date, Mark told her she was the type of girl he could make happy. And that was music to her ears.

Understanding Sue

Asian immigrants in America are subject to damaging yet palpable expectations that they will perform exceptionally, particularly academically and professionally. While the weight of this expectation has many repercussions for Asian American mental health and perpetuates various stereotypes about the "smart Asian," there are genuine expectations that many Asian immigrants place on themselves upon entering the United States. The pressure to succeed in the United States is, of course, not solely relegated to Asian people or any other race, but carrying the weight of a community left behind in one's home country can place undue and often unrealistic pressure on immigrant communities. Li and Zhou's ambition and dedication to create an honorable and worthy life for themselves and successive generations helped to create a background of increased stress before Sue's arrival into the world. Of course, all parents have hopeful expectations for their children, yet for some, when the stakes are incredibly high (as was the case for Li and Zhou), deviation from those expectations can be challenging to manage.

Sue's psychological biography shows that she's always been independent and creative and needs attention and admiration. Sue is also identified with her ability to help others and would likely identify herself as a "people pleaser." Sue has a personality structure whereby she needs to be indispensable in the lives of others to feel as though she has value, and thus, she creates relationship dynamics where she helps or supports others with the expectation that she will be cared for. This propensity is in and of itself not indicative of a personality disorder; in the Enneagram personality system, Type Two, the Helpful Supporter, is meant to play that archetypal role in human dynamics. They seek attention through emotional support, and on some level, all people of this personality style need some form of payment or validation, whether psychic or external, to uphold their sense of self. Sue, however, represents this style's narcissistic and self-gratification–oriented iteration. Very early, she positioned herself against her mother and, in many ways, cultivated a childhood whereby she did what she wanted to and expected others to adjust to her desires. Her issues with her mother stem from her not feeling seen or emotionally validated. She resented her mother's insistence on intellectual development and more pragmatic means of reaching success.

On the one hand, Sue isn't unwarranted in her rebellion because she was not allowed to fully be herself lest she disappoint her mother, a reality that although shaped by cultural expectations, is no less rejecting to any child. On the other hand, many first-generation people grow up with similar expectations and don't develop narcissistic personality traits. So what happened with Sue, seeing that her cultural experience wasn't uncommon? We could postulate that perhaps Li passed along some genetic narcissistic predispositions.

Indeed, Li modeled narcissistic interpersonal strategies by becoming cold or dismissive and openly disdainful of Sue's interests, social affability, and intellectual aptitudes. The result is that Sue internalized her mother's shame, which is a tough pill to swallow for anyone but particularly devastating for Sue, whose personality type is dependent on acceptance.

Sue compensated for her shame and inferiority by becoming socially desirable, vivacious, superficially generous, and larger than life. Her persona, which she cultivated throughout her childhood into her early adulthood, becomes the mask that hides her deeper feelings of being inconsequential. Because Zhou showered her with attention and praise, she finds male attention more desirable since men are more likely (in her mind) to capitulate to her whims. Women, or anyone who might present to her like her mother, are to be treated as competitors and, therefore, must be dominated, as reflected in her relationship with her best friend, Jenny.

By becoming somewhat of a surrogate nonsexual wife to her father, Sue competed, often successfully, for her father's attention despite her mother. Because she found Zhou easier to manipulate, Sue learned that a transactional relationship could be leveraged for either material goods or emotional validation, both of which she received from her father. Sue developed an identity predicated on the idea that giving attention to selected others should be enough to receive whatever she deemed necessary to satisfy her desire. Because of this dynamic with her father, she also equates being materially supported with being loved. This creates a dynamic she will repeat throughout her relationships, particularly with romantic partners. Her promiscuity is both a rejection of her mother's rigid standards of what should be pleasurable to her and a way to feel the temporary satisfaction of validation from others.

As *The Entitled Caregiver*, Sue would prefer to receive attention and validation for what she brings to the table, which is often simply her presence. Entitled Caregivers frequently take on personal projects, which are frequently people who give them a sense of superiority. They like to control their environments and the people within them. They often play interpersonal chess to maximize what they receive from others (e.g., material gain, attention, praise, or validation). Their "narcissistic supply" comes from being people who make things happen, and thus, they repeatedly put themselves at the epicenter of people's lives to show they are indispensable. Unfortunately, as Sue demonstrates, they often overestimate the extent to which their contributions are helpful and underestimate how others often notice that their care, concern, attention, or support is self-serving and a means to secure what they deem necessary for survival.

Possible Strategies for Change

The Prideful-Flattering narcissistic subtypes (which include *The Entitled Caregiver*) are not likely to present in any clinical or therapeutic setting of their own accord. Unlike some of the other narcissistic variants, the intense pride these types have about their value and necessity in the lives of others makes them exceedingly difficult to treat. Like Luke, Sue would balk at any suggestion of introspection. However, because Sue sees herself as an emotionally expressive person (and, in many respects, this is accurate), she might view a therapeutic or coaching relationship as an opportunity to receive more validation of her persona. Many people of this subtype spend an inordinate amount of time complaining about everything they've done for others. They often feel deeply aggrieved, resentful, and even melancholic because they see themselves as offering others love, support, attention, and care, while they are not afforded the same. Validating Sue's natural ability to grace others with her "fairy godmother"–like touch could help soften the defensive response one will receive when giving her anything but positive feedback.

While Sue's affability, charm, and superficial concern for others may provide her with temporary relational returns, she would likely realize that those returns diminish as others notice how her attention shifts to more promising prospects for attention or validation, upon which they probably begin to distance themselves. One might help Sue recognize that her intentions for assisting or supporting others are noble; viewing others as "projects" or removing her warmth and attention as a punishment for inaccurate mirroring inevitably pushes others away.

Steering Sue toward expressing her creative and performative traits could help her channel her high need for attention and validation into a more appropriate arena. Prideful-Flattering types do reasonably well in high-visibility roles where they can be the center of attention and receive validation for their contributions. Unfortunately, unlike the Ambitious-Deceptive types, they prefer mining the interpersonal realm for validation. Sue's creative endeavors and propensity toward dance, music, and other art forms could allow her to explore her emotional landscape safely. Since vulnerability is problematic for all narcissistic personalities, she would likely feel exceedingly unsafe revealing her feelings of shame or rejection, even in a therapeutic environment. If she were willing to discuss her emotional disappointments, it would likely be tinged with a heavy dose of resentment, blaming, and expecting others to fix or compensate her feelings. Creative outlets would allow her to express some of the pain she's likely experiencing (however buried) over her feelings of inferiority and shame from her childhood.

Like others of this subtype, Sue would benefit from living a life where she is largely financially independent so she doesn't need to depend on someone else to tend to her material needs and doesn't feel like she must give something to get something. Ironically, people with this subtype tend to seek out others they believe will satiate their whims, because they enjoy becoming a proverbial fount of support for others and, thus, feel more deserving of what they receive. Sue's entitlement would be challenging to break because of this deep-seated association between what she gives others and what she believes she deserves in return.

Very often, with narcissistic adults, the best one can hope for are modifications to behavior and interpersonal strategies that increase relational harmony. Helping Sue express gratitude to others and become mindful of her entitlement might help her feel less misunderstood when people push back against her diva-like behavior.

CHAPTER THREE

Also, expressing gratitude for the abundance in her life, preferably in a journal or diary, can help her take more realistic stock of what she has received (and, conversely, what she offers others) rather than believing that she is constantly owed something for overextending herself in ways that may not match up against reality.

Joe

The Charismatic Bully (SX): Charismatic, bold, and uncompromising, this subtype wants to wholly possess the object(s) of their affection. They offer protection and power in exchange for others' total submission and surrender to their dictates, whims, and demands. They are more emotionally aware than other Powerful-Aggressive subtypes and use their charisma and audaciousness to engender admiration. They can be unreasonable, unscrupulous, and demanding.

Dana's being pregnant came at a time in her life that was less than ideal for having a baby. Her ex-boyfriend Curtis was no longer in the picture and wanted nothing to do with Dana or the baby, and she knew she would be on her own. Dana was only 18 years old and terrified for her future. Her parents were wholly unsupportive of her current predicament and decided that she needed to suffer the consequences of her "poor choices." Coming from a highly conservative Christian background, having a child out of wedlock was seen as sinful, and the family frequently pleaded with Dana to repent for her sins and return to God.

Dana stopped attending church at 16 years old because she found it to be a punitive and abusive environment. Dana endeavored to build a secure and stable life for herself and her unborn child. Working three jobs, she dropped out of her senior year of high school and worked full-time as a clerk at a local grocery store. She also took babysitting and maid service jobs on the weekends and evenings. The immense pressure she felt was undeniable, but she was determined to survive despite her parents' condemnations. They often tried to persuade her to return home (and, subsequently, the church), and in turn, they would help support her financially. She always declined, knowing the psychological repercussions of allowing them to control any aspect of her life.

A few months before giving birth, she met Tyrell, a 34-year-old man who frequented the grocery store she worked at, whom she found protective and financially stable. He gave her a sense of security, although he occasionally displayed an intense and sudden temper. By the time she had Jolyn, she had moved in with Tyrell.

Jolyn was a happy baby girl, and for a time, she enjoyed security and peace with her newly formed family. Tyrell provided some financial security, but he became increasingly controlling and domineering, a feeling Dana was all too familiar with because of her upbringing. However, fearing the economic repercussions of breaking up with Tyrell, she decided to stay in the relationship for Jolyn's sake.

When Jolyn was 4, Tyrell and Dana's relationship had grown increasingly more toxic, with Tyrell often being physically abusive to Dana. His anger and rage used to be relegated so that he wouldn't display his full temper in front of Jolyn, but he was increasingly becoming verbally and physically abusive in front of Jolyn. While he was never physically abusive to Jolyn, he frequently hurled insults and screamed at her, particularly if she was in the line of fire during his tirades against Dana. Eventually, recognizing the situation was no longer tenable for her or her child, she separated from Tyrell when Jolyn was 5 years old. Dana had worked her way up the management chain as an assistant manager with a meager but sufficient salary. Although losing Tyrell's support would mean a significant decrease in financial security, it was better than subjecting herself and Jolyn to his temper.

Jolyn's protectiveness was present, even at an early age. When Tyrell would rage, she would run toward him, hurling her tiny fists or throwing toys to get him to stop his abuse against her mother. Even though Tyrell was the only father figure she had ever known, she didn't feel exceptionally connected to him due to his temper.

Dana enrolled Jolyn in a nearby elementary school and almost immediately began receiving calls about her aggressive and dominating behavior. Teachers frequently reported that "Jo" could be

CHAPTER THREE

incredibly loving, protective, and kind but then become irate and explosive at the slightest provocation. Dana knew this had to be because of the behavior Jolyn witnessed as a child, and Dana would often apologize profusely to the teachers and staff. Jo gained a reputation by first grade as being the toughest girl in the schoolyard. She also vehemently refused anything she deemed as "girly" or "feminine," preferring to dress more tomboyish. Jo seemed preoccupied with looking strong, and she viewed femininity as weak and ineffectual. By 6 years old, she often told other kids at school to refer to her as "he." Dana frequently received frustrating calls from teachers and counselors complaining about Jo's noncompliance and "gender confusion." It was suggested that Jo be put into a counseling program for kids who displayed features of "oppositional defiant disorder."

While Jo's behavior could be quite aggressive, she was undoubtedly intelligent, strong-minded, and precocious. She was particularly protective of her mother, and at 10 years old when Dana began dating a police officer named Richard, she became deeply resentful. Since Dana's breakup with Tyrell, it had been Jo and Dana against the world; with the sudden appearance of a new man, the security the two had built was profoundly threatened. Richard was kind but firm and took a more decisively disciplinarian approach to Jo's antics. Dana was relieved to have a healthy, strong influence in the home since she struggled to discipline Jo when she became defiant. There were many times that Jo's aggressiveness and adultlike confidence were intimidating to Dana, even at Jo's young age.

Richard's influence was immediately seen as threatening. He was more decisively conservative and convinced Dana to start attending a new, more open-minded church than the one she grew up with. Jo was confused by Dana's sudden interest in religion because she'd already heard many stories about Dana's unpleasant experiences with religion growing up. Dana married Richard after only eight months of dating, and they quickly moved into his home. However, Jo refused to comply with virtually any of Richard's directives, no matter how reasonable. In one particularly heated exchange, an 11-year-old Jo squared up to Richard after he requested she clean her room. Jo boldly and resolutely told him he could do it himself if he wanted it cleaned. Enraged by the insubordination, Richard spanked an unemotional and stoic Jo, who promised Richard he would be sorry he had done that.

Jo began using male pronouns when he reached fifth grade because he felt more like a man and demanded his name be changed to "Joe." Joe's revelation was nothing new to Dana, who had long suspected that her daughter had a different gender conception than the one she was born with. Yet Richard struggled to accept his stepdaughter's gender identity. Dana, still harboring some of the religious ideologies she grew up with, agonized over how to deal with Joe's revelation but knew that it didn't matter what her thoughts were about Joe's gender. Joe was so willful that he would live according to his prescriptions and no one else's. Richard was less open-minded about Joe's gender identity proclamations and stated that if he lived under his roof, he would go by his God-given gender and sex identification. Joe remained defiant, confident, and steadfast but grew increasingly angry and cantankerous with both parents.

By middle school, Joe had gained a reputation for being both a "badass" and extremely confident. He didn't give a second thought to challenging a teacher, mainly if he felt they were wrong, and would often intimidate anyone who stood in his way. He was unaffected by punishment, shame, or ridicule and would double or triple down if anyone tried to force him to do something he didn't want. By seventh grade, he began taking an interest in young girls and was surprisingly sophisticated and charming if he was attracted to someone. However, because he was still navigating the uncertainties of sexuality and gender identity, if things progressed to a physical relationship with any young woman (a relative rarity given his age and the cultural ideologies of his hometown), he felt insecure. He often broke up with love interests coldly, particularly if they wanted to reciprocate any sexual act.

Interestingly, Joe picked partners who were passive, kind, and loving, like his mother. Since sixth grade, he was never without a girlfriend (or several), and despite (and perhaps because of) him

CHAPTER THREE

being the only transgender person in his school, he was popular with young boys and girls alike. His confidence, boldness, and no-nonsense attitude earned him respect despite his relative difference from the other kids.

As adolescence progressed and Joe's body became increasingly more feminized, he grew more reactive, aggressive, and insensitive. He asked Dana if he could begin taking hormone blockers, to which she responded that she would need to talk it over with Richard. Joe flew into a rage, saying that Dana was weak, that she'd always been weak, and that he'd figure out how to get what he wanted no matter what. Joe threatened to lie, cheat, or steal to get the blockers, which shocked Dana, who was usually not on the receiving end of Joe's aggression.

In defiance of Dana and Richard's refusal to allow Joe to take hormone blockers, he began skipping school and frequenting a local arcade. Despite being arrested for truancy several times, Joe became more resolute in his refusal to comply with any requests made by Richard or Dana. By eighth grade, Joe was enrolled in an alternative school for children who exhibited frequent oppositional defiant behaviors. The strict disciplinary focus of the school seemed only to strengthen Joe's refusal to comply with any demands. Alternately, Joe exhibited high scores in standardized testing in virtually every subject, further frustrating Dana and Richard.

By high school, Joe had found refuge in music and had begun singing for a local punk band. He had an undeniable knack for songwriting and an equally compelling stage presence and confidence uncharacteristic for a kid his age. Joe found that music and performing helped him deal with the rage and anger of his gender dysphoria but seemed only to strengthen his resentment toward his parents and the world overall. However, by the time Joe was 17, he had become so independent that Dana and Richard realized the futility of trying to control him. He dropped out of school his senior year and moved to New York City with two bandmates and his girlfriend to try to "make it big." Being savvy and resourceful, Joe saved enough money from local gigs and his part-time job of doing odd jobs to make the move.

Despite Joe's distance from Dana, he remained protective of her, and when Dana told Joe that she found out Richard had been having an affair, Joe became irate. Dana told Joe they had decided to stay together and "make it work," to which Joe began admonishing Dana for her weakness and being a doormat, leading to a yearlong hiatus in their relationship because Joe tended to cut anyone off whom he found weak or "lacking honor." Joe eventually cut off his mother and stepfather, calling only on holidays and rarely visiting. Sometimes, he even fabricated an origin story whereby he was an orphan who had to figure out how to make it independently without guidance. He preferred to think of himself as a lone wolf rather than acknowledging that anyone had played a role in his development. His distance from Dana remained particularly difficult for her.

For as long as Joe could remember, he always felt like a boy despite knowing he was supposed to be a girl. He also remembers feeling incredibly protective of his mother. His first memory was of his mother singing while feeding him and Tyrell walking in and "changing the mood." He remembers admiring Tyrell's strength at once and hating him because he was cruel to his mother. He also remembers feeling furious that his mother even needed Tyrell, believing he could be (and had been) the man of the house before Tyrell appeared in their lives. His rage was constant, and he felt compelled to stand up for "weaklings." In first grade, he recalls calling himself "the green knight" because of a film he enjoyed that depicted a strong but rugged knight who protected the ladies of a village. He graduated from thinking of himself as the green knight to coining himself as "The Emperor" because emperors ruled everything. He loathed being told what to do, and even more than that, he hated being challenged.

Joe has never shirked from conflict and even found that at times, he enjoyed getting into a good fight, whether with his parents, some "idiot" at school, or a teacher. He wholeheartedly believed that even as a child, he knew what was best for him and not even adults had

CHAPTER THREE

his best interest at heart. This was particularly exacerbated by his parents' response to his gender identification. He took it upon himself to look out for himself, realizing that despite his mother's love for him, he also pitied her "spinelessness." He found Richard to be annoying and refused to acknowledge his authority. Later, Joe would develop a hatred for police officers and disdain for "organized law enforcement" or any institutional authority, inspired by his hatred of Richard and his work as a cop.

Joe rarely, if ever, experienced self-doubt, except around sexual relationships, which were, of course, exacerbated by his gender dysphoria. Because of the unfamiliar feeling of insecurity that cropped up in relationships, he found that he both clung to love interests and felt compelled to dominate and wholly control women as well. He began dating Adele in 11th grade when he saw her at one of his band's shows. Cocky and full of bravado, he approached her, claiming that by the end of the night, she would be going home with him. She was 22 years old, five years his senior, but his confidence made him appear much older. He lied about his age, suspecting she wouldn't have given him the time of day had he been honest about being 17. Adele didn't find out Joe's actual age for a year and a half and was shocked when he revealed his age since they frequented many bars and clubs and were never asked for his ID.

Joe was a smooth talker, and he believed that telling a lie "here and there" wasn't a big deal. He was often philosophical, eloquent, and charismatic but could quickly become tense, threatening, and insensitive at the slightest provocation. Many people were as intimidated by Joe as they were drawn to his raw animal magnetism. However, Adele occasionally saw glimpses of extreme vulnerability and sadness. To some extent, Joe was aware of his sadness. Nonetheless, he was uncomfortable with the vulnerability and feelings of weakness inherent in softer emotions and preferred to express rage, sarcastic humor, or cold indifference instead. His maudlin and surprisingly artistic nature would seep through his song lyrics and poetry, where he frequently exhibited a palpable mixture of anger, self-pity, and grief.

Joe convinced Adele to forgo going to nursing school to support him in his quest to become "a rock star." He always felt the world would know who he was, and he was determined to become rich and famous. Seeing it as his responsibility to take care of Adele and his bandmates, he learned various streetwise tricks of the trade. In his mind, while he detested criminality for the sake of it, he didn't mind running a hustle or two to make some extra cash to pay rent or buy Adele something she wanted.

Joe demanded loyalty from people he considered "his" and felt personally affronted by people keeping secrets or concealing even minor details. He felt secret keeping and concealment indicated being "squirrely" or "evasive," which he found "spineless" and "useless." Occasionally, Joe would become sadistic and launch into brutal but quietly threatening tirades against anyone he felt had betrayed him. He became cold, caustic, and dismissive when angry and noticeably more arrogant than usual.

Joe's relationship with Adele was tumultuous. He would break up with her over the slightest perceived infraction, launching into deeply personal admonishments of her neglect and mistreatment, only to surprise her with an extravagant gift the following day without apologizing. When confronted with his behavior, Joe had an uncanny way of making the other person feel they had transgressed him, which often elicited an apology. Despite their stormy relationship, Adele (in Joe's estimation) was the only woman who really "got" him. Despite his professed love for his only "soulmate," Joe was a notorious flirt and philanderer. He was particularly drawn to women who were his or his band's fans. Despite his frequent infidelity, Adele, unable to resist his charm and apologetic promises, would always take him back.

By the time Joe was 21, he had carved a name for himself in the New York City punk rock scene and garnered attention from record label execs who saw undeniable star power and earning potential. He made enough money at this point to pay for top surgery and testosterone therapy, a change that increased his bravado and self-confidence in such a way that he felt invincible. Upon beginning his transition, he found Adele to become less supportive. In his mind, she was no longer "ride or die," and he began to feel like she was mimicking some of the wishy-washy behaviors he associated with his mother. Joe's low tolerance for others' emotional expression (particularly when it related to something he did) and his belief in his benevolence, protectiveness, and unending devotion to others made conflict resolution nearly impossible.

When Adele finally got the courage to voice her concerns about the state of their relationship, Joe assumed she was no longer attracted to him and, instead, accused her of wanting only a cis-sexual male partner, which he could never be. One cold January day, when Adele returned home from her work as a nurse's aide, she arrived to find all her belongings outside of their shared apartment and a note that simply said, "fuck off." He refused to answer her calls and instructed his bandmates to do the same, an order they didn't dare violate lest they incur his formidable wrath. Joe had decided it was time for someone who understood his spiritual and professional journey and that he would finally make the world respect him like the emperor he was.

Understanding Joe

The psychological, emotional, and financial pressure of an underemployed single parent preparing to give birth creates an environment that can have a noticeably stressful effect on both the parent and the unborn child. Dana was determined to raise her child free from the confines of the religious pressure she experienced in her own family of origin. However, the result was that she had to endure the trauma of childbirth as a naive teenager. While we can't know the extent to which the stress of working multiple jobs, processing familial trauma, and growing a human life created for her on a physiological level, it's improbable that Dana wasn't affected by these conditions, which were undoubtedly flooding copious amounts of cortisol into her bloodstream. However, as with most things in nature, adversity tends to strengthen certain defenses, and it appears that little Joe came into this world with an innate understanding that life had been tough and would continue to be. Joe also intuited that despite the male influence early in his life, Dana was all they had, thus exacerbating his protectiveness over his mother.

Children who grow up in homes where abuse is present, whether emotional, financial, psychological, or physical, demonstrate higher stress responses that continue to be elevated throughout the lifespan.[3] How the child reacts to that stress depends on various factors, including how they're emotionally and physically regulated and whether the stressors are pervasive. While some children become hyper-empathic, attuned to others, and fearful, other children become emotionally insensitive, aggressive, and domineering. Joe developed along the latter lines and seemed to have fortified his emotional sensitivities quite early to avoid feeling vulnerable to what was perceived as the chaotic influence of unjust men.

Joe simultaneously cultivated fierce protectiveness and rage at his mother. On the one hand, Joe recognized Dana's vulnerability from a young age when they attempted to protect him from Tyrell's tyranny. On the other hand, Joe felt that Dana's inability to separate herself from Tyrell's domination demonstrated a potentially fatal weakness that could endanger them both. Joe took it upon himself to become "the man of the house," a psychological position that people with Joe's personality adopt very early. In the Enneagram personality system, Joe is a Type Eight, The Powerful Protector. Like all Eights, Joe's core fears are being at the mercy of injustice or being weak, vulnerable, or harmed. Like many people with the same personality style, Joe internalized that to avoid becoming prey, he needed to adopt a cynical, predatory-like persona that communicates to others "Don't mess with me!"

Very early, Joe demonstrated oppositional defiant tendencies because he could not easily be controlled by any authority figure. Quite often, Joe felt like he was the only authority figure that mattered. The gender dysphoria he experienced at a very young age and the social pressure to adhere to ascribed gender norms likely exacerbated both Joe's feelings of being misunderstood and mistrusting other people's directives. Being told you must behave and identify with a particular gender identity when you unequivocally feel it doesn't match your experience is a challenge for any person, no matter what their personality style. However, Joe's personality structure set up a highly adversarial relationship toward supposed authority and a relentless tenacity that would allow him to forge his path according to his internalized rules of engagement.

Joe felt abandoned by his mother when Dana met and eventually married Richard, who represented the ultimate expression of authority, a police officer. This final abandonment seems to have solidified Joe's "me against the world" orientation toward life. However, there is a deep desire in Joe for him not only to express his protectiveness (particularly with a woman) but also to regain a lost sense of union with the abandoning mother figure. Thus, Joe begins to pour his considerable psychic energy into seducing and ultimately possessing a surrendering partner. Psychodynamically, Joe wants to find a "good mother" to accept him wholeheartedly without stipulations. And while Dana did relatively well managing Joe's noncompliance, she was no match for his fierce independence.

Joe's rage about feeling unprotected, particularly from overbearing masculine figures, undoubtedly contributed to a desire to become an authoritarian masculine figure in the lives of others. Power and autonomy became of the utmost importance, and demanding loyalty and obedience from those in his life became an unnegotiable prerequisite for entrance into his inner circle.

Joe is the *Charismatic Bully* narcissistic subtype and, as such, is focused primarily on seeking loyalty and power in interpersonal relationships. As Joe aged and began to reconcile his gender dysphoria by claiming his proverbial space in the world, he sought validation in other relationships and venues. Because of Joe's narcissism (which I would argue was exacerbated due to adverse social and cultural conditions), the abject fears of inferiority and powerlessness become amplified due to his personality structure.

Joe's sense of morality becomes skewed by his necessity to maintain power and subvert or even pervert others' needs, desires, and boundaries. In the following chapter, we'll further analyze his interpersonal relationships, but here, it's essential to understand that narcissistic rage is the engine that drives Joe's treatment of others. No one can ever live up to Joe's conception of "loyalty." He will undoubtedly always see himself as fighting for his autonomy and avoiding being dominated by an overpowering father figure or attempting to force a perceived weak mother figure into submission.

This subtype often requires empathy and understanding from others and can be, at least on the surface, quite soulful and emotionally expressive. While vulnerability is avoided at all costs, people with this subtype often sniff out others' vulnerability to shore up power. They can be spiritually astute, brilliant, outgoing, and interpersonally savvy and utilize their natural charisma to pull people into toxic relationships full of power plays and damaging emotional games.

Possible Strategies for Change

Joe has admirable qualities that have already taken him far in forging his path in the world. His creative expression, ambition, and fearlessness have led him to pursue a music career where he can express some of the anger and disappointment he experiences internally. It's improbable that someone of this subtype would present for any therapeutic intervention because they prefer being in the "power seat." However, they frequently show up involuntarily due to legal interventions or court orders. Interestingly, this subtype often has a keen understanding of human psychology. Unfortunately, they tend to underestimate and ignore their psychological shortcomings and, as such, underestimate others' intelligence or savvy due to overconfidence in their abilities to manipulate and control. Joe has had a lifetime of being largely misunderstood and unfairly labeled by well-intentioned adults who could not fully appreciate the pain underneath his defiant behavior. The result was a hardening of Joe's belief that he must forge his path of fire and take no prisoners regarding his destiny.

Because Joe is a performer, helping him access more of the sadness behind his rage could be transformative. Sorrow and grief are primarily dismissed by this subtype (and its non-narcissistic iterations) because those emotions do not carry the same galvanizing charge and could render them helpless. A romantic partner like Adele, bandmates, close friends, or even his mother could help him get in touch with some of the sadness in a safe way simply by suggesting, in a matter-of-fact manner, that he might be sad. Directness is critical with this subtype, as they quickly become cynical and suspicious when they feel others are trying to manage them covertly, which activates their rage and fears of being controlled or harmed.

Accessing any semblance of vulnerability is highly fear-inducing for this subtype (and any of the Powerful-Aggressive narcissistic types) and exceedingly difficult. They harden themselves to feel invincible and see their lives as a battlefield they've had to fight their way through. Acknowledging Joe's grit, determination, and strength will fortify his ego messaging but could, in the right moment, also help him consider (however briefly) letting down his guard to access more tender emotions. These emotions would certainly be more accessible to him with a romantic partner, but even small moments of empathetic understanding from a trusted intimate can soften the hardest of shells.

Helping Joe learn the value of diplomacy can also go a long way in smoothing some of the rough edges he's cultivated throughout his childhood and early adulthood. Very often, those hard-won rough edges tend to become harder and harder to smooth, and at some point, neither charm nor intimidation go very far in getting his needs met. Helping Joe see the pragmatic value of diplomacy and, more importantly, honoring others' boundaries can potentially help lessen inevitable conflicts. The key word here is *pragmatism* because it would be exceedingly challenging to appeal to any sense of care for other people's emotional sensitivities since he would likely feel like nobody cared for him. However, helping him see that he can catch more flies with honey will inadvertently reduce at least superficial altercations that could arise due to his reactive or abrasive communication style.

This subtype often has a powerful propensity toward feeling aggrieved and misunderstood. They frequently take opportunities to complain to others that others don't appreciate their originality, strength, or devotion. For those in their orbit, it's easy to reiterate their lamentations because they often make convincing arguments and use this method well when trying to connect with others since it mimics vulnerability. Many people feel special that someone so strong and self-assured shares how others hurt or harmed them. This creates a trauma bond that hides their true vulnerability and invites the other to share their weaknesses more readily. This serves a couple of purposes; first, it helps them to find out what your trauma points may be, and second, it tests your willingness to enroll in their self-aggrandized, persecuted narrative and makes you more sympathetic. While this seems highly manipulative (and it is), it also reveals the extent to which the small, disempowered child needs to prepare others for their eventual transgressions (e.g., rage outbursts, indifference, or temper tantrums) almost as if saying, "Will you still leave me? I told you why I'm so messed up." The trick is to validate the presence of the pain without endorsing the negative behaviors that spring up because of the pain.

CHAPTER FOUR
WHEN "WE" BECOMES "ME"

Luke and Kerri: The Frivolous Flaws of Fantasy

On his second date with Kerri, Luke knew he had found the woman he would spend the rest of his life with, and he intended to sweep her off her feet. Luke also knew that his reputation preceded him with women, so he endeavored to win her over despite any preconceived notions she may have about his past. Like many of his fraternity brothers, Luke had associated with various women during his college tenure. He knew that Kerri was very good friends with an ex-girlfriend, Laurie, who had begun telling people he was emotionally abusive, a claim he found "ridiculous" since he felt that she was mad that he dumped her for being a "crybaby" and "emotionally weak." Luke knew that to combat some of his "negative press" (as he affectionally referred to any criticisms of his behavior), he would have to put some distance between Kerri and Laurie if he was ever to have a shot.

Kerri, a soft-spoken but quietly self-assured nursing major, was initially attracted to Luke because he was good-looking, confident, and funny. However, she also noted some of the warnings her friends had given her about Luke's selfishness because he had a reputation around campus for being a womanizer and a bit of a clown. Kerri trusted Laurie, because Laurie had always been reliable and trustworthy in Kerri's experiences with her, so when Laurie warned her that Luke could be quite "toxic," she believed her but decided to give him a fair, unbiased chance by going on a date and discerning his character for herself.

CHAPTER FOUR

Before Luke and Kerri's first date, he researched and discovered through polling mutual friends that she loved poetry. While he couldn't care less about poetry, he thought it would be impressive if he showed up with the newest book by her favorite poet. When Luke arrived to pick her up for their date, she saw a wrapped gift on the seat when she got in the passenger side. She flushed with excitement since she considered it unusual for men in her generation to be so considerate on a first date. Luke smiled and coyly said, "I don't know if you'll even like it, but I saw it at the bookstore and thought of you for some reason." Kerri was deeply impressed with his thoughtfulness and the simplicity of the romantic gesture. He even earmarked a poem toward the middle of the book titled "Love Story." Luke knew by the look on her face that he'd already won her over.

Luke took Kerri to a lovely restaurant and spared no expense in wining and dining her. He asked her every possible question to learn "what made her tick" and listened intently to her responses. In the middle of Kerri's talking about her childhood, Luke interrupted and exclaimed, dreamy-eyed and expectant, "You're going to be my wife one day!" The statement stunned Kerri, and she immediately turned red and dismissed his comment as silly. Kerri suddenly felt like she was the leading lady in a romantic comedy and felt a sense of derealization. She was sitting with this handsome, popular, and thoughtful man on a fairy tale–like date, and he was already professing his love.

Luke told Kerri he loved her after one week of dating, and although it was fast, she said it back. Their relationship progressed quickly, and after only three months, Kerri could definitively say that Luke was the most attentive, loving, and thoughtful boyfriend she'd ever had. After he professed his love to her, she began imagining their wedding day, a ridiculous exercise given the amount of time she'd known him. Kerri's lingering apprehension about his previous relationships had dissolved in the face of the romantic fantasy that had become her love life. Kerri had always been attracted to men who were dismissive, emotionally immature, and insensitive, and Luke appeared to be the opposite.

When Kerri finally worked up the nerve to ask Luke about what happened between him and Laurie, he revealed that Laurie had been emotionally abusive, insisting that he honor all her emotions, no matter how "frivolous" or "unreasonable." He used the term *emotional bullying* and spoke about his six-month relationship with Laurie in a way that Kerri felt revealed some of his vulnerabilities, which she found refreshing. Luke, however, felt he was "training" Kerri not to repeat problematic emotional expressions or processing patterns that he found annoying in his previous relationship. He positioned Kerri as the superior partner due to her "chill" and relaxed relationship approach. Luke liked people who let him do whatever he wanted, and Kerri wasn't seemingly concerned with controlling him. Over time, Kerri grew further away from Laurie as she began to see her in an entirely new light. She wanted to distance herself from the woman her Prince Charming found so "difficult to get along with."

After a few months, Luke began refocusing on his active social life, and Kerri noticed a shift in his attentiveness. One of Kerri's most impressive relationship achievements in the year she and Luke had been dating was that they hadn't had any fights. Of course, they bickered about what to eat or watch on TV, but there had been no significant conflicts to speak of, something her mother and sister found "weird." Kerri felt like others were jealous of the ease of their relationship so she could ignore the warnings that others gave, preferring to live in the idyllic fantasy of her made-for-television romance. Kerri was naturally conflict-avoidant and affable and enjoyed Luke's "easy, breezy" style of relating.

Luke and Kerri's first big fight occurred on Valentine's Day just before leaving to attend a formal function for his fraternity, for which he was the chapter president. Kerri purchased a short, flirty red dress that she knew Luke would find sexy. When Luke arrived to pick her up, the smile she typically expected when he greeted her was met with a dismissive and flat "hey." She thought perhaps something had happened to shift his mood (a rare occurrence that typically lasted a short time).

"What's wrong?" Kerri asked worriedly.

CHAPTER FOUR

"Nothing. Is that what you're wearing?" Luke clipped.

"Um ... yeah. What's wrong? You don't like it?" Kerri was already holding back tears and felt pangs of fear as she experienced a coldness from him she'd never felt before.

"I don't know; I'd think you would've thought a little bit more about how it would make me look if you showed up in a slutty dress. I am in a leadership position, and I just thought you got it." Luke sighed, seemingly disbelieving that he even had to tell her the problem.

"Slutty?! I have never been accused of that in my whole life, and why are you being such a jerk?!" Kerri immediately started crying, mainly due to the abrupt shift in tone from the man she'd come to see as her Prince Charming. "Fine, I'll change." She conceded, starting to walk upstairs.

"Oh, here we go. You're so sensitive now that you can't take any honest feedback. You sound just like Laurie. I just thought you knew the pressure I'm under. You don't have time to change at this point. Let's just go." Luke stood motionless, simultaneously unfazed and deeply angry. His eyes were cold and feelingless and lacked any of the jovial brightness she had come to love.

Kerri stood there, staring at him, looking for any semblance of the man she'd come to know over the past few months, and he coolly stared back at her. Briefly, at that moment, she considered breaking up with him. She then reasoned with herself that they'd have to fight eventually and that this wasn't that bad in the grand scheme of their relationship. To her surprise, Kerri found herself apologizing for not thinking about how her dress might make him look. Her anger and hurt shifted into an abject panic as she looked at him for absolution. After a moment, he smiled, kissed her on the cheek, and said, "You look great. Let's go."

For the remainder of the night, Luke behaved as though nothing had happened, but Kerri was left feeling destabilized and with more doubt than she'd had at any other point in their relationship. He spent the rest of the evening thanking her for accompanying him and being a "good girlfriend."

The night after the party, Kerri decided she wanted to discuss the fight with Luke because she still felt unsettled. When Kerri broached the subject, he immediately rolled his eyes, sighed, and dismissed her attempt to "dredge up old demons." He insisted that he had "moved on," a sentiment that made her feel guilty for even wanting to discuss it further. She had seen him do this with his friends, particularly his best friend, Jack. She chalked his dismissal up to his discomfort with negative emotions. She eventually convinced herself it was healthier to drop it and move on rather than risk being labeled as a "Debbie downer" or further compared to her old friend, Laurie.

Things evened out after Valentine's Day. Aside from occasional quibbles, Luke seemed back to his normal effervescent breeziness, and Kerri was back to making sure he got his way to avoid unpleasantness. While Kerri was happy their relationship was solid, she craved a deeper emotional connection. At times, she would try to talk to Luke about his feelings around his mother, since he seemed ambivalent about her, or the strange anxiety he exhibited when around his father, with whom he had a complex relationship. Unfortunately, Luke found retrospective or introspective conversations to be "exhausting" and assured her "not everyone is a head case" and that he didn't need "analyzing." Kerri, a naturally curious and empathetic person, was planning to get an advanced degree in psychiatric nursing (a profession Luke was less than thrilled about), and he would frequently make disparaging comments about those with mental illnesses or "therapy hacks." Kerri repeatedly ignored his dismissal of her interests, reminding herself that her line of work was not for everyone. However, she often made a concerted effort to listen to him gossip about his law school classmates or political interests.

The two were married a year after graduating college, and as they pursued professional degrees in nursing and law, respectively, their lives became increasingly busy and less intertwined. They were fine if they came together for fun date nights or occasional weekend getaways. Still, she felt Luke was disinterested in her day-to-day existence, preferring instead to spend time at his law clerk internship or with other law students, many of whom were women who she knew

CHAPTER FOUR

had crushes on him. On the rare occasion that Kerri would address her concerns, reminding him that only two years prior, they'd spent as many moments together as possible, he'd dismiss her concerns, saying, "You don't want to get tired of each other, do you?" before he'd flit off to have a drink with the guys (or girls) or go work on a brief for his boss.

Three years into Kerri and Luke's marriage, they had settled into a dynamic that mainly consisted of living separate lives due to work schedules and professional obligations. However, Luke insisted that Kerri accompany him to most of his work functions, while rarely joining her for outings with her coworkers and their spouses.

Luke began working in the governor's office as a legal adviser and had already started positioning himself for a state legislature run. Kerri was expected to accompany Luke to help present his desired image to potential donors and voters. Kerri found herself without many close friends, and her relationship with her family became increasingly strained the longer she was married. She chalked this up to the normal individuating process of being in a marriage, and she also grew tired of hearing her mother's and sisters' "unfair judgments" of Luke. They believed he was selfish and self-absorbed, and after he chose to have Thanksgiving dinner with the governor rather than her family (as he'd promised), their belief was further solidified that his primary concern was for his aspirations rather than creating closeness or getting to know her family in any meaningful way. Kerri's sister felt she had become "less and less herself" and that she was expected to behave like a "Stepford wife."

It was true that Kerri had learned how to become increasingly presentational, but she understood that this came with marrying someone like Luke. Kerri spent a fair amount of time making excuses to others for Luke's flippancy, arrogance, and often antagonistic "jokes." She felt other people didn't "really" know him and that he always "meant well." She even tried to mediate a massive fight between Luke and Jack when Jack had finally had enough of Luke's cruel jokes and backhanded comments. When Luke refused to apologize (something he rarely, if ever, did), she knew that Jack had had enough, and he distanced himself for good. After that, Luke never mentioned his oldest friend again unless it was to call him a "pathetic loser."

Despite Luke's demanding career and social schedule, he found time to go on "mini adventures" and frequently planned weekend trips with his buddies from college or coworkers to "blow off steam." Kerri's schedule at the hospital was intense, and she rarely found time to go on impromptu vacations to Key West or pub crawls in Boston. Luke began referring to Kerri as "Kerri-puss" because he felt that her "practicality" and tendency to be unspontaneous made her a sourpuss. And, like all of Luke's jokes at others' expense, there was an undercurrent of disdain and superiority. Kerri increasingly began to feel like she would be a drag on his good time and resigned herself to the fact that she just "wasn't that fun." If she voiced her anxieties to Luke, he would frequently dismiss her. She hated arguing with Luke because he refused to recognize the effect of his arrogance and emotional callousness. She always knew Luke was uncomfortable with any emotion that wasn't positive, but this "quirk" gave way to a full-on disdain, particularly regarding Kerri's emotional concerns.

After being married for five years, Kerri gave birth to their first child, Brooklyn, and for a couple of years, creating new memories with their child helped them breathe new life into their relationship. Luke was a fun father but struggled to deal with the day-to-day responsibilities of parenting, which created occasional tension. His refusal to do anything he didn't want to do made delegating parental tasks difficult because he would work late or schedule meetings or other engagements to avoid dealing with menial tasks. The result was that Kerri had to serve as a disciplinarian, taskmaster, and overall "responsible" parent, while Luke could maintain his position as the "fun dad." When Brooklyn was 4 years old and Kerri became pregnant with their second child, Luke, who had already served one term in the state legislature, announced his candidacy for state attorney general without consulting with Kerri about the effect it would have on the family.

Luke's candidacy ushered in a new level of public attention to their family, and he began to increasingly implore Kerri to resign from her job since he wanted her to be a stay-at-home mom. He positioned this as a move that would improve Kerri's life since she'd have more time to spend with the children. Kerri intuitively felt that while the change may make more practical sense and give her more time with the children, it would also take away the only other thing in her life that was entirely hers and not attached to Luke. She was an excellent psychiatric nurse and quickly became the head nurse at the state's largest psychiatric hospital. She even considered returning to school to become a psychiatric nurse practitioner so she could open a private practice.

Luke understood that to achieve his political aspirations, he needed to construct a life that matched his desired constituency's "ideal family." Thus, he considered himself merely "convincing" Kerri to make the "best choices for their family." He believed she lacked the social understanding or savvy to realize that being a stay-at-home mom would appeal more to traditional, conservative voters. Besides, he always felt uncomfortable with Kerri's profession and her mental health and psychology knowledge because he knew nothing about those topics, which exacerbated his feelings of inferiority (Luke fancied himself a Renaissance man who knew a little about many issues). He felt that her stepping back from her stressful and depressing job might help neutralize some of their intellectual disparities. The deeper he got into conservative politics, the more insistent he became on adhering to traditional conservative values. He wanted to be the household's intellectual, spiritual, and financial head. He saw the culture's focus on mental health and "processing emotion" as a drain on the justice system by encouraging nonsensical explanations for lawlessness. He also felt it was bad for children's development to spend too much time thinking about their emotions and processes. Thus, he felt Kerri would be most effective and transformative in raising their children with the values he set forth. Kerri and Luke had numerous disagreements over his view of mental health, child-rearing, and many other social values, and she often felt diminished and undermined by his increasingly reductive approach to human relationships.

After the birth of their son, Braxton, Kerri experienced a severe bout of postpartum depression. Luke, who had won the election and was now the state's new attorney general, was increasingly busy, and the pressures of public service only exacerbated her feelings of isolation. Luke's disdain for emotional vulnerability gave way to palpable callousness for his wife's emotional experience. While Luke did not typically "rage" when he was angry when Kerri suggested that she spend a week in an inpatient postpartum depression recovery center, Luke flew off the handle. On the one hand, Kerri knew he would be reluctant. Still, she also felt that going to the facility would be the only way she could both get his attention and receive the help she needed since she had become estranged from her mother and sister, who had always been her primary means of support.

Luke was more concerned with the "optics" of his wife going to a "nuthouse" than Kerri herself, which only exacerbated her depression. Luke hired a public relations consultant to help them "frame the conversation" around her departure because he was afraid people would find out and it would undermine his image of being the archetype of a stable, well-adjusted conservative family. Once the consultant outlined the plan for Kerri's absence, which they called a "mommy retreat," Luke capitulated. Kerri left for a much-needed respite from what had become the pressure cooker of her everyday life.

Luke's staff generally liked him and found him funny, charismatic, and fun. Many of them had been with him since his career started in the legislature, but they noticed that his ADHD and disdain for details had become increasingly pronounced. He frequently demanded staffers pick up the slack, and his refusal to focus on "menial tasks" made everyone else's job harder. He became increasingly unwilling to admit when he'd made a mistake and occasionally became belligerent when someone suggested he was wrong or they questioned a decision. As was common in his marriage, if Luke felt inferior or challenged (particularly intellectually), he would suddenly become arrogant, dismissive, and even sarcastically mocking. In a particularly heated exchange with an aide who questioned his legal approach to a high-profile criminal case, he took the opportunity to publicly rebuke

CHAPTER FOUR

them, calling them an "idiot" and a "wetback," and questioning their education and competency in front of the whole office. The aide filed an EEOC complaint and subsequent lawsuit, which resulted in a mini scandal. Those around Luke learned to recognize his triggers. However, because of his legal prowess and considerable power, they chalked up his behavior to his brilliance and immense professional pressure as the state's youngest attorney general. Luke also developed a reputation for making inappropriate but veiled sexual comments to female staffers and showered particular attention on an assistant whom he frequently invited for drinks after work. Although very careful never to cross the line, particularly in this current culture of "man-hating" (as he called it), he liked to "have fun like any other man" and "refused to become a wuss and act as though he'd had his balls cut off just to please the snowflakes."

Luke's professional relationships often straddled the line between seriousness and sophomoric flippancy. It was common for Luke to stop work in his office in the middle of the day and demand everyone play Ping-Pong or go out for an afternoon drink. He increasingly relied on senior staffers and assistants to take care of the office's structure while focusing on the things (and people) he enjoyed. Despite the occasional chaos, Luke developed a reputation as a highly cunning legal mind and a particularly ruthless and effective prosecutor.

In Kerri's retreat, she reluctantly discovered that her anxiety and depression were exacerbated by her feelings of isolation in her marriage. When her therapist, whom she'd greatly respected, suggested Luke might have "some narcissistic qualities," she became defensive. Kerri insisted that he could be arrogant and cocky but that ultimately, he was a "good guy." She felt personally criticized every time someone mentioned his negative qualities and also felt that people were telling her "not to love him" or to "give up." She found herself repeating some of Luke's common refrains when people were "too negative" or "focusing on the worst." She had become wholly dependent on Luke financially, and he was the only other person in her life besides her children and a few acquaintances.

Eventually, Kerri returned home and settled into her everyday routine, except she insisted she continue her treatment in weekly therapy sessions with a psychologist. Luke refused to pay for Kerri's therapy. He'd prefer her to speak to their pastor since he trusted his approach to family values more than "head shrinkers." Exhausted with managing her depression, duties as a mother, and Luke's increasingly controlling and antagonistic behavior, she capitulated and instead met with their pastor (often with Luke present) to discuss their roles as a "Godly couple" and, in particular, her role as a "good wife and mother." While her depression medication had taken the edge off her emotional pain, Kerri began developing physical symptoms, such as unexplained aches, gastrointestinal upset, and a sharp decrease in her sex drive.

Ten years after they first met, their life's outside trappings seemed ideal. Luke was a prominent and respected politician; they had a beautiful family and a large house and were financially comfortable. Despite appearances, however, Kerri barely recognized herself anymore because she had, at some point, resigned herself to the Stepford wife role Luke insisted she play. She learned how to mask her authentic emotional state and perform her duties by hosting parties and serving on boards and committees with the other wives. She increasingly drowned her pain in wine and an addiction to trashy reality television, which she indulged in while the kids were at school. Her only friends were those she'd met in the gilded circle of political heavy hitters, and her relationship with her family was practically nonexistent. When Luke sat Kerri and the kids down and announced that he was finally ready to run for governor, her heart sank into her stomach. She knew intuitively that the stress would make Luke unreachable emotionally and exacerbate his arrogance.

Lose Yourself: Self-Negation, Minimizing, and Superficial Expectations

From the moment Luke had set his sights on Kerri, he began a seduction campaign. While it's entirely possible that Luke's attraction to

CHAPTER FOUR

Kerri's down-to-earth and humble approach to life could be an unconscious desire to capture some of those qualities for himself, often the very traits that attract the narcissistic person to another are deeply envied and sometimes even hated by the narcissist. Nonetheless, he was successful in love bombing Kerri. His calculated decision to purchase a book of poetry she would like while feigning ignorance might seem charming or cute in a non-narcissistic relationship when recounted as a couple's "meet cute" origin story. However, in Luke's case, the feigned interest in poetry in conjunction with his over-the-top proclamations of love and marriage virtually upon meeting her had an intoxicating and disorienting effect on Kerri.

Luke has a pervasive fear of feeling inferior and criticized due to a self-image based almost entirely on external validation. To prevent losing Kerri before he was able to establish attachment, he knew that he needed to diminish his ex-girlfriend's negative reviews of their relationship by delegitimizing her to Kerri. To assume that Luke's experience of Laurie was entirely fabricated would be unfair; rather, it was a distortion of the events of their relationship that positioned him as a victim of her overreactive emotionality and emotional selfishness. Also, in fairness, Laurie could have been insecure and emotionally inconsistent during her relationship with Luke. Of course, as with any interpersonal relationship, projections of one's shadow fears and insecurities often color the way we review unsatisfactory relationships. What differs with narcissists, and Luke in particular, is their inability to acknowledge any fault of or flaw in themselves that may have contributed to the relationship's dissolution.

Luke's charisma, drive, and confidence have afforded him many opportunities in life and undoubtedly attracted Kerri to him. However, Luke maintained a relatively evasive presence in Kerri's life, and she became a tool for his political and social ambitions. As we saw throughout the relationship, Kerri increasingly lost touch with herself and her loved ones.

Isolation is a tactic used to prevent voices critical or questioning of the narcissist from reaching those under their control. Luke fears criticism so much that he convinced Kerri that any feedback from those in her life who could provide support or perspective could damage their relationship. Many narcissistic people believe that without their control or manipulation of the opinion of those around their friendships and intimate relationships, others may recognize the narcissist's insecurity and subsequently leave or abandon them.

Although all human egos fear destruction through loss, interpersonally expressed through the dissolution of relationships, the narcissist is terrified of anything that minimizes their belief in their specialness. Often, they do not give their intimates enough credit in that they assume (because of some vague awareness of their narcissism) that if others provide an assessment of their behavior, they will be humiliated and exposed.

Luke prioritizes his career aspirations and has virtually no appreciation for Kerri's professional accomplishments despite their impressiveness. From his disparagement of her intellectual and professional interests, we saw that he's threatened since he has developed so little internal awareness. Psychology, self-help, or any other fields exploring one's inner experience are foreign to him and seem poised to offer unwanted analysis into his behavior. While some narcissistic people are more adept at navigating the human psyche (after all, psychiatry has a high incidence of narcissism), often the interior world is uninteresting for the narcissist. This is because developing internally yields little extrinsic validation and could potentially expose flaws that they'd rather keep hidden.

Luke intuitively chose Kerri for her moldability. She is accommodating and conflict-avoidant and seemed eager to please and appease her Prince Charming from the outset of their relationship. Kerri has a Pollyanna-esque orientation likely developed as a response to other stresses and traumas experienced in early life. Whatever the case, Luke made it clear that he needed a partner to support him in the life he wanted to build for himself. Kerri's people-pleasing tendencies contributed to her eventual abandonment of her autonomy and close connections in service to Luke's pressing desire to present a particular image.

Research suggests that couples merge personalities in fascinating and often surprising ways.[1] Some of this merging is due to proximity, but a great deal of molding occurs due to a mutual desire to find coherence and relational ease. In the case of Luke and Kerri, because of Luke's extrinsic values and fear of inferiority and Kerri's agreeable and flexible nature, the typical mutual-merging phenomenon is circumvented by Luke's psychological rigidity.

Most narcissistic egos lack psychological flexibility. Maintaining a fragile narcissistic psychic structure necessitates an inability to adjust one's interior world for relational harmony. Indeed, some narcissists are better equipped to make external behavioral changes to avoid constant conflict or discord, but this is very rarely accompanied by a shift in their capacity to empathize or truly understand the deeper value of those modifications. Luke is naturally conflict-avoidant and superficially optimistic; however, these characteristics belie deeper aggression and disdain for anyone who interferes with his happiness, freedom, or goals. We see this play out clearly in his professional relationships whereby his playfulness quickly gives way to ridicule or rage when he's questioned or made to appear incompetent.

His inappropriate humor and lack of professional boundaries are typical for the *Gleeful Charlatan* subtype, who often believe they deserve reverence, appreciation, and complete liberty due to their buoyant and playful energy. However, they frequently ignore social clues that indicate others' discomfort with their sophomoric, grandiose, or irresponsible behavior.

Luke indulges his libertine whims (e.g., impromptu trips and midday goof-off sessions at work), rendering him emotionally and physically unavailable in his marriage. As a result, Kerri, due to the pressures of living up to the social expectations of political life, begins to crumble under the expectations. As was apparent early in their relationship, Luke finds emotional expression burdensome at best and infuriating at worst. The internalized messaging from his unexpressive father and passive and often-fawning mother has caused him to project a toxic mix of attention-seeking neediness, emotional immaturity, and antagonism. The effects on Kerri prove to be devastating as she tries to manage the emotional weight of a loss of autonomy when asked to vacate her job position, motherhood, and emotional neglect.

Luke manipulates Kerri's emotional health and frequently gaslights her to create a reality that better suits his worldview. It is both inconvenient and undesirable for his wife to struggle with depression given his ideological standpoint on mental health. The effect on Kerri is immediately noticeable and will undoubtedly have an indirect effect on their children, who will grow up with a virtually absent and emotionally cold father and an exhausted, traumatized mother who has endured the pain of narcissistic neglect for years.

Kerri has adopted a classic enabling role with Luke in that she excuses his poor behavior to her family and even the therapist at the recovery center. It's often difficult for people in close relationships with narcissists to fully acknowledge the weight of the reality of their personalities. While it's true that narcissism isn't the entirety of a person's being, the behavioral and cognitive distortions created by narcissism can make it difficult to happily coexist with them without complete abdication of one's autonomy and preferences.

Luke's decision to run for governor represents a pattern of disregarding his wife's preferences and emotional health. By launching them further into the spotlight, Luke makes his world considerably larger, and Kerri's world becomes even smaller because she will undoubtedly be expected to present the false image of the perfect wife in an ideal marriage.

Sue: My Presence Is a Present

From the outset, Sue and Mark's relationship was characterized by Mark's prioritizing Sue's needs and catering to her material and emotional whims. Mark is dutiful, quietly confident, and ambitious; he felt that Sue would be an exciting challenge for him because he's always enjoyed winning over people who seemed inaccessible. Sue's vivacious personality and diva-like behavior were an aphrodisiac for Mark, and he knew she was the type of woman who would demand no less than the best. Sue made Mark "work for it" and wouldn't agree to be his girlfriend until he had passed through several months of intense cat-and-mouse games of hard to get. He showered her

CHAPTER FOUR

with increasingly grand and opulent gifts, culminating in a dazzling diamond necklace and a note that said, "Will you finally be my girlfriend?" Sue adored the attention and frequently bragged to her girlfriends about Mark's persistence and thoughtfulness.

Early in their relationship, Sue was quite attentive and, in many ways, fell into a similar role she played for her father. She cooked Mark meals, baked him cupcakes and cookies, showed up outside his classroom, and even surprised him with sexual favors at unusual times, such as in parking lots before tests or in between classes. Sue was also very moody. From one day to the next, Mark never knew if she would be bubbly, kind, flattering, and appeasing or cold, rejecting, aggrieved, and dissatisfied. He often told his friends he enjoyed that he never knew what he would get and that it "keeps him on his toes." However, many of his friends grew tired of her histrionic outbursts at parties. Sue had developed a reputation for getting very drunk, starting a fight with Mark, and storming out only to wait for him to follow, begging for forgiveness (often for unfounded evidence that he was "flirting with other women"). Sue displayed jealousy only while drunk. Otherwise, she appeared unbothered by Mark's popularity with other women and even had a sense of pride that she had mesmerized such a desirable man.

Sue would periodically threaten to break up with Mark when she felt he was becoming complacent and remind him that many men would die to be with her. At one point in their relationship, she flirted with and accepted dates with other suitors as if to say, "If you liked it, then you should've put a ring on it." Mark was frequently faced with a confusing dichotomy of Sue's angrily proclaiming how she didn't need him and that she was an "independent woman" and an opposite and equally intense neediness and softness that communicated "don't leave me."

After a year of dating, Sue abruptly broke up with Mark, coldly telling him that she wasn't confident he'd be able to give her the life she wanted. Sue told her friends that this was all to get him to propose because she wanted to be the first of her friend group to get engaged before graduation. The breakup, while only a few weeks, devastated Mark because the emotional whirlwind of his relationship with Sue had left him in a disoriented and depressed state. He felt addicted to the drama and her mercurial nature. While he hadn't intended to get married until he was close to finishing the first couple of years of medical school (a plan the two had previously discussed), he knew that he had to propose or he'd lose her.

The first four years of marriage were a whirlwind. Sue, who desperately wanted children, was pregnant with a son (Dylan) the first year and conceived their second child (Lilly) within a few months of Dylan's birth. Sue always had an affinity for babies and enjoyed the attention she received while pregnant. Her entitlement and demandingness increased exponentially when she was pregnant, and Mark, as much as possible, obliged her every whim. Sue became pregnant with twins (Conner and Callie) just before the two were about to move to Washington so he could begin his residency. The pressure of managing four children under four years old was overwhelming, even for Sue, who prided herself on being able to manage her household. Sue's mother, Li, insisted she move in with Sue and Mark since she had recently divorced Sue's father. Li was adamant that the children be raised with Chinese values and wasn't confident that Sue would adequately impart the cultural knowledge and discipline required.

Sue and Li's relationship had improved significantly since Sue left home for college, and Sue had matured considerably from being the "reckless" teenager Li had had such difficulty raising. Li was pleased that Sue "married well," but she still harbored disappointment over her daughter "wasting her talents" by not pursuing a graduate degree. From the moment Li moved into their home, Sue's stress increased, and she became more militant, testy, and emotionally reactive. While Sue appreciated the help with the children, having her mother "breathing down her neck," at times, made being at home unbearable. Sue started shopping and initiating expensive home decoration projects and became increasingly less interested in caring for her children.

Mark, who worked grueling hours in the hospital as a resident, had taken to completely placating Sue's whims, and even though

CHAPTER FOUR

the financial toll of Sue's shopping habit weighed heavily on him, he kept his concerns private to friends and family, instead, framing it as "keeping the Mrs. Happy." On the rare occasion when he did confront her regarding her excessive spending, Sue became coldly defiant, telling Mark, "I've had four of your children; I at least deserve to have some things that I want!" When anyone criticized or questioned Sue's selfishness or entitlement, she became similarly petulant and defiant and proudly proclaimed that she was the "queen of the house."

Sue, while typically upbeat (particularly if she got her way), could become enraged, overreactive, and punitive. She was particularly harsh with her mother, who was determined to stick around to help manage the daily tasks (e.g., cooking, cleaning, and changing diapers). Despite the often-tense relationship between Li and Sue, Li shared with Mark that she couldn't be sure the children would get meaningful attention if she weren't there. Mark agreed, recognizing his wife lacked any meaningful maternal instincts. Sue developed a vibrant social life serving on various boards and committees in the community, and Mark was busy working. She enjoyed taking the children with her while on the town because she liked the attention and praise she received for her "beautiful family."

After a few years, Sue and Mark finally felt settled in Washington. Mark was offered a prestigious surgical residency at a local hospital with a significant salary increase. Sue began volunteering at a small local children's theater and quickly became the organization's executive director due to her love of the arts and her outgoing personality. Despite daily life feeling more established, Li and Sue's relationship was no better off. Luckily, there were fewer arguments between the two, and Li had taken an adjunct professor position at a community college but remained living with Sue and Mark.

Over the years, Li had softened considerably compared to the stark taskmaster orientation Sue experienced in her childhood. Li felt her duty was to protect her grandchildren from her daughter's selfishness. Sue was deeply resentful of Li's improved mothering and softer nurturing nature compared to what she had received as a child, which gave rise to a palpable competitiveness.

Sue's relationship with her children was fraught with favoritism. She adored her firstborn, Dylan, and would move mountains to make him happy, and he, in turn, as he grew up, would defend her dutifully against his sibling's criticisms. Her second child, Lilly, was frequently ignored. Sue often commented on how her personality was "too much like NaiNai" (Li) and was constantly pushing her to be "more fun" and to "make more friends." She would also "jokingly" predict Lilly's becoming a "boring professor with no friends."

The twins, Connor and Callie, were virtually ignored, except when Sue wanted attention for having twins. Indeed, much of Sue's neglect was seen only within the home because, in public, she played the role of a doting mother, often taking credit for much of their accomplishments and barely mentioning that her mother had essentially helped raise the children for the past decade. Sue rarely made any effort to conceal her favoritism. She would shower Dylan with attention, gifts, and impromptu surprises. One summer, she took Dylan and the twins to Disneyland, leaving Lilly behind, claiming she "wouldn't enjoy it anyway." Lilly internalized her mother's obvious disappointment and became increasingly withdrawn, anxious, and sullen. She tried to compensate by excelling in school, greatly pleasing her grandmother, with whom she had grown very close.

Sue often made Mark feel guilty for his demanding job. Although she immensely enjoyed the financial and status benefits of being married to a doctor, she was deeply resentful when he wasn't home to "help her with the kids." In reality, her mother frequently tended to the children, and Sue's social calendar was full of meetings, lunches, girl's trips, and other self-serving distractions. When Mark would push back on her guilt-trip tirades or blatant contradictions, Sue would stop talking and often give him the silent treatment for days at a time (a punishment she also frequently used against the children). Mark, who had become solely focused on his career and providing the lifestyle his wife and children had grown accustomed to, preferred to smooth over difficulties with gifts and satiating his wife's desires. He erroneously believed that if he kept her materially satisfied, she would eventually become grateful and appreciative of his efforts.

CHAPTER FOUR

Interestingly, while Sue was extravagant when purchasing items for herself, she was notoriously frugal (bordering on cheap) when shopping for others, including her family. Her tendency to skimp or bargain shop when it came to purchasing things for the children or even household essentials was a point of tension between her, Li, the children, and Mark. However, Mark, and eventually the children, understood that the more she saved on groceries or household essentials, the more she could redirect her substantial weekly household allowance toward things she wanted for herself. When questioned about her spending habits, Sue would obfuscate or, more frequently, become defensive and respond by willfully and defiantly spending more money.

After one particularly heated discussion with Mark about the weekly household budget, Sue went out the following day and purchased a brand-new Jaguar without consulting Mark. Incensed, Mark had had enough of Sue's entitlement and confronted her about her diva-like behavior, saying she thought only about herself. Sue became hysterical, breaking dishes, screaming, and verbally abusing Mark. The explosive fight resulted in Mark's leaving for a month to stay with a close friend. Sue threatened divorce and to "take him for everything he has." She lamented her "ungrateful" and "absent" husband and truly believed and convinced most of their friends that he doesn't appreciate all she does for him and "his children" and felt entirely justified in her punitive treatment. After Lilly begged him to come home, Mark apologized to Sue for upsetting her and implored her to let him return home, even though he still felt his anger regarding her selfish decision was justified. She capitulated and was subsequently gifted with a new diamond ring for his "insensitive criticism." Sue never apologized, and once she had agreed to let him come home, she never spoke of the argument again. Sue was notorious for her lifelong streak of never apologizing or admitting fault. She was prideful and confident that anything she said or did was justified, even in the heat of an argument.

Other than the occasional explosive row, Sue and Mark's relationship was relatively free of conflict primarily because they stayed out of each other's way. Sue was busy as the executive director of the children's theater and other community arts pursuits, while Mark took a surgical director position at the hospital. Generally, Sue was as pleasant, upbeat, and gregarious as she'd always been, but as their prominence in the community grew, so did her entitlement and tendency toward excessive spending. Sue struggled to moderate her spending habits, and on the rare occasion that Mark would challenge her spending, she would reign in her frivolity for a brief time, demonstrating that she knew how to budget, then slowly return to her old ways or secretly indulge her whims.

The disparities in her treatment of her children had become evident to anyone who spent time around the family. By the time the children were adolescents, the twins had developed a vibrant social life, preferring to spend most of their time away from home. Lilly, leaning into her natural academic talents, excelled in school and spent most of her family time with her grandmother. Dylan's personality strongly resembled his mother's: gregarious, outgoing, attention-seeking, and entitled. Sue continued to underscore her preference for Dylan through conspicuous displays of generosity. She often alternated focusing on each of the twins depending on the whim of the day and consistently expressed disinterest in Lilly, mainly due to her close relationship with Li.

As a teenager, Lilly began to blossom. She found a friend group aligned with her values, and her previous awkwardness gave way to elegance and sophistication. For the first time in her life, she began to see (through the encouragement of her grandmother and a supportive friend group) her outer beauty and intellectual prowess and took more pride in her appearance. Subsequently, Lilly began receiving attention from young men, joined the cheerleading squad, and eventually started dating a boy she met in the engineering club. As Lilly transformed, Sue grew more antagonistic and critical of her daughter, and a palpable competitiveness developed. Sue would frequently comment on how certain outfits Lilly wore could be improved or tell her she didn't know how to apply makeup or fix her hair flatteringly despite Lilly's being noticeably more attractive than

CHAPTER FOUR

her mother. When Lilly would push back or call out her mother's critical comments, Sue would exclaim that she was "only trying to help" and then pout or give Lilly the silent treatment for a few days to regain control.

Lilly hesitated to bring friends around her mother because Sue would often find opportunities to criticize or subtly undermine her if she was around. Sue encouraged Lilly to invite the engineering club members, including her boyfriend, Travis, to work on an upcoming science fair project at their home. Reluctantly, Lilly agreed, and Sue prepared snacks, ordered pizza, and not surprisingly, played the role of "cool mom" quite well. Lilly's friends, who had often heard stories about her mother's bad behavior, were confused because they immediately liked her. Sue focused excessively on Travis, smiling and flirting with him like a schoolgirl. Lilly was humiliated and hurt when Travis exclaimed how much he "loved her mom." Lilly knew that her mom's efforts to win over her friends were simply a demonstration of Sue's likability, ease with people, and an opportunity to compete for attention. Lilly invited her friends over a few more times, and every time, Sue went out of her way to ensure she was home (a novelty since she was frequently out running errands, at meetings, or socializing) so she could entertain her friends.

After six months, Travis broke up with Lilly because he felt she was "always complaining," which caused a fight between them since this was a common refrain she received from her oldest brother, Dylan, and her mother. Lilly didn't appreciate Travis's constant implications that Lilly was paranoid because she thought her mom "hated her." Because Travis was the first romantic relationship Lilly had ever experienced, she was understandably distraught over the breakup. She found little solace or sympathy in her mother and instead confided in her brother, Conner, whom she found emotionally sensitive and understanding.

In addition to Travis's dismissing Lilly's feelings about her mother, she was able to see, in retrospect, that they shared many similarities in that he could be critical of her appearance and moody and tended to shift his attention from Lilly to her friends when he was upset, which often made her feel abandoned and lonely. While Mark was pleased that Lilly had broken up with Travis, because he thought "he was annoying," Sue expressed anger and even admonishment in her belief that Lilly had "thrown away the best thing that ever happened to her." Lilly received little empathy or attention from either parent.

With her oldest children nearing the age of leaving home, Sue accepted a more prestigious creative-development position with a larger theater company without discussing it with her family. The job would require her to travel within the state more, but she assumed her mother would continue to stay home to help manage the day-to-day parenting duties she avoided. However, Li informed Sue that she would be moving back to China to help care for her mother, who had recently become ill. This meant she would be unavailable to help cook, clean, and drive children to extracurricular activities. Upon hearing Li's news, Sue flew into a rage, claiming nobody supported her dreams and lamenting how much she sacrificed to raise her family with no appreciation or recognition.

Mark tried to mediate his wife's tantrum by offering to get a housekeeper and pay someone to help drive the kids when he was unavailable, but she was inconsolable and refused to be quelled. For a week after her outburst, she gave everyone in her family the silent treatment, moping around and indulging in shopping and eating as consolation for her life. She told the theater company she couldn't accept the job and stayed in her current role as creative director of the youth theater group. However, she was noticeably more irritable and fussier with her staff, the children in the company, and her family. Her close friends were frequently subjected to martyring narratives and complaints about those who were "ungrateful" and "unappreciative."

Sue became increasingly punitive to Mark, and from his perspective, it seemed like no matter what he did to please her, it was impossible to make her happy. Gifts, trips, words of affirmation, and any other attempts to garner any pleasantness (which was increasingly less frequent) were met with lukewarm reception at best and overt disappointment at worst. Sue revealed that Li was leaving and

CHAPTER FOUR

that she was turning down her "dream job" because her family was "mostly unsupportive of her," which made her realize that she'd spent her "whole life putting her needs aside for the sake of others." Any attempts from Mark or her friends to counter this narrative was met with derision or accusations that they were "gaslighting" her. She would often withdraw and freeze the person out or redirect any remaining pleasantness to someone adjacent to show her displeasure.

As Sue grew disappointed and dissatisfied with her life, her unhappiness produced far-reaching effects outside her marriage, family, and close friends because of her prominent role in the arts community. Additionally, her histrionic displays, vindictiveness, and entitlement, mainly contained within her home environment, seeped into her professional life.

Me First: Entitlement, Competition, and Selfishness

Sue's childlike entitlement only grew more demanding as she aged. As her and Mark's relationship progressed, Mark learned that the best way to ensure Sue's happiness was to prioritize her wishes. This dynamic is undoubtedly charming at first because Mark sees himself as a bit like a Prince Charming archetype, but it quickly becomes an enabling device that reinforces Sue's view of herself as special. Sue relishes making Mark "work for it" and plays a coy game of cat and mouse while subtly testing Mark's willingness to accommodate her. Sue is the *Entitled Caregiver* and within the psychodynamic structure of this subtype is the belief that others' willingness to provide for them materially is equivocal to their love. Any denial of their desires is thus communicated as an insult and an indication that they are not valued or loved. This belief becomes the central theme and, subsequently, the most toxic element of Sue and Mark's relationship.

Sue demonstrates superficial caretaking behaviors to establish herself as attentive and caring (e.g., baking, surprises, and gifts). Still, these acts of service fuel what will ultimately be Mark's permanent indebtedness due to Sue's "generosity." Before the two married, Sue's belief in her generosity and Mark's relative inattentiveness in comparison fueled some stark double standards whereby she continued to express interest in other men to invoke jealousy and punish Mark for not adequately tending to her needs or paying enough attention to her. Sue even manipulates Mark into a marriage proposal by dramatically breaking up with him to incite a sense of loss and desperation.

In romantic relationships, people become addicted to the emotional intensity that narcissists evoke. The human brain seeks stability and consistency, particularly when something feels good. Thus, whenever whatever made us initially feel good is withdrawn or feels inconsistent or intermittent, we develop a fear response to ensure that the stimuli, or what we believe to be the source of our satisfaction, don't leave. Narcissists are inconsistent with their affection and attention because they often intuitively understand the interpersonal power that attention can broker. Therefore, many narcissists focus and refocus their attention on various people, sometimes strategically, to show those who are not getting their attention just what they're missing.

Sue's inherent interpersonal intelligence (not uncommon in the Prideful-Flattering types) affords her a finely tuned ability to manipulate others with whom she is in a relationship. This becomes particularly damaging to children or subordinates, who often experience their parents' withholding and weaponizing their praise, attention, and approval. Sue is no exception, as we see with her daughter Lilly. Sue loves the attention she receives from being pregnant and having young children. Many of this subtype enjoy young children and conceive of themselves as nurturers. They can be attentive and loving toward infants, but the *Entitled Caregiver* tends to lose interest as the child grows and requires more complex emotional relating. This is because the expectation is that the child will grow up and, much like everyone else in their lives, tend to their whims and needs as they arise. Of course, all of this is unspoken and largely unconscious. If they have a child who is not focused on pleasing or meeting their expectations, conversely, if they are overly focused on pleasing or seeking approval, they withhold their affection. It's a constantly moving target designed to keep others in the position of trying to please them.

Sue is almost immediately resentful of her children likely because their needs trump her desires. Thus, when her mother moves in to help tend to the children, a competitive dynamic is created, building animosity in which the children are in the crosshairs. Many narcissists compete with their children. Whether it is the attention of the spouse or simply attention from the outside world, their inherently unstable sense of self causes them to see comparisons everywhere, including their loved ones, partners, and spouses. When it becomes clear that Lilly embodies many of the characteristics that Sue believes she lacks (e.g., intellectual, academic, thoughtful, or quiet), Sue equates those qualities with her mother, who values those traits. Thus, Lilly becomes the de facto black sheep for daring to stoke Sue's insecurities.

Growing up as the black sheep child of a narcissist is a dangerous and painful role for the child. These children often become the psychological dumping ground for much of the narcissist's disowned rage and shame. In Sue's case, because of her need to "help" others superficially, Lilly became a project (not unlike her best friend Jenny) that required her expert care and molding to become more like Sue. Typically, if the narcissistic person has multiple children, one child will strive to embody or naturally be more amenable to their view of themselves as a person and a parent. This creates a clear "favorite" among the children and fosters more significant sibling division, as with Sue's firstborn, Dylan (we'll see more of this dynamic in the following chapter).

Sue's refusal to engage in parenting duties that don't suit her whims creates a dynamic whereby Li, Lilly, and Mark have taken on more responsibility in the household. Many histrionic traits accompany this narcissistic subtype, making them superficially charming or alluring to others. Sue's focus on her work with the theater is a good use of her flair for the dramatic, but her inability to focus on others for too long will become increasingly problematic for her in the social world. The immediate effect of her superficiality creates an environment in which her family learns to walk on eggshells around her mercurial moods and temper tantrums.

To cope, Mark becomes increasingly resigned to Sue's personality and, in some ways, sacrifices his children on the proverbial altar of Sue's narcissism by burying himself in increasing layers of work. Of course, the less attention Sue receives from Mark, the more her despondency grows. However, because she cannot express vulnerability or manage her growing loneliness and dissatisfaction, she punishes Mark by becoming more materialistic and entitled. Despite wanting to have children early in their marriage and enjoying the attention of being pregnant and having babies that others could fawn over, Sue did not truly enjoy being a parent. The older she becomes, the more her resentment and rage grow, eroding many of the positive qualities that made her, at times, fun to be around.

As Mark and Sue's marriage progresses, Mark finds a way to exist under Sue's rules of engagement, which consist primarily of satiating and not obstructing Sue's desires. However, the toll of Mark's enabling Sue's petulance is most evident with their children. While the twins took on the role of invisible children, they appear to be largely disconnected from the overall family dynamic. At the same time, Dylan embodies the role of the good child because he mirrors Sue's desirable qualities back to her.

Sue's relationship with Lilly is deeply problematic. Sue has projected her mother's critical voice onto Lilly, exacerbated by the fact that Lilly and Li are close. Li's living in the home and adopting the role of surrogate mother to Sue's children exacerbated Sue's resentment toward her mother and propagated a competitive environment in which the children become collateral damage. However, Sue's blatant criticism, disapproval, and rejection of Lilly profoundly affect Lilly's self-esteem. Often, the most sensitive child is the one who receives the narcissistic parent's negative projections due to their inability to acknowledge their vulnerability. Lilly serves as a proverbial garbage receptacle for Sue's deep feelings of inadequacy and dissatisfaction.

The disturbing dynamic between Sue and Lilly reaches a zenith when Lilly finally individuates and forms social relationships that align with her interests and aptitudes. Sue's jealousy of Lilly's academic interests and flowering beauty creates a situation in which Sue feels that to regain a sense of superiority, she must denigrate and humiliate any semblance of her daughter's growing self-worth. The effect will be profound and pervasive because Lilly already experiences the dissonance of people (including her boyfriend) who cannot reconcile Lilly's perception of Sue's calculated manipulation with her energetic, nurturing, fun image. Travis, Lilly's boyfriend, thus becomes a template for future relationships whereby she will not only choose relationships with people who mirror her mother's disapproval and criticism but also set up comparisons between her and her more outgoing, extroverted mother.

While some narcissistic subtypes are more evidently antagonistic or challenging to the social world, many let the breadth of their antagonistic traits shine only with those closest to them (usually their family or primary relationships). The split between the narcissist's public persona and their relationships shows a level of cognizance that their more challenging behaviors are not desirable. This is an essential distinction between those whose impulse control is compromised and thus struggle to modulate their reactivity or anger due to some other factor (e.g., brain injuries, mood disorders, or trauma) and narcissists, who have relative awareness of when and with whom they can misbehave. That said, emotional impulse control and narcissism can and do coexist in some people, which can complicate matters. However, in Sue's case, her acute awareness of her image, unlike her private tantrums, implies a willful refusal to modulate her behavior.

The interpersonal and social implications of narcissistic abuse on children cannot be overstated. Children of narcissistic parents are more frequently diagnosed with depression, anxiety, PTSD, OCD, and substance abuse disorders.[2] The effects of narcissistic parenting styles have long-lasting effects on relationships and help reproduce intergenerational trauma due to learned behaviors, particularly if the child of the narcissist never receives the support or validation to make sense of what they experienced as children. It can be difficult to reconcile that your parent, whom you often love, is also incapable of mirroring unconditional love due to their feelings of inadequacy and fear of intimacy. The implications of narcissistic parenting styles on children's integration into the greater social world are profound, and we'll explore some of the ways that narcissistic interpersonal abuse and neglect shape familial environments in Chapter 5.

Joe: Lust, Insight, and Domination

Joe gained attention in the New York City music scene as a soulful and talented maverick. His musical style shifted, and he began composing more acoustic works and developed an equally impressive representation as a singer–songwriter. His work was lauded as "emotionally honest," "raw," and "unapologetic." It had been four years since Joe completed his gender-affirming surgery, and he had had a couple of significant romantic relationships that had become the guiding force behind his artistic expression. Joe met Josie after a tumultuous breakup with another woman and a challenging period of feuding with his mother and stepfather. Josie became his spiritual muse, and through her, he discovered transcendental meditation and became deeply interested in esoterism and Eastern spiritual philosophies. Josie was the opposite of Joe; she was compassionate and vulnerable and embodied a soft feminine finesse. Josie worked as a bodyworker and holistic therapist. They enjoyed a relatively peaceful and healthy relationship for the first two years compared to Joe's other love affairs.

Josie taught Joe "nonviolent communication," and the two attended various workshops on spiritual development, healing, and psychoanalysis. Joe had a knack for understanding people, and at workshops, he made a strong impression on others with his bold and often insightful pronouncements, tendency to "call out bullshit," and charismatic and electrifying energy. Teachers in the workshops would even capitulate to Joe for insights, and at healing workshops, he demonstrated a strong aptitude for effective physical and emotional healing. With his music career stalled, Joe saw more lucrative opportunities for recognition and financial success by becoming a spiritual teacher and healer.

CHAPTER FOUR

Throughout Joe's spiritual awakening, he had taken some considerable steps to heal some of his gender dysphoria and early childhood trauma growing up as a trans man in a conservative community. However, he remained primarily unwilling to allow himself to be fully vulnerable. Because of his commanding nature, he dazzled his teachers and healers and subtly switched roles so that he became an authority to avoid revealing his actual vulnerabilities. While his relationship with Josie was relatively calm, he often took opportunities in workshops or courses to demonstrate his prowess and magnetism relative to her quiet and gentle approach. Josie frequently held workshops in somatic healing, where Joe would often interject and, in many cases, take over. Josie occasionally asked Joe to allow her to conduct her workshops without interference and eventually requested he not attend them. He would capitulate and eventually conduct his own seminars, which would sometimes siphon attendees from Josie who were entertained by his charismatic approach to healing.

Joe earned several certificates in psychospiritual healing and energy work. He took courses with many prominent healers and teachers and took great pride in being friendly with the heavy hitters of the self-help community. He branded himself a "spiritual psychotherapist" who specialized in healing childhood trauma through "confrontational insight." Because he was effective and powerful, he quickly gained a following with people who had heard about his no-nonsense and penetrating approach to healing.

Joe's larger-than-life personality quickly overshadowed Josie's work, and in a few years, he had wholly reinvented himself as a self-help guru in New York. Joe charged three times what the average psychotherapist or coach charged and, because of his confidence, had little trouble getting others to pay his fees. He often inflated his accomplishments and didn't hesitate to drop the names of well-known spiritual teachers or authors he'd associated with to increase the perception of his greatness. When Josie suggested, in her characteristically tactful way, that perhaps he was "overstating" some aspects of his resume and he didn't need to do that, he would retort that she was trying to control his business and thwart his success because she was jealous of his gifts in a spiteful and vicious way; then he would quickly bookend his anger with a spiritualized response by stating something like, "which is understandable given the history of trauma of being overlooked by others. But don't make me the bad guy. This is your shadow work." Josie often had little recourse to respond when he'd use his newfound understanding of psychology and spiritual concepts against her. When called out, he had a way of being spiteful and deflecting any blame onto the other through weaponizing self-help language, much of which he had learned from Josie.

Early in Joe and Josie's relationship, he often complained of a lack of intensity and passion. He would frequently display an overbearing possessiveness and protectiveness over Josie, which she initially found intoxicating. Additionally, Joe's physical appearance changed considerably as he underwent hormone therapy. He gained significant muscle mass, which he enhanced by frequent weightlifting and which made up for his relatively short stature. His jet-black hair contrasted his cobalt-blue eyes, which made him striking and intimidating. Joe was particularly intriguing to women, and he enjoyed the attention he received, particularly now that he felt he "passed" as a cisgender, heterosexual man almost without exception. He frequently flirted with women, including clients and workshop participants. At times, he would even indulge in affairs with workshop attendees and clients. Josie made efforts not to make her jealousy or insecurity Joe's problem given she never had proof of his infidelities.

Upon feeling tortured by her intuitive knowledge that Joe was cheating on her, she asked if Joe wanted to have an open relationship, having observed his penchant for women, at which he became irate. He took her request as a "projection of her desire to sleep with other people." After his initial rage at Josie's attempt to accommodate his sexual appetites while trying to create some transparency and honesty around Joe's indiscretions, he adopted the role of psychotherapist. He had become exceptionally skilled in obfuscating and spiritualizing interpersonal conflicts. At times, he could be incredibly insensitive, refusing to acknowledge any emotional investment in Josie's concerns. At other times, he could be immensely insightful

CHAPTER FOUR

and empathetic and facilitate profound emotional breakthroughs. The latter kept Josie engaged and intoxicated, feeling something akin to an addiction to him that often superseded her appropriate anger at his insensitivity or emotional manipulation.

Joe's spiritual awakening smoothed many of his rough edges as he learned to be more diplomatic, particularly in business and with clients. He also learned how to conceal his characteristic rage and instead utilize his ability to charm or weaponize his intuitive understanding of others' motivations and desires to his advantage when necessary.

Joe extolled the benefits of compassion, honesty, and authenticity in his workshops and work with clients. He was an exemplar of spiritual and psychological health for those who didn't know him well. He learned how to conceal his many vices, from sex to drinking and gambling. However, if for some reason, someone did challenge his excessiveness (or any character flaw) in the face of his spiritualized persona, he adeptly turned the situation around, challenging them to look at their puritanism and judgment.

Joe considered Josie his soulmate, and after four years of being together, he asked if she would marry him, and she agreed despite some reservations. Joe insisted that even if she denied his request, they were meant to be together and she would always find her way back to him. He also suggested that their karma dictated that she be unfailingly loyal to him no matter what he did because of her past-life indiscretions. He always ended those conversations by assuring her he forgave her for hurting him in those other lifetimes.

Their relationship was peppered with Joe's indiscretions. Still, the two had enjoyed meaningful psychological, spiritual, and emotional improvements in their lives, and their romance was quite often intense and fairy tale–like. They traveled extensively together, attending various retreats, workshops, and courses around the world, and gained some recognition as a spiritual power couple.

While Joe was an effective and dynamic healer for many of his clients, he was also possessive and territorial. He enjoyed his ability to exert control over the emotional and psychological lives of his students and clientele. He subtly demanded they reveal all their secrets to him if their healing was to be successful. He often demanded that his clients abandon other therapists, coaches, or clinicians because it would "interfere with the transformative process." Even though Joe became quite skilled at working with others, he lacked the formal education to deal with official clinical psychological diagnoses. Josie was a licensed professional counselor who offered to treat clients who needed mental health assistance. Still, Joe refused to refer them, which resulted in legal liability when a disturbed client attempted suicide after a particularly intense session with Joe. Unable to admit wrongdoing, Joe severed ties with the client and adopted a lengthy liability waiver, assuming no responsibility for the client's well-being or mental health despite advertising himself as a psychotherapist. Though undeniably respected, Joe inspired fierce loyalty, admiration, and at times, fear from others.

Joe believed boundaries were for the weak, but his mandate often worked only one way. For example, he implicitly insisted on Josie's complete transparency with him, while he would frequently withhold or refuse to offer information to her, claiming she was "too nosy." He struggled to maintain a healthy professional relationship with clients and, if so inclined, would socialize with them and invite them to his and Josie's home. The blurring of professional boundaries was often confusing for clients who never knew what to make of this dynamic.

Iona, a beautiful young woman with a strong desire for spiritual development, had become one of his favorite clients because of her willingness to learn and her lighthearted and gentle demeanor, and she quickly became his mentee. As his work with her progressed, so did her enmeshment into his personal life. He began their relationship within the confines of an appropriate client–coach dynamic. He helped her work through some residual anger and resentment toward her father, who sexually abused her as a child. In only two years, Joe had learned virtually everything about Iona's life and successfully helped restore her self-esteem, reverse a long-standing autoimmune disease, and recognize an innate gift she had for healing. Eventually,

CHAPTER FOUR

he began offering Iona gratis sessions, inviting her to observe his coaching with other clients and bringing her as his helper to workshops he facilitated, often replacing Josie (a dynamic that incited considerable jealousy in Josie given her suspicion of Joe's past indiscretions). Over time, Joe began confiding in Iona and sharing details of his and Josie's marriage and his feelings of being trapped due to her emotional manipulation.

During a spiritual retreat to Chile, which Joe and Josie hosted, he asked Iona to join him as his apprentice. During the trip, he asked if Iona wanted to have a threesome with him and Josie, now his wife, before having consulted with Josie. Flattered and intrigued, Iona agreed since she had developed a strong attraction to and increasingly found him and the mystique surrounding him irresistible. Iona enjoyed the attention that Joe paid her, and her confidence in her abilities as a healer had grown immensely because he had assured her of her "specialness" and "unique gifts." Josie was immediately insulted when Joe proposed the ménage à trois with Iona. She expressed her concern not only for their relationship dynamic but also for Iona's mental health because she would undoubtedly be confused by the unclear and shifting relational dynamics.

Joe dismissed Josie's concerns and discussed the spiritual importance of bringing Iona into their relationship, insisting that the three had "important work" to do together and stating that if Josie weren't into the dalliance, he would proceed with Iona anyway. Josie erupted in anger, telling Joe that his manipulation and coercive tactics were toxic and that he was deeply out of alignment with his spiritual values of doing no harm. The two had an intense fight in their room, which was next to Iona's. Hearing the conflict and sensing that it must've stemmed from Joe's proposition, Iona went next door and attempted to mediate the dispute. Josie was horrified that Iona had overheard their fight, but Joe took it as an opportunity to convince Josie that the threesome and, ultimately, a "throuple" between them was what "their karma demands."

"Josie, you have to understand that the universe brought Iona into our lives and that she holds both the masculine and feminine polarities to balance out my strong masculine and your soft feminine," Joe said in a calm, rational voice only moments after screaming at Josie.

"I'm just not comfortable with this. I love Iona and think she has wonderful potential, but this could be a real problem for her development. There's no boundaries here," Josie said, holding back tears of anger and disappointment.

"I hate to see the two of you fighting about me. Even though I'd love to share in a relationship with both of you, if it's going to cause conflict, I don't want to hurt anyone, so maybe it isn't the best idea," Iona said, tears welling up in her eyes.

"Josie, I'm really disappointed in your lack of maturity here. We can all sleep on it and discuss it later. I've made my intention known, and I think you'll both find that, ultimately, this is what will happen anyway." Joe left the room smugly, leaving the two stunned women staring at each other in confusion.

The next day, after the intense exchange, Joe facilitated a workshop of over 40 people in which he was teaching the importance of integrity and brutal honesty in spiritual development. The whole time, he acted as if the drama from the evening before had never happened.

After the Chile trip, Joe felt he had lost authority over Josie and Iona and was distant and cold for several weeks. He dialed back warmth with Iona and ceased inviting her to social gatherings. However, he continued his paid sessions with her, although Iona noticed he had adopted a slightly harsher, more pointed way of indicating her shortcomings. He insisted that Iona work on her "loyalty issues." He suggested that she reconcile with her father, whom she hadn't spoken to in 10 years due to previous physical and sexual abuse. When Iona pushed back against the suggestion, she pointed out that Joe was contradicting his previous guidance about maintaining healthy self-care boundaries and having no regrets about leaving those behind who had hurt her. Joe would become cold and unflinching, stating that his guidance on the matter had changed. He said that under no uncertain terms, she needed to forgive if she wanted to grow.

CHAPTER FOUR

Thereafter, in sessions with Joe, Iona became increasingly anxious and depressed. She felt that she had disappointed her mentor, and despite her best efforts to repair the relationship and get back in his good graces, it appeared she was only further disappointing him. The suggestion that she reconcile with her father weighed heavily on her mind, and she began having nightmares and flashbacks of some of the abuse she had endured as a child. Iona reached out to a therapist she had worked with in the past to help her deal with her increasingly unstable emotional condition. However, because she knew of Joe's policy of not having other practitioners while working with him, she also experienced immense guilt because she knew she couldn't tell him lest she risk his terminating what was left of their relationship.

After several months of attempting to get Joe to address some of their relationship problems, Josie requested that the two see a couple's counselor to help save their marriage. Joe agreed to see a clinician he chose because he didn't trust her selections, believing she would choose someone who didn't understand his personality; he also insisted that their counselor be a man. Josie reluctantly agreed after Joe selected a psychotherapist the two had met at a retreat who specialized in "reclaiming masculinity."

Joe was charming, calm, and authoritative in their first session with Dr. Finn. He insisted that Josie share her concerns about the relationship first and sat quietly as she outlined her belief that a double standard exists in their relationship and that Joe demands complete loyalty and transparency without giving the same. When she finished stating the problem from her perspective, Joe began eloquently discussing the difficulties he experienced in showing vulnerability and how, as a transgender man, he feels that she is trying to squelch his masculine expression. Dr. Finn, who was famous for his ideological assertions of defined gender roles, particularly in emotional relating, agreed that Josie had unfair expectations of Joe given his gender dysphoric trauma. Joe shared that he felt judged and stifled by Josie, who "takes every opportunity to demonstrate his insensitivity from her feminine perspective," and that he had plenty of judgment from his mother and stepfather growing up. Josie left the therapy session feeling guilty and apologized to Joe for not realizing the extent of his pain. However, she also felt that many of the issues, such as infidelity, dismissiveness, and lack of respect for her relational boundaries, were superseded by his pain. Even though she felt that Dr. Finn had taken Joe's side and against her better judgment, she agreed to continue the sessions.

After the initial session, Joe shared with Josie his love and appreciation of her and his heartfelt expression that she was his only "true soulmate" and that all he needed was her. Joe's seeming vulnerability and openness was something Josie hadn't seen since the two had begun dating, so she was thrilled to experience his romantic side again. They had a wonderful two weeks filled with romantic dinners, extended intimate talks about their shared interests, great sex, and plenty of laughs.

At their next session with Dr. Finn, Joe began by discussing his desire to open their relationship to experience greater pleasure and satisfaction and his feeling judged and criticized by Josie's refusal to discuss the issue. She was blindsided, asking why he hadn't brought this up to her again since their trip to Chile, to which he responded that she often comes across like a scolding teacher and that he'd rather not deal with it. The session was contentious, and Josie passionately defended her boundaries with Dr. Finn and Joe, calling out the rampant double standards in the expectations of conduct.

After the session, Josie felt exhausted. While she felt justifiably angry with Joe, he broke the silence between them by stating that he felt "extremely disrespected" by her "dramatic display," then coldly told her he had already spoken with an attorney and wanted to file for divorce. Both shocked and relieved, Josie agreed.

When they returned home, Joe told Josie he wanted her to move out as soon as possible since he had paid most of the rent. Josie called a close friend, who agreed to let her stay while she found a new place. Joe's coldness and indifference were stunning, given his warmth and expressions of love just a few days prior.

"Why are you doing this? Why are you being so cruel to me?" Josie finally asked before packing a few of her belongings.

CHAPTER FOUR

"That's the problem. It's always about you and what you want. I've protected you from many things, and you don't have my back. You'll always be tied to me spiritually, but I need room to be myself," Joe replied coolly.

Josie opened her mouth to protest but decided against it. She realized that the more she said, the more disturbing the interaction would become.

A few weeks later, after Josie had completely purged herself from the apartment with Joe, she saw on social media that Iona had moved in with Joe. As she looked at the photograph of the two in her old bedroom, she saw that the life seemed drained from Iona's eyes in much the same way that hers had faded over the years.

She spent the following year in intensive therapy as she negotiated an unusually contentious divorce in which Joe refused to pay any alimony or separate their assets fairly. Despite asking for the divorce, he seemed to relish in prolonging finalizing the agreement. On several occasions, he quibbled about minute details outlined in the decree, demanded financial retribution for his pain and suffering, and threatened to sue her for stealing clients and other business contacts. Over the eight years of their marriage, the two had made a considerable amount of money through their coaching practice, and although she was entitled to half of the assets, Josie decided to walk away from it all to free herself of Joe.

After two difficult years, they finally finalized the divorce. Josie relinquished her practice client lists and their dog and received no alimony, but she felt free for the first time in many years. Joe had spent the time since their separation maligning her to all their mutual friends, clients, and workshop participants, and she found herself with few allies. It wasn't uncommon for former friends to lecture her about her "treatment" of Joe, knowing what he's been through. She decided the only way to rebuild her life was to move away.

Josie moved across the country and, while reading a popular New Age magazine a few years later, ran across a picture of Joe, with his brooding yet piercing eyes staring back at her, in an article titled "The Confrontational Controversial Guru." She shuddered and instinctively closed the magazine and threw it across the room. Weeks later, she finally read the article, learning that he had relocated to California. The article offered a positive review of Joe's growing spiritual community and the fantastic transformations inspired by his "confrontational and deeply empathic" leadership style. One of the photos featured Iona, whom he had married; she looked tired and sad despite her young age. Josie breathed a sigh of relief knowing that Joe was now someone else's problem while also feeling regret that she hadn't been able to protect Iona from his manipulation and control.

Power, Control, and Triangulation

Joe's charisma, power, and magnetism are not uncommon when narcissism meets a generous dose of psychopathy. While it would be a bit hyperbolic to identify Joe as a "psychopath," he, along with the other Powerful-Aggressive subtypes, share some characterological traits that exaggerate his "dark triad" behaviors and motivations.[3] Joe's primary avoidance is vulnerability and powerlessness, which he shares with other narcissistic subtypes; however, his efforts to dominate and blatantly, as well as covertly, control others around him render him a more destructive force compared to some of the other more seemingly benign subtypes.

Psychopathy, as discussed by somatic psychoanalyst Alexander Lowen, is a psychological and somatic defense strategy that has internalized a disgust and, subsequently, fear of weakness. The result is someone who adopts a self-image as being strong, formidable, and in control of themselves and others in their environment. Joe's early experiences with his mother, the significant trauma from gender dysphoria, and the lack of acceptance he received as a trans man codified an inherent belief that others will victimize and control you if you don't victimize and control them first. His relationships with his wife, Josie, and clients reflect this internal dynamic.

In many ways, Joe's spiritual journey softened some of the blunt edges of his presentation and started as a genuine desire to lessen his internal suffering due to early trauma. It's important to remember that many narcissistic people can have authentic and meaningful spiritual experiences because the part that seeks spiritual union exists outside of (or despite) the human egoic concerns (we'll explore this further in the final chapter). However, it is not uncommon for spiritually inclined narcissists to be unable or unwilling to resist the temptation of their ego to usurp their spiritual wisdom for personal recognition, dominance, or power.

In *The Narcissist in You and Everyone Else*, I outlined several overarching narcissistic types before describing in detail the 27 subtypes. In my classes and workshops since publishing that book, I have received the most feedback and questions about the Dark Empath type. The Dark Empath differs from the other more commonly understood types of narcissism (such as the malignant or vulnerable narcissist) in that they possess a high degree of cognitive empathy. They are unusually attuned to others' motivations and emotional states, making them very effective counselors, therapists, spiritual leaders, and coaches.

> They're adept at reading others' emotional cues and have a talent for reading people's motivations and vulnerabilities. Research shows that they demonstrate more affective and cognitive empathy and have lower levels of physical aggression. They appear intuitive, wise, emotionally mature, and inspiring. They intuitively understand others' psychological, spiritual, and emotional experiences and utilize their understanding of the human psyche to manipulate, coerce, control, or abuse people.[4]

Joe's charisma, paired with an innate understanding of human motivation, was only strengthened by his spiritual and psychological education. Meeting Josie opened a world of possibilities that deepened and sharpened his innate intellectual and spiritual aptitudes. However, because there is so much potential for power and domination when one learns how to understand, analyze, and manipulate others' emotional world, the temptation to utilize his skill set to strengthen his ego was impossible to resist.

What likely started as Joe's admiration for Josie's ability to empathize with her clients genuinely and then employ compassion to transform and heal others turned into disowned competitive envy. Many narcissists know they cannot connect with others on an emotionally deep level. Affective or experiential empathy is not second nature. Thus, those interested in healing or assisting others physically or emotionally must rely on cognitive empathy to compensate for a lack of affective empathy. Joe saw the potential glory and financial gain from being a healer by attending workshops and witnessing Josie's gifts. His admiration shifts to a need to demonstrate his prowess and aptitude over Josie's. In essence, Joe could not allow himself to be upstaged, and he eventually leveraged his charisma and confidence to surpass Josie as an authority figure.

Narcissistic people loathe being one down, and even as they acquire knowledge from experts, they harbor fantasies of surpassing those who taught them as a demonstration of their superiority. Joe also demonstrates a common narcissistic need to associate with only the best. Thus, he manages to befriend those he deems worthy of his attention and, therefore, grows in importance by association. His tendency to insert and assert himself as the "real" authority, even in learning environments with established teachers, illustrates this subtype's intolerability of subordination or any semblance of inferiority.

Because of Joe's intelligence and savvy, he reinvents himself as a spiritual self-help guru. His confidence and powerful energy instill trust in others, and he facilitates meaningful change because of his straightforward style and ability to ferret out inauthenticity and fear in others. However, the darker consequence of his involvement with clients is that his issues with trust, loyalty, and power are unconsciously acted out through toxic transference with his clients. He insists on being the others' sole source of guidance and authority. Joe engages in coercive control by implicitly or explicitly demanding obedience to his methods and implicit trust in his intuitive and intellectual wisdom. His effectiveness, charm, and authoritative aura create a relational dynamic where others do not want to disappoint him, thus increasing his power and influence.

CHAPTER FOUR

Joe's relationship with Josie offers an excellent example of how the Dark Empath, particularly *The Charismatic Bully*, weaponizes their strength and above-average emotional intelligence to manipulate intimates. Joe spiritualizes his and Josie's connection, creating an intoxicating fantasy that reinforces a belief that Josie will never be able to escape. He also plants the idea that Josie must endure any abuse he throws her way due to her past-life indiscretions while also positioning himself as the benevolent father figure who forgives.

The Dark Empath utilizes psychological, spiritual, or emotional connection to help ensure the other's devotion, decreasing the likelihood that the person will abandon them. Because they fear rejection, they often expertly mine the other's interior landscape for gems that can be used later. This type of emotional manipulation is common among cult leaders and other charismatic leaders who employ their emotional intelligence for coercive control.

Joe spends a lot of time eroding Josie's confidence in her craft so that she eventually relinquishes control over her professional destiny. One-upmanship and professional showboating make Josie doubt her ability and thus fall in line with his agenda. Her professional self-esteem was damaged, even though she ultimately drew a boundary regarding his interference in her workshops. Joe's inability to recognize boundaries and to push others through his confrontational method and overt contradictions positions him as a rebel to some and a menace to those closest to him. He is blatantly possessive of those he considers "his" while expecting complete autonomy and independence from the influence of others. Like most narcissists, Joe cannot handle criticism and punishes, rejects, or abandons anyone who would challenge his self-image. He sees himself as benevolent, magnanimous, and powerful and cannot fathom why anyone would see his actions or behaviors as anything but virtuous.

The Powerful-Aggressive subtypes are an augmented version of the Enneagram Type Eight personality styles. When Eights are healthy, they embody generosity and valor and see themselves as the protector of the weak. However, even non-narcissistic Eights can become so fixated on maintaining their autonomy and independence and avoiding weakness that they become too aggressive and even paranoid about losing their power. However, perhaps with some coaxing or enough interpersonal drama under their belts, non-narcissistic people with this personality style can see that they've hardened themselves to such a point that they have become impenetrable and unapproachable and begin to soften and allow their vulnerability to deepen their compassion for others' weaknesses. As a narcissist, Joe may ideologically have a self-conception of himself as benevolent and lacks the accurate self-awareness to sense the discrepancies in his behavior and treatment of others and his self-image.

We see the full scope of Joe's toxic behaviors reach a fever pitch in his attempts to triangulate his mentee, Iona, into his relationship with Josie. Joe has an insatiable sexual appetite, and, as is common with many narcissistic people, he sees no real reason to mitigate his desires because he believes he should always have what he wants when he wants it. Intellectually, Joe must be aware that his boundary-crossing professional style is unethical. He sees himself as above the rules. However, because he is intelligent and understands that immediately muddying the waters with Iona with his domineering relational style, he takes his time grooming and love bombing her to establish trust and loyalty. In the process, he also triangulates Iona into his relationship with Josie by creating a competitive environment whereby the two women are forced to compete for his attention.

When Joe felt he had sufficiently garnered enough trust from Iona, he increased the intensity of the triangulation during the trip to Chile. Joe likely knew that introducing the idea of Iona's joining his and Josie's relationship would result in Josie's anger and likely create a cascading relational effect whereby he could justify exiting the relationship. However, he seemed unprepared for Iona's empathetic response to hurting Josie, which signified weakness and a lack of loyalty. When the conflict reached a fever pitch, Joe went cold and regained his position as the mighty father, expressing his disappointment in Josie and Iona. By becoming indifferent to the proverbial bomb he released on these two women, he also regained emotional control of the situation, proving to himself and the women he was in charge.

CHAPTER FOUR

We could speculate that Joe's toxic behaviors within intimate relationships are an opportunity for him to regain control over his parents, who he felt didn't protect him or consider his autonomy or interests. The incessant intensity seeking and lust for power and dominion over others' emotional, sexual, and spiritual lives in his mind represents a fear of control and abandonment at the hands of women. He became the omnipresent male figure he saw in his life who controlled a weak and impressionable mother, thus replaying his early childhood rage and disappointment.

When Josie reaches her boiling point and finally attempts to heal the relationship, he agrees to couples counseling, not necessarily because he wants to fix the relationship, but because he wants to prove to Josie that he's not the problem. He insists on choosing a therapist who he knows will cosign his perspective of the relationship and the toxic masculine expectations therein. He continues the triangulation pattern with the therapist, who, perhaps knowingly, perhaps not, helps reinforce Joe's moral superiority. Joe's expert use of a victim narrative by evoking his gender trauma with the woman who has demonstrated immense patience and empathy for Joe's journey has a devastating effect on Josie's self-image. To make matters worse, after an apparent improvement in the relationship, Joe creates further chaos by suddenly returning to the romantic, charismatic man who initially attracted Josie before pulling the rug out from underneath their relationship and coldly demanding a divorce.

Joe becomes cold, dismissive, and rejecting to regain control over Iona, making her work to return to his good graces. Iona's regression into depression, due to the breakdown in her relationship with Joe and subsequent fear of the consequences of betrayal, has a catastrophic effect on her mental health. By selectively giving approval, attention, and care and pushing Iona back into the traumatic abuse dynamic with her father, he also creates a situation where he can build her back up by shining his light back on her when he chooses. As we saw with Sue, the on-again, off-again emotional roller coaster of the narcissist creates an addictive response in the brain that makes others crave stability through the consistency of the stimuli. The narcissist's attention creates a dopamine response in a person so that they begin to rely on the narcissist for their feelings of happiness or satisfaction.

Despite Josie's eventually being freed from the drama of her dynamic with Joe, we see the aftereffects of the recovery from narcissistic abuse in that even when the relationship seemingly ends, the narcissist often seeks to continue their control over others. In many ways, they never fully relinquish control over those in their lives because they either want to keep their options open should they run out of *narcissistic supply* or punish the other for betraying, leaving, or otherwise individuating from them.[5] Josie relinquishes her rightful financial stake to avoid continued acrimony with Joe, who consciously drags out the divorce he sought to punish Josie. The emotional toll of picking up one's life after narcissistic abuse can often strip abuse survivors bare of their psychological (and sometimes financial) reserves and requires the knowledgeable care of a narcissistic abuse-informed therapist. It's also worth noting that Josie's mental health education did not preclude her from falling victim to what was a toxic relationship and that narcissistic abuse can and does happen to those who should "know better." In Joe's case, Josie's spiritual and psychological expertise likely made dominating and controlling her even more enjoyable. In the case of Josie, the best thing she could've done was to walk away from the continued conflict, which fuels Joe's rage and energizes him by the power struggle. A person's ending the power struggle with a narcissist can, at times, be difficult and often takes a significant toll on their inner and outer resources, but for many, it is the only way out.

In the following chapter, we'll explore how the narcissistic psychological landscape doesn't stop at narcissists' interpersonal relationships and, because of the interconnectedness of human affairs, often seeps into communities in surprising ways, helping to reinforce dysfunctional social messaging and support a sort of narcissistic abuse-by-proxy by those who begin to model and unconsciously re-create toxic dynamics.

CHAPTER FIVE
OH, WHAT TOXIC WEBS WE WEAVE
Broadening the Scope

Undoubtedly, narcissistic people do a considerable amount of damage to significant others, children, family members, and friends. However, their behavior has a ripple effect on increasingly broader human ecosystems because no relationship exists within a vacuum. The complicated nature of human connections necessitates that anything that happens within a microcosm will certainly affect a larger community. In this chapter, we'll explore the frequent phenomenon of narcissistic people's resonating with and finding sympathetic company in other narcissistic individuals and the effects of their antagonistic strategies on the social world. While it may seem at first glance that the social dynamic between two narcissists would be, at least theoretically, easier to manage given that they often share similar essential personality characteristics, it is equally as likely that the dynamics can be even more toxic, as we'll see, if not for them, then for those in their orbit.

To give us a more dynamic perspective of the various iterations of the 27 subtypes of narcissism, we'll meet a supporting "cast of characters" that illustrate the different flavors of narcissistic personalities. In my research and experience with narcissistic personalities, I found that most narcissistic people, particularly in social settings, tend to unconsciously or subconsciously gravitate toward others that mirror their worldview. Like non-narcissists, they enjoy the company of those who think, feel, and behave similarly to them, even if those gravitations sometimes exacerbate interpersonal challenges.

As we explore Luke, Sue, and Joe's broader social world outside of their primary relationships, we'll see how, in some instances, supporting characters help mitigate the negative effect of their narcissism on those around them and, in most cases, encourage or enable toxic behaviors. We'll also see how the proliferation of narcissistic social dynamics and community relationships builds an insidious foundation for the more systemic and ideological effect that we will explore in Chapter 6.

A Tight Operation

Preparations to launch Luke's career on the national stage were well underway. Early, he received important endorsements from high-profile senators and congresspeople. He had already raised $300,000 in campaign funds from a prominent conservative super PAC that believed in his promise and ideological stance and desperately wanted to unseat the incumbent, who had fallen out of favor with the electorate. These early achievements helped bolster Luke's confidence and added considerable momentum to the campaign.

At 38 years old, Luke was seen as dynamic, energetic, and a political wunderkind. As a result, prominent national party members felt it was essential to give him ample party support and a well-oiled infrastructure to ensure a successful and efficient campaign, so they sent him Bruce.

Bruce was a legend in political circles because of his shrewd and savvy political intelligence. To coach Luke and his wife, Kerri, the state party's chairman sent Bruce to a dinner at the couple's home to strategize how to build the optimal image for public consumption and maximize Luke's chances of winning. When Bruce arrived for dinner, Luke was taken aback. Bruce was a small, stout man in his mid-50s. He was balding; wore thin, oval-shaped glasses; and had small, cold, penetrating green eyes. Generally, his face revealed no emotional resonance, except the occasional eyebrow raised when posed a question, and his mouth was small, cruel, and thin. He was quiet at first and answered Kerri's small talk with short, clipped answers. There were long breaks in the conversation, which made for an awkward dinner. When the meal was over, Kerri asked if he was ready for dessert; Bruce interjected brusquely, stating, "We don't have time for that; I'd like to get down to the business of how Luke's going to win this race and how you're going to help him." The sudden turn surprised Kerri, and she sheepishly set the expensive cake she had bought to impress him down on the table and sat back in her chair. Kerri replied, "I'll do what I can to support Luke, but I'm no politician—"

"Oh, but you are; your whole family has to learn how to politick," he quipped, then turned to Luke.

"Luke, you ran a decent DA campaign, but that's small potatoes compared to what you're about to embark upon. I ran some preliminary polling numbers, and people find *you* (glancing at Kerri) to be underwhelming; you code as a liberal. I think the clothes are a bit granola, so we have to change them. I've scheduled an appointment with Lana, an image consultant we've used in previous campaigns. She's the best in the business."

"See, this is exactly what we need, sweetie! He knows what he's doing. We got this in the bag!" Luke exclaimed.

Kerri sat at the table, staring at the two men in disbelief as a sinking sense of dread took over. She had learned over the years that when this feeling presented itself, to dissociate to avoid feeling the anxiety and to snap into the more manageable role of the supportive wife of a politician. She poured another glass of wine and sank further into herself.

Bruce continued with an eerie, monotonous drone, "While I admire your enthusiasm and youthful exuberance, you have a long way to go before anything is 'in the bag.' I'm good, but I'm not a miracle worker. You'll have to pull it back on the campaign trail a bit; if you continue with this frat-boy-turned-lawyer act, people won't take you seriously. You have some good ideas to inspire the electorate, but I

CHAPTER FIVE

have also pored over the data and polled for your public sentiment. People can find you a bit annoying and, at times, reckless. So we're going to have to do some damage control. I set up a meeting with Ron, whom I've worked with for years, to help coach you on the new direction." It was Luke's turn to be stunned; he wasn't used to anyone talking to him with such candor, and while the criticism stung bitterly, he felt a strange desire to please him.

"I dunno, Bruce; I think this state needs to laugh a little. Everyone is so serious and sensitive. Have you ever seen the movie *Beetlejuice*?"

"I'm going to stop you right there. I don't watch movies and am not really in the mood for funny anecdotes," Bruce continued coldly.

"I was just going to say that I relate to the character because he—," Luke said, determined to win Bruce over before being cut off.

"Here's something I want you both to know about me. I'm very good at what I do. They don't call me 'the mastermind' for no reason. I don't mess around, and I expect you to listen to me if you want to win. I don't enjoy people much; data is much more interesting. So you can save your cute jokes and anecdotes, at least, the ones I approve, for the campaign trail, but I have no use for them. I also think most people in this country are idiots. Frankly, I think liberals and conservatives are all stupid, but the touchy-feely stuff doesn't get anything done and is for irrational, non-thinking humans. So I agreed to take this job because I believe most of your ideas are decent; they just need to be polished. I'm assuming a man of your ambition doesn't want to stop at the governor's race, right?" Bruce surmised, matter-of-factly.

"Right. I'd like to run for the House or Senate after this," Luke quietly replied.

"Then you have to learn how to play the game, the big game, not the small-scale operation you've been running. And if I know anything, it's how to manipulate people's minds, and we do that with your charisma and my brain. So let me lay out a rough sketch of the plan."

Luke and Kerri listened to Bruce lay out his plan for the campaign, which included directives on how to speak, where to eat, and how to utilize language to hypnotize the masses during a speech.

Luke, riveted and slightly frightened of Bruce's clinical communication style, took notes, something Kerri had never seen him do. Bruce promised to hire a chief of staff who shared his skill set and political prowess and emphasized that the community he was about to build around Luke was a community of "vetted winners." Bruce left four hours later. Even more despondent than before the meeting, Kerri sat on the sofa, staring into space. Luke, unaware—and uncaring—of his wife's exhausted, emotional state, cut a slice of cake, grabbed a beer from the fridge, plopped on the couch, and began watching ESPN.

"He was pretty cool, right?" He chirped, staring at the television. "I'm excited; we're going to win this. He's a dick, but he's smart. And that's what we need."

Kerri got up, nodded silently, and went upstairs to check on the kids.

The following week, when Bruce showed up at the new campaign headquarters, Luke's current staff, many of whom had been with him since the beginning of his district attorney career, felt uneasy, knowing that changes would be made that could alter their livelihood. Bruce asked everyone to stand in a line, introduced himself, and then coldly stated, "Thank you all for everything you've done up to this point for this campaign. Your services will no longer be needed. You'll be given a small severance and a recommendation letter. Please gather your things." He then motioned with his hand, and several new faces appeared in the small office space. They began placing their personal belongings and computers on the desks provided. The staff was stunned. Amy, who had been with Luke since he had started his private practice after law school, looked at him with disbelief. With an air of flippancy, Luke awkwardly stated, "It's been real, everyone. If you want to come out for a drink later, I'm buying!"

Stunned at Luke's lack of emotion, Amy asked, "Did you know about this?"

"Amy, you know better than anyone; it's not personal. We're still friends, right?!" Luke proclaimed with an innocent smile and a little shoulder nudge.

CHAPTER FIVE

Amy left the office, feeling blindsided and betrayed by Luke's flippancy. Bruce briefed the new staff on the day's business and introduced James, who would serve as the campaign's new chief of staff.

James was a tall, biracial man with a pleasant smile and sleepy brown eyes. He was congenial and seemed friendly and gentle. Bruce handpicked James to manage the staff because of his ability to deliver difficult and often upsetting news with seemingly unflappable grace. James was laid-back, diplomatic, charming, and deceptively ruthless. He assured everyone, in a nonchalant yet authoritative manner, that he was there for them and that with him steering the ship and them as his "co-captains," they would win this election and most of them, if they cooperated, would have a job in the governor's office once all was said and done. James was a true professional who managed multiple campaign staff through a mixture of laissez-faire management and an uncanny ability to minimize conflict and discord.

The campaign office was productive, jovial, and efficient for several weeks. Luke enjoyed touring the state and giving speeches, interviews, and talks to professional organizations, news outlets, and other state institutions. His charm and humor were often irresistible, and he enjoyed positive media attention due to his likable and easy manner. With the day-to-day management of the office and its staff left to James, he was less testy and prone to outbursts. He was far more well suited to life in the public eye. The only annoyance was the constant criticism of Bruce on the way he spoke, dressed, and even moved. Bruce, attempting to craft a polished political candidate who would, at some point, be primed for the national stage, took crafting Luke's political career personally.

Bruce was often cantankerous and misanthropic and lacked any real sense of humor, and the two frequently butted heads. Ultimately, Bruce always won with his dry, sardonic insults and threats to have all his funding and party support pulled. Luke, unused to being at the mercy of others, found himself acquiescing more often than he would ever allow in any other relationship. Even Luke found Bruce's frequent derision of the "idiot" electorate and the constant inflation of his intellect and power to shape people's minds and ideas distasteful.

In one particularly tense exchange, Bruce demanded that Kerri have a limited role at campaign functions because she was "dour," "dull," and "uninteresting." Although Luke might use the same adjectives at times to describe his wife, he nonetheless reacted poorly to someone he had just met disparaging his wife, believing it reflected poorly on him.

The campaign honeymoon period ended when Amy came forward with allegations of sexual harassment and inappropriate conduct while under Luke's employ. After filing a discrimination and harassment lawsuit, she made damning comments to the media detailing her time working with Luke and his unprofessional behavior. Amy alleged that Luke frequently texted her after hours, asking her to go to the bars to "party." In one instance, Amy alleged that Luke, while drunk at work, asked if she wanted to see why they called him "Lucky Luke." She claimed that she hadn't quit because Luke had engaged in coercive language, frequently affirming, "You're my number two" and "You get me and wouldn't ever betray me." Amy believed that her firing from his campaign staff was also an effort to eliminate any potential damage she could cause to his reputation. She worried about the other female staffers who worked for him, stating that she knew of others with similar experiences working for Luke who were afraid to come forward.

The allegations shocked the campaign and the state overall as the scandal dominated the local and national news cycle. Bruce, who received the news of Amy's allegations before it broke, waited to tell Luke to see how he would respond. Upon reading the story, Luke flew into a rage while waiting to speak at an event for agricultural workers. Bruce, who now routinely enjoyed criticizing Luke, knew he would react poorly and often used those opportunities as "teaching moments."

"Can you believe this bitch?!" Luke exclaimed. "She's not even that hot. I gave her a job when nobody else would because she's so unlikeable. Why didn't we get prior knowledge of this? I thought we had contacts at the court who would leak to us before something like this broke?"

CHAPTER FIVE

"I did know about it. Yesterday," Bruce said flatly while looking at his phone.

"What?!" Luke exclaimed, stunned. "Why didn't you say anything?"

"Because I wanted to see if you'd learned anything, and I knew it would come out while we were here and that you'd act like a complete ape. So calm down. You forget sometimes you're always on," Bruce continued.

"Stop talking to me like I'm an idiot! You're supposed to prevent stuff like this from happening. You're not doing your job!" Luke raged, unable to control his reactions despite the room full of potential voters and press waiting eagerly on the other side of the wall.

"You are an idiot—a lot. Listen, I've already mapped out a plan. Nobody will believe her because she's acting like a typical angry woman. I need any text messages and photos of her you may have. We will ruin her credibility, which won't be hard. I've called some media contacts, who are already digging up dirt, like her drinking problem. This won't be around long," Bruce calmly stated. "I just can't believe you didn't make anyone sign NDAs. This is why you're still more stupid than I would like, but you'll learn that this is what happens when you're sloppy. You can do anything you want when you have power, as long as you're not sloppy."

Bruce, Luke, and their legal team spent the next two weeks disparaging Amy in the press and leaking private information about her troubled romantic past, her substance abuse issues, a brief stint in rehab, her depression, and even information about an abortion during her college years to help turn the predominately conservative audience against her. Bruce knew that emphasizing her mental health issues would help to underscore Luke's campaign agenda and hard-line stance on the ineffectiveness of mental health services and the need to reroute state funds to more worthwhile outlets.

Luke provided much of the salacious information to aid in Amy's public defamation despite previously considering her one of his closest friends and allies. At times, he felt slight pangs of guilt for going in so hard on her, knowing her struggles with alcoholism and depression, but making this case and Amy go away was far more critical than sparing his coworker and friend of over 10 years.

With the weight and funds of a powerful political machine bearing down on Amy and her sobriety and mental health at risk, she decided to drop the case after relapsing one weekend when embarrassing videos of her drunk at an office birthday party were released to the media.

Meanwhile, Chief of Staff James subtly pressured the campaign staff to speak highly of their experience on the campaign since national and local reporters were hounding employees to dig up dirt. James was an expert at finessing conflict and assuaging others' discomfort and was well-known in political circles for his nonchalant manner of gaslighting. Before the scandal, Luke had already taken a liking to a couple of the young volunteers on the campaign and had begun inviting the college-aged women (one of whom was underage) to bars; James felt he needed to protect his and the campaign's interests. When one intern expressed some discomfort over Luke's repeated social invitations, James worked his magic. He began obfuscating the primary issue, implying that she must've misunderstood the request and that with her political career aspirations, she didn't want people to think she was "difficult."

James became well-known for ignoring most issues, placating others with seemingly proactive phrases like "I'm on it" or "Don't worry about it," while having little intention of making any actual adjustments to the status quo he'd established. Many staff complained about the egregious hours they were being asked to work. James would pacify them with pizza and beer while implying that they would be rewarded if they pushed themselves further. Predictably, the "rewards" never came. Eventually, most people ceased approaching James with any issues because of his apathy and minimization of anything he deemed "people's little dramas." However, he could also be insensitive, callous, and glib. When the campaign's press scheduler needed to take a few days off to tend to her dog's death, James flatly told her, "Well, if your dead dog is more important than your job, by all means, take a few days." When asked if he was threatening her, James, able to evade culpability with his predictably vague responses, said, "Of course, not. Why would you assume that's what I meant? You tend to think the worst of people, don't you?"

While the campaign got back on track after the scandal had abated, the previously superficial, upbeat positivity around Luke grew tense, disgruntled, and laced with unease. Under the direction of Bruce and James, the staff was afraid to voice concerns for fear of retaliation. The few employees who refused to sign an NDA (non-disclosure agreement) were assigned menial tasks, such as licking envelopes or taking coffee orders, no matter what their skill level or experience; however, to avoid the appearance of retaliation, they were told that given the highly sensitive nature of working on a political campaign, they must think of themselves as "working at a lower security clearance."

The employees who excelled could either "play the game" well and minimize or eliminate any complaints or were so aggressive and status seeking that they demanded the attention of Bruce, Luke, and James. When Luke was in the office, it was often to "boost morale," and James would instruct staff to laugh at his jokes and make him feel amazing since he needed that to keep the campaign momentum going. James fawned and became an obsequious "yes-man" when Luke was around, agreeing with every word he uttered, no matter how foolish, and laughing uncharacteristically at Luke's sophomoric humor.

Kerri was often expected to host campaign staff at her home and excuse the growing toxicity that had increasingly constellated around her husband. She would attempt to offer empathy and compassion to a beleaguered staff member. Now, fully accustomed to her role, Kerri made excuses for Luke, who many felt was largely absent as their leader, except when he wanted an audience to test out his newest campaign stump speeches or jokes. She explained away his absence of parental or spousal presence on the stresses of the campaign, pushing herself to have empathy for the immense pressure he was under (a refrain he often lodged at her when she voiced any grievances). Still, she struggled to find adequate excuses when he would blatantly forget the name of one of his staffers with whom he'd interacted several times or when he made some smart-assed remark or unsophisticated gaffe that she or James would later have to smooth over.

As the year-and-a-half-long campaign ended, Luke's team rotated several times due to excessively high turnover. However, the culture of silence and superficial sense of loyalty cultivated by James kept staff from leaking any more negative press that could affect his polling. Due to his undeniable charisma, humor, and ability to win over an audience, Luke was slated to win the governor's election with a 14% lead over the incumbent. In fact, due to Bruce's masterful spin on the Amy scandal, he was able to leverage the fallout to argue further why the mental health industry in his state was ineffectual and that until they found better ways of "dealing with" people, they should receive reduced state funding, which should be redirected to state defense, industry and commerce, and entertainment, things that "make the people feel good." Luke also spent considerable time railing against the foolishness of soft-hearted teachers and the "feminized education system," which placed too much emphasis on subjects that are invariably useless (e.g., art, English, and psychology). He gained considerable traction among male voters by playing to their feelings of grievance and efforts to make them more sensitive. One particularly compelling campaign gimmick was abolishing the term *toxic positivity* since it represented the unhappy "losers" who hate fun, progress, and improvement.

When Luke won the election, Kerri was both relieved and horrified. He had become increasingly callous, and most of his remaining softness had given way to a cynical and ruthless approach to people, including her and her children. He rarely spent time with the kids unless it was a photo op or "fun." She knew the family would receive even less of his time with his responsibilities and newfound national fame, but in some ways, she felt his decreased presence might be better for the children.

Kerri felt that the one bright spot in the campaign process and her newfound role as governor's wife was the friendship she forged

CHAPTER FIVE

with the lieutenant governor's wife, Laura, and the camaraderie she'd fostered with James's fiancé. Both women shared similar criticisms of their husbands' ambition and egos. Laura reinforced Kerri's defense of blocking out most of Luke's behavior and tried to help her appreciate "the good" in him despite their relationship's devolving into a public display for political optics. They barely spoke when he was home, and they often communicated through his assistant or James, who had grown quite accustomed to placating Kerri, the children, or anyone else for Luke's unfulfilled promises, missed dinners and holidays, and harsh language, chalking it up to "the immense pressure he's under."

Once Luke was elected, his ideological positions became increasingly more extreme, and his anti–mental health funding agenda was increasingly replaced with a hypermasculine, anti-sensitivity platform that resonated with a particular subset of the state and national electorate, which would later have ramifications for more than the residents of his state as he continued to progress in his political career. He imposed harsh regulations on those going through mental health court and partially defunded the three most prominent state mental health hospitals. He also spent considerable state resources going after teachers and educators he believed were indoctrinating children with "woke" political ideologies. He became known for his "stand-up comedy"–like pressers, where he would frequently refer to various "snowflake myths," including the high incidence of depression and gender dysphoria and the prevalence of autism spectrum disorders and ADHD (despite being diagnosed with ADHD as a teenager). His message began to resonate with many parents, and he endorsed and mentored a young state superintendent who promised to adhere to Luke's ideologies to help strengthen America's "weakening constitution." After four years in office, he challenged one of the long-standing incumbent senators and was elected to the Senate. Subsequently, Kerri suffered two more severe bouts of crippling depression and struggled increasingly with alcoholism and substance abuse, all of which, of course, was hidden from public view.

We the People

It'll come as no surprise to anyone that the political world is populated with a fair degree of narcissists and narcissistic enablers. Often, people who find their way into politics want to make meaningful contributions to the social world, having observed structural or social problems they believe they can shift or change through their influence. Many, however, seek glory, fame, power, and influence with a touch of civic-minded idealism thrown in for good measure. Most politicians lie somewhere between these two poles. Therefore, it would be patently unfair to say that "all politicians are corrupt," which is a common societal refrain that reduces politics and those who work in politics to rotten, no-good scoundrels. That said, even those with the best intentions frequently become engrossed in a world teeming with opportunities to strengthen individual ego identification because of the tantalizing potential for power, money, and influence.

As we'll explore in Chapter 6, politicians' political or ideological concerns are often shaped by their values, which are inextricably linked to their psychological landscape just as much as their cultural or social conditioning. Thus, if one's inner landscape does not understand or value compassion, empathy, or consideration of others' needs, often their adopted ideologies reflect this reality. There is always the potential (and expected) split between a public figure's forward-facing ideological positions and their inner life or interpersonal strategies. The cliché of the megachurch pastor who espouses charity, poverty, and the transcendence of the material who lives in a mansion and owns three Bentleys is an archetypal example of this paradox. Indeed, in politics, there can be a stark contrast between one's inner reality and espoused beliefs, but in Luke's case, the two align nicely.

Luke's lifelong drive to prove his superiority and value began in early childhood, partially in response to his perception of a disapproving and emotionally unavailable father and a contrastingly permissive, libertine approach to discipline by his mother. Together, they created Luke, who strives unceasingly for social relevance, influence, and power to prove his virility, paired with a dichotomous rebellion

CHAPTER FIVE

against structure or control. We see this juxtaposition playing out in Luke's career as a district attorney (a typically somber position), where, while effective and bullish in his approach to the work, he also demonstrated an immature, irreverent nonchalance unbecoming of the position. His flippant approach and unprofessionalism toward others created a working dynamic that lacked boundaries, which would later come back to bite him when confronted with the reality of his carelessness.

When Luke runs for governor, he's thrust into a world where he no longer fully controls his domain. The demands of running for a high-profile state governance position are raised when, because of his ingenue-like boyishness, Bruce imposes the same kind of critical, joyless structure he experienced with his father. As an older male figure, Bruce represents the emotionless, anti-empathic masculinity Luke has adopted throughout his life. While he reels against his callous criticisms, he ultimately falls in line to achieve the power and influence he craves.

Bruce is cold, intelligent, calculating, and remote and lacks interpersonal warmth. As the *Intellectual Elitist* narcissistic subtype, his primary concern is broadening his power and influence through the application of what he believes is his superior rationality and breadth of knowledge compared to virtually everyone around him. On the one hand, his focused, no-nonsense approach and willingness to unemotionally challenge Luke helps Luke achieve a goal that he would've been unlikely to achieve without proper molding. On the other hand, Bruce's demeaning and bullying tactics only reinforce and solidify Luke's belief that any semblance of vulnerability or emotional awareness toward himself or others is a liability. He's not incorrect in his assumption because Luke has entered a world where vulnerability and emotional sensitivity are weaknesses and could cost him an election. One must have thick skin in politics because it is a dirty game and benefits those willing to roll around in the proverbial dirt to win.

Bruce's disregard of both Luke's and Kerri's opinions or feelings in service to the goal of winning illustrates the tendency for narcissistic people to objectify others. Additionally, it illustrates how even narcissists can be hurt by the erosive interpersonal strategies employed by other narcissists. Many narcissists are initially attracted to other narcissists because, as the universal law suggests "like attracts like," they seem to recognize each other's emotional frequencies and feel like kindred spirits. It's easy to forget as we're perusing the social and interpersonal world of narcissists that they are also humans with emotional needs and most have an excessive need for validation and approval, in some ways, making them more sensitive than non-narcissistic people. Therefore, the self-centeredness, objectification, and lack of empathy inflicted on them by other narcissists can be equally hurtful, which is why they often demand others' understanding and compassion, while they are unable to give it.

Once James is hired to manage the campaign staff, the culture of indifference and emotional silence is further strengthened. James is the *Ambivalent Avoider*, and because of this subtype's nonconfrontational, easygoing but quietly ambitious nature, they are frequently found in middle management or management positions. In a political campaign fraught with potential negative publicity (particularly when the candidate is a narcissist), maintaining the status quo, placating or diminishing others' concerns or problems, and forestalling others' anger are necessities. James's brand of narcissism often goes undetected because this subtype at first seems free of the same hard edges and self-inflation of some of the more extroverted narcissistic subtypes. However, the erosive power of neglect is particularly damaging to those who find themselves at this subtype's mercy. With Bruce as the calculating strategist, Luke as the archetypal "fools king," and James as the chief toxicity placater, tensions run high, as will the potential damage to those in their orbit.

The use of the NDA[1] is commonplace with high-profile businesses, celebrities, or political machinations to prevent not only the sharing of proprietary information privileged by the organization or contract holder but also to prevent unfavorable publicity from spreading without legal recourse. While using NDAs does not necessarily imply nefarious or salacious dealings or behavior (often, they are boilerplate protections to protect exclusive information), many use NDAs to silence those with less power and often hamstring those who have been the victims of abuse, discrimination, or harassment. Legally, NDAs cannot be invoked to cover illegal activity. However, many legal laypersons aren't aware of the confines of the contract and are thus bullied into suppressing their free speech rights or reporting abuse or mistreatment.

For those who are in toxic work environments, the imprinting of the narcissistic or unconscious people who helped construct the cultural norms becomes part of everyone's conscious and subconscious conditioning. There are various ways to manage working within a toxic system, which run the gamut from assimilation, which includes adopting strategies and ideologies out of necessity for survival, to revolt, which is an attempt to expose or destroy toxic social ideologies. In either case, the emotional, physical, and mental toll those strategies take on those within the environment can be erosive. In Luke's world, this was exemplified by Amy's attempts to fight the toxic machine, only to find herself spiraling into substance abuse relapse and depression. For those with the temperament to withstand the toxicity, there are often tangible rewards for "playing ball." Promotions, raises, affirmation, and appreciation from those wishing to maintain and bolster the status quo can be nice consolation prizes for those who don't "rock the boat" but ultimately reinforce and preserve the toxicity, which at some point poisons everyone in the end.

People like Chief of Staff James represent a category of narcissistic subtypes that flies under the radar for most. James is a Type Nine in the Enneagram personality typology system, and many believe that because of their inherently conflict-avoidant and ease-seeking temperament, narcissism is improbable or even impossible. However, as outlined in *The Narcissist in You and Everyone Else*, no personality style (no matter how superficially pleasant) is exempt from developing narcissistic traits. James's primary antagonistic strategy lies in his ability to placate and minimize others' problems, thus contributing to the proliferation of a toxic work environment. His ability to gaslight and lull other people into a false sense of security can be maddening.

They accomplish this by diminishing, admonishing, and punishing those they believe to be problematic, complicated, or "drama queens." Their desire to maintain their peace and equilibrium at the expense of others' peace can make them ironically challenging to get along with. All three Ambivalent-Neglectful narcissistic subtypes fly under the radar because they do not typically exhibit the same kind of braggadocious, attention-seeking bravado as the Powerful-Aggressive, Hedonistic-Exuberant, or Ambitious-Deceptive types. Instead, they conceal their lack of vulnerability, callousness, and empathy deficits through a superficially placid and easygoing persona. In many ways, the damage created by some of the less extroverted narcissistic subtypes can be more insidious and pervasive because it is quieter and less overtly threatening.

Volumes of books could be written on the inherent narcissism built into the corporate and political structures in any given country. Anywhere the potential for power, influence, and notoriety exists, the potential for narcissism, exploitation, and objectification isn't far behind. Access to endless streams of validation and approval will always attract people like Luke, who, because of their conditioning and psychological and physiological makeup, seek opportunities to exploit others for their gain. As we'll explore in Chapter 6, the key to reprogramming and thus healing some of the indignities of social toxicity amplified by narcissistic and otherwise antagonistic personality styles is examining the ideologies that become part of the cultures they influence.

Family Ties

Once the last of Sue and Mark's children were grown and out of the house, Sue increasingly focused on finding satisfaction in her volunteer work and social life. She had become well-known in their affluent community for her contributions to children's arts and was increasingly in demand for various nonprofit boards and community initiatives. Once she redirected most of her frustrated energy into public acts that gained her recognition and respect, she became

CHAPTER FIVE

moderately less tempestuous at home. However, another by-product of her redirected energy was that her children and other family members received considerably less of her attention, which was already minimal. The one exception was her "golden child," Dylan, who had continued his trajectory as "mommy's bright light" (as he was affectionally named), earning a golf scholarship to a prestigious university and graduating with honors and a future burgeoning career at a software start-up company. Sue focused most of her parental attention on Dylan, with the twins a close second. However, her complex and often fraught relationship with her middle child, Lilly, became more complicated as the years passed.

Mark's behavior toward the children was detached, and over the years, he had developed a slight drinking problem and corresponding cantankerous temper that often erupted toward Lilly. During her final year in the home, Lilly grew more vocal and critical of the various inequities she observed at the hands of her parents. For example, when Dylan turned 16, he was gifted a brand-new Ford Mustang. However, when Lilly turned 16, she was given a used Honda hatchback and told she would have to tote around the twins to various extracurriculars. At the same time, Dylan was afforded no such responsibility. Lilly was often punished for slight indiscretions, such as staying out past curfew on one occasion. At the same time, Dylan was rarely, if ever, reprimanded or reproached by either parent for anything, including a dangerous night of drinking and driving with his friends when he totaled his car.

Lilly's anxiety and depression worsened. Although she was able to soldier through high school and maintain her 4.0 GPA, the pressure of trying to receive the same praise and attention as her siblings and keep the approving eye of her grandmother was overwhelming, resulting in burnout.

Lilly moved out of the house at 18 to live with her boyfriend, Darius. Her bright academic career was cut short when she decided she no longer wanted to go to school, feeling exhausted by how hard she'd pushed herself in grade school to gain her parents' approval to no avail. Instead, after a year in college, she took a sales job at a pharmaceutical company, abandoning her full academic scholarship. Darius was several years older and was the first man Lilly had met who made her feel seen and important. Lilly's choice shocked the family, particularly Li, her grandmother, who was disheartened to hear her favorite had, in her opinion, gone off track. Li kept close tabs on Lilly since she had moved back to China and felt some guilt for leaving Lilly to fend for herself with her daughter Sue.

When Lilly met Darius one night at a friend's party, she found his attention and protective energy comforting, and he gave her the courage she felt she needed to drop out of school and attempt to find a life path more aligned with her true desires. Lilly had never tried any drugs and had drunk alcohol only a few times before meeting Darius. However, he introduced her to "partying" in a new way, and she experimented with all manner of drugs and alcohol as part of her emancipation as the unrewarded "good girl." While she was always a bit too nervous to use any drugs but marijuana consistently, she did enjoy drinking and the way it helped her forget her pain, particularly her crippling anxiety and depression. Despite not attending college, Lilly found decent, well-paying jobs that gave her a wealth of experience in various industries. Darius, however, was less ambitious and had long periods of unemployment, whereby Lilly helped support the two of them.

The two were married when she was 22, and they had their first child when she was 24. Their relationship was fraught with periods of conflict because he was prone to infidelity and, at times, could be incredibly jealous and controlling. At the age of 26, Lilly experienced a severe bout of depression and attempted suicide by overdosing on sleeping pills and drinking wine. Darius found her in time, and the EMTs were able to pump her stomach and save her life. The psychiatrist attending her in the ER recommended a week or two of inpatient mental health rehabilitation. Darius, who knew of Lilly's complicated relationship with her family, felt he needed at least to inform his in-laws about Lilly's suicide attempt and to ask for financial help supporting her recovery. When he called her parents' home, Sue answered. She liked Darius and was friendly. However, when he

CHAPTER FIVE

delivered the news about Lilly, she coldly replied, "She'll be fine. She can be dramatic." Stunned, Darius sat, unsure of what to say next. He then asked to speak to Mark. Mark picked up the phone cheerfully, and Darius delivered the news again, hoping to receive a different reaction. Instead, he was met with an equally dismissive but pleasant response.

"We really appreciate your letting us know. Please tell me when she's out of the hospital. Also, in the future, you can call me directly; it's best not to upset Sue with news like this," Mark said in a businesslike tone. Confused, Darius inferred that Sue wasn't upset; neither could care less. There was no offer to visit her, nor did they ask to speak with her. He did, however, know that her brother Conner would be supportive and was the only member of her family to express concern for Lilly's well-being.

Over the years, Lilly's mental health endured many ups and downs. At times, she was able to retain a stable, well-paying job until the depression, panic attacks, and subsequent self-medication using alcohol and prescription drugs would inevitably necessitate extended periods of sick leave, often followed by termination and worsening depression and bruises to her self-esteem. Darius, who had taken a job in construction management, took on the brunt of helping manage his wife's tenuous mental health and supporting the family during periods when she was unable to work. However, tensions between them were never far beneath the surface. Eventually, after a particularly violent fight due to Darius's difficulty managing his temper, Lilly filed for divorce after 10 years of marriage at the encouragement of her mother, who grew to resent his "influence over her." The two had one child, Brock, who would continue to live with Lilly after the separation. Brock and Lilly became very close as he now assumed the role of surrogate husband and caretaker for his mother.

Lilly continued to have periods of varying functionality, alternating between relative stability and emotional dysregulation and addiction. At various times, Brock would turn to his grandparents for help or guidance with his mother. Unfortunately, he often received the same cold dismissal and refusal to assume any responsibility or assistance for their child's emotional or physical condition. However, Sue would occasionally feign concern and make empty gestures of help without any genuine attempt to ease his or his mother's financial pain. At various points when Lilly was between jobs, Mark and Sue would claim they didn't even have any extra money to help pay bills, allowing Brock and Lilly to be evicted on one occasion. At other times, depending on her mood at the moment, Sue would offer to let Brock and Lilly move back into her home. However, this was often just a way to control the two. She always loved having an audience with which to play hostess or create the appearance of being a loving mother or grandmother. Sue enjoyed being needed because it made her feel significant, but her influence was always more detrimental to Lilly's mental health than helpful. After a while, when Sue felt Lilly and Brock had overstayed their welcome, she would instruct Mark to ask them to leave or suggest they find an apartment and offer some marginal financial support to "get them on their feet."

By design, Dylan's life was the opposite of his "failure" sister's. Dylan always fancied himself the winner of the family and took every opportunity to let anyone around him know that he came from an affluent, well-known family. His tendency to lead with his familial clout and academic and professional accolades afforded him an illustrious career in the tech industry. Dylan was a workaholic and focused primarily on climbing the corporate ladder and becoming rich before age 35. From a young age, Dylan fancied himself the golden child because of his mother's adoration and special treatment. He was intelligent, ambitious, attractive, athletic, and hard-working. Many people found Dylan arrogant, brusque, and a bit glib, but overall, he was well-liked and popular. After graduating from college, he married a beautiful young woman, Emily, whom he, not surprisingly, called his "trophy wife." He always indicated he wanted to find a woman "like his mother," and Emily was similar in many ways, albeit far more passive and accommodating.

From the time he was a child, Dylan focused his life on money, success, and looking good. He and Emily built the "perfect family" as if on schedule with their peers. By the time Dylan was 35, he

CHAPTER FIVE

had made his first million dollars after selling a proprietary code to a large software developer. Dylan always positioned himself above his siblings, except his sister Callie, who he felt most like him. He and Lilly always shared an antagonistic relationship when they were younger. He enjoyed taunting and teasing her, believing her to be weak, uninteresting, and fearful, and she would retort that he was vain, empty, and mean-spirited. Of course, some of this behavior was not uncommon for siblings. However, sometimes Sue reiterated his criticisms, believing Lilly could "learn something" from her more fearless and gregarious brother.

Interestingly, none of the children, besides the twins, had a close relationship, and neither parent tried to foster healthy relationships among their children. Because of his busy work schedule, Mark frequently checked out of the home dynamics. Sue seemingly enjoyed compartmentalizing her children and often found their sibling rivalry "interesting" since she grew up as an only child. The result was a household where each child was parented with wildly different standards and expectations and little care or effort to reconcile differences among the children. The home environment thus exacerbated the primary rivalry between Dylan and Lilly and helped Lilly to feel more alone.

As adults, Lilly reluctantly asked Dylan to loan her money when she was in a bind, to which he acquiesced. Then he would shame and admonish her for not being able to take care of her family responsibilities and demand that she repay him. Dylan seemed to relish having a financial advantage over others. He took every opportunity at family functions to flaunt his wealth, a display often championed and reinforced by Sue and Mark. At one Christmas celebration, Dylan made a big show of giving each of his three children brand-new electric child-size cars in a year when he had gotten wind of Lilly agonizing over being unable to buy her son one. She and Brock were then forced to watch Dylan's children ride around the spacious yard in their new toy cars while Sue and Mark admired how happy Dylan's kids were. To contrast this display, Brock would often receive meager gifts compared to the other grandchildren, which Lilly could only assume was a de facto punishment for Brock's being her son. All of this had the effect of exacerbating her shame at not measuring up to Dylan's success.

Callie's and Connor's experience was very different from their older siblings'. Being twins, they were often treated as one entity by their parents. Sue was particularly proud that she had twins, and as children, she frequently paraded them around town to garner attention and admiration from those who were fascinated. Being the youngest children in the family, they became observant of their older siblings' varied treatment. Connor was sensitive, quiet, empathic, and caring. He acted as an emotional sponge in his family, silently absorbing the unspoken emotional turmoil. As a result, he experienced frequent illnesses as a young boy, including severe asthma, allergies, and unexplained headaches. Connor's sensitivity and empathetic sensibilities contrasted with his twin sister, Callie, who was stern, rational, and stoic. Callie was a strong-minded, opinionated, and willful perfectionist from a very young age. Callie, always focused on appropriateness, ethics, and etiquette; frequently corrected her family members' manners at dinner; and often enjoyed lecturing or teaching others. She was also uncharacteristically religious and became involved in church youth extracurriculars despite her family's not attending church except for Christmas, Easter, or other special events (a tendency for which she routinely admonished them).

Connor was a natural mediator and often tried to mitigate conflict between Dylan, Lilly, and his parents. He would frequently sneak into Lilly's room to comfort or spend time with her when Sue unnecessarily punished her for something petty or unreasonable. He always felt guilty for Lilly's treatment. But being a child, he also didn't want negative attention turned on him, so he often avoided being present when Sue was on the warpath.

When they were children, Callie's and Connor's opposite personalities were amusing to adults. Connor's gentle, free-spirited, and kind approach to others contrasted with Callie's dry, almost dour criticality and rigidity. Connor was artistic and creative and had difficulty ignoring his or others' emotional pain. Annoyed by her twin brother's sensitivity, Callie often teased and rebuked Connor for being a "bleeding heart," "too soft," and "undisciplined." Callie also enjoyed tattling on Connor if he broke the rules. Although the two were rarely punished, she hypocritically held herself to a different standard of conduct and regulations than others, excusing her indiscretions, contradictions, or lapses in judgment and becoming righteously angry at any perceived criticism.

Callie always gave herself ample leeway to circumvent protocol or procedure while policing others' decorum and behavior. Ironically, Callie had high theoretical standards for how to treat others and often talked about being kind, polite, and considerate. However, her manner of speaking and behaving was the antithesis of her self-proclaimed values. She was exceedingly harsh and judgmental, particularly when she perceived someone's violating her conduct rules. In school, she was often picked or volunteered as a teacher's aide because she presented herself as wise beyond her years, organized, and willing to forgo loyalty to her peers if given a chance to exercise power to control or punish others. As a result, Callie was not particularly well-liked among her peers but achieved a great deal of respect and notoriety for her perfectionism and high-achieving nature. In this way, she was very similar to her brother Dylan, with whom she shared ambition and drive. However, she was often critical of his vanity, need for external validation, and materialism. The two frequently ganged up on the "sensitive" children, Connor and Lilly, forming an unspoken alliance that remained throughout their adult lives.

Callie went to college on a full academic scholarship, maintained a 4.0 GPA, and received a scholarship to study educational leadership. She earned a Ph.D. in education by age 28, accepted a professor position at a prestigious school in the Northeast, and became the youngest associate dean of students by age 36. Callie enjoyed her job immensely because she was primarily tasked with managing academic misconduct claims and facilitating the expulsion and suspension processes, which aligned well with her propensity toward punishment and procedural conduct enforcement.

Interestingly, Sue's orientation toward Callie was less than ideal because she found Callie to be a "stick up the ass" and "bossy"; thus, the two would often find themselves in intense conflicts, typically when Callie would correct Sue on a particular issue or how to do something. Nonetheless, Callie was always unafraid of Sue and her temper tantrums. Sue's manipulative tactics didn't affect Callie as much as they did the other siblings because, as Callie explained, "she didn't care" how her mother treated her. In many respects, Callie's calloused emotions did protect her from Sue's selfishness. She was strongly critical of Lilly and Connor, who could not dismiss or ignore Sue's histrionic displays, unfair treatment, or blatant selfishness.

Connor, after a rough patch in early college with untreated ADHD (a condition that was identified in elementary school but left untreated due to Sue's refusal to acknowledge his limitations), finally graduated college with a degree in psychology and earned a master's degree in marriage and family counseling. Connor continued to foster closeness with his older sister Lilly. He also became very close to his nephew Brock, serving as a surrogate father figure since Darius had started a new family several states away. However, he also fell into codependent caretaking behaviors, often enabling her to avoid work during one of her drinking binges by babysitting Brock and even going to the liquor store and purchasing her alcohol. Brock also gave his sister informal therapy, further blurring the line between brother and social worker. Connor also tried in vain to mitigate the frequent conflicts between Lilly and Sue or between Lilly and Dylan.

Callie rarely spoke to her sister and felt little connection to her siblings except Dylan, who she felt was the only "reasonable" one. At family holidays or other events where the family was gathered, she would admonish Connor and Lilly for "focusing on the negative" aspects of their family when they tried to discuss their experiences with Sue, Mark, or Dylan. She would strongly rebuke Lilly for her irresponsibility with her child and suggested that her mental health and substance abuse issues were to elicit attention.

As the years went on, the family's prominence in the community grew, and everyone was expected to attend awards ceremonies for

CHAPTER FIVE

Sue's or Mark's contributions to the arts and medical field, respectively. Sue always wanted the appearance of the perfect family that supported her unconditionally. Despite having virtually no close relationship with anyone, she also felt more like a true matriarch with all her children and husband around her to contribute to the idyllic family portrait. At times, however, she felt inferior to Dylan, whose success was a source of pride to others when he was absent but a source of competition when his success overshadowed her accolades.

When Mark filed for divorce after 25 years of marriage, it shocked Sue and the community, which had grown accustomed to believing in the image they had constructed over the last 30 years. Immediately, lines were drawn in the sand, and familial tensions reached a fever pitch, further entrenching the toxic dynamics. Sue immediately became vengeful and began spending extraneous money from their joint accounts. She called the children ritualistically to complain and admonish their "piece of shit" father. Sue fabricated numerous stories about affairs and infidelities and even told Dylan she believed Mark was gay. If any child, in particular Lilly or Connor, expressed a desire to remain neutral in their parents' divorce proceedings, Sue would lash out and verbally berate them or threaten to remove them from the will. In a particularly nasty fight with Mark, after throwing all his clothing, watches, and framed medical diplomas in the backyard, she visited the family attorney, partially drained Lilly's trust fund, and went on an extravagant weeklong trip to Aruba. When confronted and rebuked by Mark's attorney, she falsely claimed that he had been withholding the amount agreed upon for her living allowance and needed cash to send to Lilly because she struggled to pay her rent and "needed to help her daughter."

Sue managed to prolong the divorce for four years while she quibbled endlessly about every item in the home. She frequently roped the children and grandchildren into the dispute, expecting them to lie to protect her and defame Mark. During those periods, she was uncharacteristically kind, showering them with gifts, praise, and sympathy, which was alluring, particularly to Connor and Lilly, who craved their mother's positive attention. However, if at any point they deviated from her expectations, expressed an opinion that differed from hers, or refused or failed to uphold falsities surrounding their father, she'd cut them off for weeks or months. During one such period, she refused to see Connor and his wife or acknowledge her new grandchild because he wouldn't write a statement claiming she was "always financially responsible" with the family's funds when they were children.

Sue's constant defamation of Mark resulted in a significant reduction in his patient load, which, of course, negatively affected his income. She successfully managed to turn most of their friends against him, exaggerating his treatment of her and claiming years of financial and emotional abuse because of his negligence. By the time the divorce was finalized, due to Sue's relentlessness, Mark was resigned to giving her whatever she wanted to be free of the continuous conflict, which had resulted in his developing prostate cancer and his rheumatoid arthritis worsening. Connor, who gave up trying to mediate between the two, developed signs of lupus and severe inflammatory bowel disease, and Callie and Dylan stopped speaking to their siblings altogether. Instead, they shared family holidays with each other's families and occasionally Sue, who managed to keep their support throughout the process. However, Callie remained closer to Mark than Dylan, who was angry at his father for "breaking up the family."

At 45 years old, Lilly died suddenly from a heart attack on Christmas Eve after receiving a phone call from Sue, who was admonishing her for not "checking on her" more often during the divorce. The coroner believed that she developed a heart condition likely due to her alcoholism and substance abuse and the stress on her body due to her panic disorder. Sue demonstrated little emotion upon hearing about her death from Lilly's son, Brock. She demanded complete control over the funeral preparations, mostly because she wanted attention, sympathy, and condolences from friends and extended family. Mark, Connor, Sue, and Callie attended her funeral, but Dylan was overseas on a business deal and found it "inconvenient" to return. He sent a flower bouquet and a card to Brock that read simply, "I'm sorry for your loss." Two years after Lilly died, Connor suffered a stroke, lost control of the left side of his body, and spent years in rehabilitation to regain his health. Callie was appointed senior dean of students, and Dylan was featured in *Forbes* magazine as one of Silicon Valley's "power players." Mark remarried a few years after the divorce and worked hard to develop a stronger relationship with his children. However, Callie and Dylan remain unforgiving and blame him for "destroying Mom." One year after the divorce was finalized, Sue married one of Mark's fraternity brothers, moved to southern Florida, and lived happily ever after.

Intergenerational Trauma

Narcissism is just as erosive to a family system as alcohol, drugs, or any other potentially toxic external influence. Substance abuse and narcissistic abuse within a family system have virtually the same cluster of outcomes and produce the same scars as heroin or violent crime. The difference is that narcissistic abuse and the propagation of narcissistic family systems are not seen as nearly as threatening to the healthy development of a family system as drugs or alcohol. Thus, people have fewer tools to recognize and manage the trauma, and often, when it is identified, the suffering has laid waste to many psyches and relationships.

In families where substance abuse is prominent, there are various archetypal roles that people play to help manage the effects of the chaotic influence of addiction. Many scholars, including most notably Sharon Wegscheider-Cruse, have posited six primary roles that are unconsciously adopted in family systems touched by addiction, including the hero, the child, the mascot, the clown, the enabler, and the scapegoat and, of course, the addict.[2] Many have expanded upon and tweaked Wegscheider's archetypal roles to include other iterations that point to common positions within a family system that are intended to mitigate the turmoil of addiction. While the accuracy and global application of Wegscheider's roles have been refuted by many (since not all roles can be occupied and cultural and societal influences significantly affect the performance of some roles), there is wisdom to be gleaned from understanding family systems theory as it relates to addictive and narcissistic family systems.

As the family matriarch, Sue's selfishness, competitiveness, manipulativeness, and empathy deficits helped create an atmosphere of neglect, antagonism, and developmental disruption for her children and marriage. Sue's mother, Li, recognizing her daughter's deficits, attempted to mitigate the potential upset of "healthy" familial relating. Still, her exit to China heralded a significant shift in the breakdown of order toward chaos. These effects were subtle at first, and as is common in many narcissistic families, the true effect of the narcissistic foundation of the family system wasn't felt until the children were grown. Li was the family system's first enabler. Whether born out of her inherent and long-standing disappointment in Sue due to her narcissistic projection of the ideal daughter or a genuine desire to protect her grandchildren, Sue was afforded a lifestyle whereby she never had to develop interpersonal strategies that nurture healthy psychic or relational development. This is not to say that without Li, Sue would've spontaneously developed empathy and a deep concern for others, which was not already present; more than likely, it wouldn't have mattered. However, Li's presence in the home allowed Sue to abdicate many basic adult responsibilities that accompanied parenting and live in an almost perpetual adolescence.

Being the *Entitled Caregiver*, Sue believes she is nurturing and self-sacrificing. Indeed, because of her narcissism, any concession to others' needs, wishes, or desires would be seen as self-sacrificing, so from the perspective of her reality, she indeed has sacrificed herself repeatedly for her family. However, her overestimation of her contributions created a schism between her actual care, love, and concern and what her family experienced. As we already saw in Chapter 4, Sue's unconscious rejection of her daughter Lilly stems from her complicated relationship with her mother and a dynamic of competitive comparison to Lilly as the intelligent, studious child she felt she could never be. Li's favoritism of Lilly undoubtedly exacerbated Sue's disdain while providing at least some kind of nurturing influence for Lilly, who, in early childhood, had already internalized her mother's disdain. Like many children, and in particular daughters of narcissistic mothers, Lilly developed a complicated self-image that included messages of being rejected by her mother who gave birth to her and in the awkward (and unnatural) position of being the target of a narcissistic mother's competitive rage.

The effect of Sue's neglect and subtle undermining of Lilly's goals, gifts, and aptitudes eventually took its toll on Lilly, who, upon leaving home (after enjoying an academic career punctuated by success and accolades), rebelled against trying in vain to be valued by her mother. In rejecting college scholarships and opting instead to put her energy into the safe harbor of a romantic relationship with an equally emotionally unavailable man, Lilly, in an effort to heal the trauma of being the scapegoat, instead continued to sabotage herself in the same way her mother thwarted her development.

The unprocessed pain of the rejection and emotional abuse Lilly experienced from her mother took root in the form of substance abuse because it promised an immediate escape. Substance abuse disorders are not uncommon in children of narcissistic abuse.[3] Many also have a challenging time recognizing or maintaining healthy romantic relationships. Lilly married a man who, although not likely narcissistic, showed significant deficits in his ability to demonstrate love and care appropriately and who, at times, mimicked her mother's emotional neglect. Drinking and prescription medication abuse were externalizations of her low self-regard and likely low dopamine receptor sensitivity due to 18-plus years of feeling fundamentally wrong in the eyes of her primary caregiver. It's worth noting that Mark's implicit abdication of care for his children only watered the seeds of trauma. Not uncommonly, spouses of narcissists participate in the proliferation of abuse through enabling behaviors designed to keep them in the good graces of the love-rejecting spouse.

In larger families, there's typically more than one casualty from narcissistic abuse. While some family members may appear relatively unscathed, their scars are likely more aptly hidden under heavier armor. The incidence of narcissistic parents' producing a narcissistic child is heightened due to the partially genetic component of narcissistic personality features. Both Dylan and Callie are narcissistic but personify different subtypes. Dylan, who was given "golden child" status, internalized his mother's admiring gaze. It's difficult to say whether Dylan might've developed into a narcissist without his mother's excessive praise and effusive attention compared to his siblings. Whatever the case, Sue saw something in Dylan that mirrored her perceived desirable qualities and nurtured him accordingly as an extension of herself.

Dylan best fits the *Ruthless Workaholic* subtype. He is vain, competitive, and convinced that his extreme work ethic, ambition, and desire to be rich and famous are all necessary to succeed in the world. Indeed, in Western culture, these characteristics can afford someone with a considerable degree of success, particularly those from a privileged background like Dylan's. While we don't know much about Dylan's internal processes, it's safe to assume that Sue's overvaluation of him supported his character armoring as being "the star" and, as is familiar with this personality style, the need to be seen and validated for one's external contributions, accolades, talents, and productive output can become all encompassing. The *Ruthless Workaholic* is immensely superficial and cutthroat and openly rejects emotions that threaten their ultimate desire for money and power.

To continually receive the glow of Sue's approval, Dylan naturally developed a disdain for his sister Lilly, who represented what he framed as "loser" qualities (i.e., her sensitivity and relatively quiet demeanor). Thus, to survive within the family system and maintain and support his burgeoning ego, Dylan needed to position himself as the antidote to Lilly's disappointing ineffectiveness. He also took it upon himself to mimic and even amplify Sue's antagonism toward Lilly by becoming a deputy bully. Very often, narcissistic people feel threatened by those who exhibit or experience greater emotional sensitivity because it highlights their deficits. Of course, they frequently position the more emotionally sensitive person as weak or otherwise deficient, which is a projection of their inferiority fears. Conversely, for those narcissistic types whose emotional sensitivity is a source of pride, proving themselves or competing with others in the emotional sensitivity Olympics is often preferred.[4]

For twins Callie and Connor, two very different personality styles and methods of managing the narcissistic familial dynamics developed. Callie, a rigid, perfectionistic, self-directed rule follower, created an identity that rejected her mother's overbearing, effusive need to imprint herself on her children. Instead, Callie, self-directed and strong-willed, was the antithesis of Dylan's boastfulness, Lilly's unassertiveness, and her twin brother's softheartedness. On the other hand, Connor is the family's resident "empath" and, being more naturally attuned to the emotional dynamics in the family system, seems to internalize the dysfunction of the family unit, taking it upon himself to play the role of healer and mediator. This role would shape his professional trajectory and inform his ongoing enmeshment with his vulnerable sister, Lilly, who is also highly empathic. Callie is the *Moralistic Inquisitor* subtype. She delights in pointing out and exploiting others' mistakes, errors, and unethical behavior to bolster her sense of moral and ethical superiority. Her career as the dean of students reflects this subtype's tendency to excel in professions where they can arbitrate justice. She sadistically relishes punishing others who don't adhere to her internal standards of correctness. However, any suggestion that she had less than altruistic motives would be offensive to her righteous self-image. Callie exhibited this behavior early on and acted as the rational, measured balance to her brother's emotionally resonant interpersonal role. In both cases, the twins flew under Sue's radar. Very often, in narcissistic family systems with multiple children, the desire to stay out of the proverbial eyeline of the narcissistic caregiver is a desirable position. Too much positive attention often means unrealistic expectations and bearing the brunt of excessive projection by the parent. Too much negative attention means risking excessive criticism, judgment, unrealistic expectations, and increased punishment or ridicule.

The family's affluence and community notoriety only exacerbated the necessity to keep the private reality of the emotionally chaotic, neglectful home environment separate from the social environment so they can appear to be the model family. The schism created between the reality and the image of their lives is an unspoken expectation but one that, over time, has subtly erosive effects and only strengthens the expectation of suffering in silence present in dysfunctional family systems. This also allows any addiction (e.g., Lilly's alcoholism) or any other mental health problems to remain untreated and fester under the weight of toxic positivity. The shame many narcissistic parents have for their children's struggles (whether physical, emotional, or mental) prevents effective and timely intervention. Their need to maintain an exceptional image in the eyes of their chosen audience is often upheld at their own and their loved ones' expense. That said, there are vulnerable narcissistic subtypes who exploit and leverage their loved ones' difficulties for sympathy or to suit some other goal. *Entitled Caregivers* like Sue are typically quite neglectful of other people's emotional needs, and while they project an image of nurturance to the outside world and, in many cases, may even be extraordinarily generous to those outside of their immediate circles, the reality is that through withholding their care and attention, they manipulate and control those in their orbits who seek their gaze.

Although largely distant and absent from the crumbling family dynamics long ago, Mark abandoned hope for Sue to change and, in many ways, left the children to fend for themselves in an environment that was more often a stage for their mother's histrionics. Mark and Connor also enable Sue's abuse either by failing to protect those she abused or reinforcing her negative messages, as is Connor's preferred method of coping. Narcissistic relational strategies are undoubtedly toxic, but those who enable their toxicity are often complicit in reproducing the abuse. However, we can't necessarily blame them for their enabling strategies. Enablers have adopted a coping strategy designed to survive in a dysfunctional system. Enablers also play a role in ensuring that the ecosystem isn't disrupted, and in some cases, when enablers step out of their role, the system falls into further disarray. This dynamic plays out in tragic form when Mark decides to divorce Sue, leading to a cascading degenerative effect on the family's tenuous equilibrium.

CHAPTER FIVE

While Dylan's and Callie's lives seem to thrive due to their narcissistic defense strategies and the socioeconomic privileges afforded to them, Connor's and Lilly's lives become increasingly fraught. Lilly's tragic, unexpected death, because of mental illness and substance abuse caused by the emotional neglect and psychological abuse of her mother and her own choices, is a reminder of the rotten roots of trauma. The fractured sibling dynamics and the competitive environment only helped to erode the social support that could, under normal circumstances, have helped to save their sister's life. Connor could not single-handedly rescue Lilly from the degenerative effect of familial trauma, nor could he see the harmful effects of his caretaking on his health, leading to the development of lupus. Not surprisingly, chronic illness in abuse survivors illustrates the interconnectedness between humans' emotional and psychological experiences and their physiological stress, as Bessel van der Kolk's seminal book *The Body Keeps the Score* outlines expertly.[5] What is less discussed, and worth noting briefly, is that narcissists often experience a higher incidence of chronic illness, depression, substance abuse, and other mental health disturbances likely due to their unprocessed emotional trauma and extensive armoring strategies. In one particularly apt exploration of this topic, researchers refer to the phenomenon of chronic illness in patients with narcissistic traits as an externalization of the proverbial Achilles' heel, pointing to a crack in the otherwise impenetrable armor of the narcissistic defense strategy.[6]

Depending on the severity of the trauma, neglect, or abuse, healing family trauma is often a lifelong journey. In many narcissistic family systems, many people don't exactly know what to call what happened to them, not to mention others' parroting trite but well-meaning statements like "families are hard" or "no family is perfect." For many familial narcissistic abuse survivors, these statements only serve to gaslight them further into believing that their oversensitivity to their mother's, brother's, sister's, or father's relational tactics is overwrought or dramatic. Finding a narcissistic trauma-informed therapist could've been the determining factor in saving Lilly's life. Still, without fully appreciating the full force of Sue's toxicity on every level of her family's experience and the enablers who perpetuated the damage, it isn't easy to heal.

Anyone who is in a narcissistic relational dynamic long enough begins to unconsciously adopt some of the narcissist's strategies either into their internal self-talk or in relationships with others. For example, in Lilly's case, she adopted Sue's disparaging and condescending view of her as an inner critical voice, which fueled her negative self-talk. To make matters worse, this unhealthy self-relating is projected into the world, and negative relationship dynamics feel familiar, thus reinforcing the person's negative self-perception.

Reprogramming negative self-talk and building a healthy and nurturing relationship with oneself in recovery from narcissistic relationships is paramount to healing. The narcissist, unable to fully integrate their flaws and vulnerability, thus spits their proverbial poison into their relationships with coworkers, family members, children, spouses, friends, and significant others, perpetuating a kind of social epidemic of skewed self-perceptions, manipulative relational strategies, and unnecessary competitiveness.

The antidote to the poison is awareness of the dynamic and a conscious rejection, often through gray-rock techniques, boundaries, and self-imposed distance from the narcissistic person (and frequently their enablers). Unfortunately for Lilly and the other members of her family, the relational toxicity had already taken hold of their psyches and, without recognition of the offending toxin, would continue to erode body, mind, and spirit. The almost Sisyphean irony is that Sue, due to the impenetrable narcissistic armor, will likely live the rest of her life relatively unscathed by her psychic contagion.

An Enlightened Community

Joe's rise to spiritual prominence was swift. After moving to Northern California and purchasing a 4-acre plot of land, he quickly attracted a spiritual community, many of whom had been attending his dynamic and controversial "Radical Truth" workshops. Joe's business was twofold: a spiritual mentoring program, available only through

CHAPTER FIVE

application, and seminars open to the public. Joe charged an excessive $450 an hour for his spiritual mentoring services and upward of $3,000 per person for a 3-day workshop and spiritual retreat. Joe's business model was always to attract influential and wealthy clientele, and by positioning himself near Silicon Valley, he could attract many wealthy seekers to his work.

Via a ghostwriter, Joe self-published an autobiography about his travels and meeting various unnamed "masters," who anointed him with spiritual power. Joe's book was generously exaggerated and was a marketing tool to attract spiritual seekers looking for a Western spiritual master. Joe implied he had been enlightened during a particularly intense yoga retreat in India but knew that stating his spiritual status outright would alarm most people; he wanted to maintain a sense of humility. It was accurate that Joe had many significant spiritual insights during his training, and when he could temporarily suspend his ego conditioning, his spiritual guidance was indeed profound. Nonetheless, his severe lack of self-awareness countered his total and permanent ego annihilation claims. Nonetheless, he achieved a spiritual awareness and power that many found alluring and aspirational.

Joe had a keen business sense and secured an investor to build a small spiritual center that would be the home base for his work. After moving from the East Coast and burning many bridges with previous clients, his fresh start in California taught him to have those closest to him sign NDAs to prevent "secrets" about his "methods and spiritual technologies" from leaking to the public.

During a fortuitous workshop in Sedona, Arizona, Joe met Trent, who would become instrumental to his continued rise to spiritual stardom. Trent was mysterious, aloof, shy, and off-putting to many who encountered him. He mostly sat in the back of the room during the workshop, quietly observing the other participants. When it came time to participate in what Joe called "The Process" and come to the front of the room to allow Joe to give him real-time spiritual coaching, Trent refused, stood up, and left the room. The other participants were amazed at Trent's bold refusal since most had a "healthy fear" of Joe. However, Joe laughed and told the group that he respected his courage.

Joe caught Trent at lunch and patted him on the back, telling him he had some real "balls" to disrespect him like that. Unintimidated by Joe's aggressive style, Trent laughed arrogantly and said, "I don't need a room full of losers judging my emotions when I know I've already done enough spiritual work for a thousand lifetimes." Trent's glib, cocky, and sarcastic style resonated with Joe, and the two developed mutual respect at that moment. When another participant told Joe that Trent was a wealthy tech investor, he thought it was advantageous to try to foster the connection more deeply. However, as was his customary manner, he acted unfazed and unbothered. Toward the end of the retreat, while walking out of the room, Joe casually mentioned that Trent should book a session to "process the many lifetimes of being ignored and undervalued." Joe's hook was compelling, and two weeks later, Trent emailed him to request a personal healing session.

Joe worked with Trent in several sessions to help him uncover and heal some of his "core wounds." Trent spent most of the sessions telling Joe about everyone in his life who hadn't recognized his genius and exquisite taste and appreciated him only for his money. Joe convinced Trent that it was his karma in this lifetime to be a benefactor, a payment for many lives spent stealing from others. Trent, highly intellectual and even more spiritually focused, fancied himself a rare, old soul and felt he had finally found someone who could see the "real him." Despite his aloof demeanor, Trent was emotionally sensitive and terrified of criticism or shame. When talking to others, he spent most of his energy lamenting his problems and blaming his parents and family for not understanding him and his intellectual superiority.

Trent believed that his three failed marriages were all due to his ex-wives' gold-digging tendencies and that nobody understood his unique gifts. After a few months of intense psycho-spiritual work with Trent, Joe began to mention his desire to open a spiritual center in Silicon Valley because the area needed its vibration raised and he

CHAPTER FIVE

felt called to go there. Trent, fully convinced of Joe's spiritual power, offered to fund the project if he could direct the business operations. The two had numerous conversations about how their combined spiritual power would be transformative. Joe agreed to allow Trent to manage the day-to-day business operations, but ultimately, as a consummate micromanager of every detail, Joe would make the final decision for everything.

The early stages of building the business were difficult because of Joe's meticulousness and obsession with control. Trent wasn't used to having someone dictate his decisions, and Joe's tendency to require approval was a source of early tension between the two. Despite Trent's financial leverage, Joe's position as the guru helped solidify his ultimate authority.

Trent was uniquely able to draw people in through his aloof mysteriousness. He was instrumental in recruiting people to work for the "Center for the Process," as the retreat center was called. Because of his connections, Trent was instrumental in garnering publicity and buzz about the center. He felt it imperative to market Joe and the organization as an "elite, progressive, spiritual technology community" because he knew how much Silicon Valley tech types craved early adoption of the latest and greatest technologies. He even acquired a trademark for Joe's spiritual process called "advanced spiritual technology." He even purchased a billboard on a busy street near Stanford University that read, "Spiritual Tech Is Coming . . . ," followed by a web address that allowed interested people to sign up for a waiting list to experience the emerging spiritual community.

When the Center for the Process opened, there was a waiting list of 1,200 people, and they accepted only 50 (wealthy) people for the "inaugural class." The organization was structured as a multistep spiritual school that promised to teach participants the latest spiritual technologies to help foster greater abundance, health, wealth, and peace. Joe led workshops on meditation, holistic eating, enlightened exercise, and awakening one's intuitive faculties. He also led one-off "supplemental" workshops on creating wealth and manifesting fame and conducted classes on spiritual influence and power for which he charged anywhere from $9,000 to $15,000 per class and required all students to participate in one-on-one spiritual coaching for a minimum of 4 hours a month at $450 per hour. Despite the excessive pricing, the center was an immediate success with the who's who of Northern California and grossed over $1 million in its first year. Joe quickly became known as the "guru's guru" in Silicon Valley, and at Trent's insistence, admission to the school came only by invitation.

Trent enjoyed gatekeeping the organization because, in his mind, it kept out the "riffraff" and "low-consciousness" people and allowed the organization's energy to stay bright and productive. Trent managed the day-to-day operations and the center's employees, including café workers, yoga and Pilates teachers, three masseuses, and a few Reiki and energy healers.

Joe's wife, Iona, oversaw the healing arts at the center; however, she and Trent rarely agreed. When Joe proposed moving to California to start the center, Iona believed she would play an integral role in shaping the direction of the center; however, as Trent became more involved, he continually diminished her ideas and suggestions as "pedestrian," "trite," or "basic." Iona hated conflict and rarely pushed back, but she privately insisted to Joe that she be given domain over the healing work, a request he eventually obliged (of course, with the implication of his final approval on all decisions).

Iona and Joe seldom fought during the seven years of their marriage due to her sedate temperament. He quickly learned that her demands were few and, often choosing the path of least resistance, would ultimately acquiesce when she did express a specific need. Conversely, Iona had learned from the mistakes of his first wife, Josie, and let Joe do whatever he wanted. Iona, however, found Trent to be snobbish, rude, and condescending to her and the employees, and she felt that it was in Joe's best interest to rein him in.

Trent's snobbishness became a point of contention for the center's patrons and employees, both of whom often avoided him. He frequently made comments to people about their clothing, hair, or other superficial aspects of their appearance, and when anyone challenged his judgments, he would often lash out and either publicly

CHAPTER FIVE

humiliate them with a sanctimonious tirade about how someone's outer appearance affected the energy of the group overall or fire or ban them from the center under the guise of keeping "the energy clean." Because everyone in the center had signed an NDA, there was little recourse to expose the toxicity. Curiously, Joe seemed to avoid confronting Trent about his behavior, not necessarily because he didn't believe that it was potentially damaging to the center's reputation (which it was), but because Trent's emotional outbursts and the potential for the money flow to end if Trent were criticized were too much of a risk.

Joe became increasingly challenging to reach as he rose to power and prominence, and he spent most of his time and energy mentoring his wealthiest and most influential clientele. When Iona mentioned that it seemed like he favored the rich clients, he said it was because their focus on wealth and power needed the most work spiritually and that he was in a new "phase" of his spiritual work on the planet and was called to work with the elite to transmute the energy. Joe's spiritual persona became larger than life, and he truly believed himself to be one of only a few "true" conduits of universal spiritual energy on the planet. To some extent, given his massive charismatic sway over very powerful and influential people, one could understand why.

Joe also became increasingly paranoid and cynical of everyone around him. The more power, money, and influence he attained, the more convinced he was that others were out to undermine him, steal his ideas, and poach his clients. He often instructed Trent to file copyright claims on catchphrases, training ideas, and course materials. He would fire a client or student for any perceived disloyalty, including attending another spiritual retreat or workshop or obtaining another teacher's guidance. He publicly humiliated one student for attending a talk given by renowned spiritual teacher Eckhart Tolle, believing that by doing so, he was deviating from his school's tradition and that he'd been karmically tainted.

At the request of Ahmed, one of his longtime students, Joe hired his wife, Donna, to serve as his assistant. She and Ahmed, a successful app developer, were early members of the center, and she believed wholeheartedly in Joe's method for spiritual and emotional healing. While Joe did need someone to help him manage his day-to-day schedule and comply with his constant requests to tweak his training booklets and presentations and to micromanage the company's most minute details, he also wanted someone to help him manage Trent, whom he began to find annoying and high maintenance. Trent became increasingly displeased with his role and demanded to teach and offer spiritual guidance. He thought that he deserved to be designated as the next in line of succession to Joe's burgeoning empire (a sentiment that was endlessly annoying to Iona). Because Joe felt he could no longer fully trust Trent, recognizing his tendency toward envious undermining or passive-aggressive sabotage, he believed Donna could help him track Trent's actions and mediate between the two because their relationship had become increasingly less amicable.

Donna was clever, organized, superficially pleasant, and seemingly timid. Initially, Joe liked that he felt he wouldn't have to fight too much to get her to do his bidding, but he quickly found out that her anxiety, sensitivities, and fears would have to be navigated. Donna shared Joe's suspiciousness and tended to believe everyone was out to undermine or sabotage him. She enjoyed working for Joe because being near "The Teacher" was a highly coveted position. However, Donna had always been skeptical of anyone in power; she would proudly tell stories of previous positions where she uncovered coworkers' "plots" and "plans" and reveled in one particular instance where she exposed a supervisor of a nonprofit for adultery. Even though she admitted his adultery had nothing to do with his performance on the job, she found it indicative of his "true character." Most who worked at the center found Donna to be funny and charming in a quietly neurotic kind of way, and thus, she could build trust with others easily. Unfortunately, her inherent mistrust of others and general desire to have others cater to her many anxieties created significant obstacles to her forming meaningful relationships.

Initially, Donna enjoyed assisting Joe. She liked seeing her influence over his business decisions and felt comfortable enough with

CHAPTER FIVE

him to be pushy and arrogant about how she believed things should be done. She would gladly spar with him on his directives, particularly if what she was being asked to do made her uncomfortable or, as was quite frequent, made her anxious. For example, Donna refused to make phone calls to anyone she hadn't met because she found the phone awkward and would pout, resist, or become punitive and stubborn if she couldn't simply email whomever he was asking her to contact. Donna hated being wrong and would argue mercilessly with anyone she felt was trying to make her look stupid or incompetent. Ahmed warned Joe that she could be particular and had "a lot of anxieties" but assured him she was a hard worker and fiercely loyal. Ironically, Joe found her antagonistic behavior annoying but loved that he could gather intel about his employees and students because of her unthreatening and unassuming personality. Therefore, Joe tolerated her occasional quarrelsomeness or neuroticism since she proved herself a loyal assistant.

Over time, however, Joe and Donna's relationship became fraught with frequent power struggles. Donna became deeply resentful of Joe's power over her and, as was the case in most of her past relationships, became mistrustful of Joe. She began to undermine him by talking about him to other students and employees, acting as a double agent. Indeed, most of the issues she highlighted to others were toxic and problematic, such as his insistence on loyalty; the necessity of NDAs; the exorbitant price of the workshops, classes, and coaching; and his questionable coaching methods and increasingly grandiose guru persona. At first, Donna would do this jokingly, but the simple act of sowing doubt had a corrosively damaging effect. Strangely, however, her loyalty to Joe, whom she still strove to please, and her mistrust and resentment of him created an even more tense relationship between the two.

Over the course of five years, the center grew in prominence, and Joe reached a level of self-help stardom that he both enjoyed and hated because it increased scrutiny of him and his business. A small critical piece was printed in a local newspaper accusing Joe of running a "high-end cult," which infuriated him and only increased his secrecy, paranoia, and extreme expectations of loyalty. Although many of his students felt indebted to him for his transformative power, they also felt increasingly fearful of saying anything remotely critical about him, even to each other, for fear of being labeled disloyal. While no one was ever officially kicked out of the school, many who questioned Joe, particularly around his intuitive insights; guidance; or the exorbitant cost of classes, workshops, and services, were iced out by other group members who saw the person's justified concerns as a "dark" or "unconscious" influence. The result was that the person felt increasingly unwelcome and ultimately stopped attending coaching or classes.

The atmosphere around Joe was tense between Donna and Trent, who acted as gatekeepers and progenitors of toxic workplace dynamics. Trent resented Donna's influence because he found her simple, unrefined, and undeserving of her position, and Donna felt Trent was snobbish, hateful, and sneaky. All of this bubbled under the surface because the two often behaved amicably enough, particularly around Joe, who had become very conscious of his reputation and critical of anyone acting in an "unprofessional" way that made him look bad.

Joe became furious when a popular tech industry magazine published an exposé of the center. The article referenced several "insiders" and "students" who, under the cover of anonymity, violated the extensive NDA preventing discussion of the activities at the center. Aside from the damning criticism of Joe's larger-than-life guru status and the rules of engagement enacted to protect him and his image from harm, a particularly salacious and illegal detail was exposed, which outlined the center's recent practice of asking for cash payments for retreats and workshops, setting off investigative scrutiny for the business' financial recordkeeping and allegations of tax evasion.

Joe's aggressiveness and suspicious disposition reached a fever pitch when he decided to fire most of the center's employees and sever his business relationship with Trent, with whom he'd been feuding for months over his expensive desire to expand the center to other markets and Trent's insistence on more control. Endlessly litigious and hopelessly aggrieved, Trent sued Joe for a return on his

CHAPTER FIVE

investment, beginning an acrimonious and complicated legal drama. Many of Joe's students left in the ensuing months after the publication of the exposé. However, some die-hard loyal students remained and helped with damage control.

Those who still received spiritual coaching from Joe saw a substantial increase in their hourly coaching rate, which he justified because of the "unfair and dark" influences seeking to take him down. They also saw a substantial decrease in the effectiveness of Joe's insight and contentious process. They spent significant portions of their sessions listening to Joe complain about the attacks on his character and urging others to "speak their truth" about the situation, which was code for attacking his dissenters. He also spent significant time sharing (and exaggerating) ex-clients' confidential content to help bolster his attacks. Many understood the implicit request behind his nonchalant invitation to speak the truth, and some long-standing friendships and relationships were ruined in a matter of days over their defense of the flailing guru.

Donna remained working for Joe until one of his former students, furious at Donna's attempts to have her cast out of the community, sent an email outlining Donna's behind-the-scenes and duplicitous undermining of Joe's methods and pricing and suggested that she was at least one of the informants behind the article and subsequent articles that were published about Joe. After a particularly explosive conflict, Joe fired Donna, hurling expletive insults and threats of legal action for stealing proprietary secrets and information.

As Joe's mini spiritual empire imploded, many were left with gaping holes in their sense of spiritual community and camaraderie, not to mention a loss of guidance from their teacher, with whom they'd developed a seemingly deep and intimate connection. Many former students found themselves in therapy, attempting to reconcile their belief in their spiritual teacher's divine guidance and transformative healing power with his caustic, accusatory, cynical attacks on anyone he believed to have betrayed his trust.

Iona and Joe's relationship became increasingly fraught as his anger, distrust, and controlling behavior reached a fever pitch. Many of the friends she made while helping manage the center had abandoned her due to Joe's cantankerous behavior. She was left to bear the brunt of his self-pitying rants and tantrums about the unfair treatment he was receiving when "all he ever did was devote his life to caring for others' spiritual and emotional benefit." Iona found that no matter her response to his complaints, it was never right. Sometimes, he would go days or weeks on end, ignoring her, preferring to talk to his most loyal, sycophantic students, who would spend hours fawning and reinforcing his self-righteous, all-powerful spiritual image.

Joe created fake email addresses and alternate social media accounts (or encouraged his remaining "inner circle" to do so), intending to spy on the activity of former students and employees so he could gather evidence against those who were betraying him. He sent cease and desist letters to former students for utilizing any concepts learned during their time with him or in his classes while refusing to back down from any conflict or accusation. He often doubled or tripled down on controversial or bombastic statements. The result was that even those who managed to separate themselves from the center and Joe were frequently pulled into a never-ending conflictual environment instigated if not by Joe, then a request for an affidavit by Trent or requests for statements by Donna or some other employee or student seeking retribution amid the fallout.

After the massive scandal had settled, Joe and Iona moved to Southern California. Their relationship had degenerated significantly, and Iona eventually left him and moved back to the East Coast. Joe opened a small spiritual coaching practice, rebuilding his reputation and brand, and established a relationship with another former student who had become his primary confidant during his crisis, with plans to plot a comeback and revenge tour of those who had wronged him.

The Kool-Aid Man

As the Dark Empath subvariant of the *Charismatic Bully* subtype, Joe represents a paradoxical space in the narcissistic cannon. Possessing a greater-than-average degree of cognitive empathy and undeniable spiritual intelligence, he wields the power he seeks over others in a particularly mesmerizing way. Unsurprisingly, he could successfully leverage his magnetism and particular blend of audacity and emotional intuition into a loyal following.

The word *cult* evokes different images for everyone. The public's fascination with cults has produced numerous books, films, and podcasts about famous and obscure cults and their charismatic leaders. Generally, a cult is a sect of people with a particular ideological or spiritual perspective outside the mainstream. Not all cults are necessarily sinister. In fact, the world's largest religions began as cults before receiving more widespread influence and membership. Most cults constellate around a charismatic leader responsible for dictating the cult's ideological perspectives and deciding who accurately adheres to the prescribed ideologies.[7] Charisma is a necessary tool of persuasion, which, in most cases, is relatively harmless. However, when charisma and narcissism collide, the potential for abuse, manipulation, and coercion is heightened.

Joe's ability to leverage his natural magnetism with his spiritual and psychological knowledge helps enlist even the most intelligent people into his spiritual spiderweb. Joe's philosophies and ideologies are nothing groundbreaking. Borrowing liberally from Eastern and New Age spirituality, he seduces others by suggesting their soul is special compared to the souls of other people he has not anointed. Often, there is an implicit suggestion that by working with Joe, who has achieved the desirable spiritual status, others can one day be as spiritually exalted as he. This tactic has been used for eons by pseudo-spiritual teachers. That is not to say that in some instances, the wisdom they have attained doesn't help others progress on the spiritual or psychological path, but the damage their ego unconsciousness inflicts on others often outweighs the benefits.

As human beings, we have a natural desire to believe in our specialness over others. This helps to assuage our fears of being another proverbial cog in the universal machine. While each human possesses unique gifts and plays an individual role in the fabric of existence, many cult leaders play on the fear of being mundane, dull, or basic. Joe's financial and business savvy helps him recognize and seize on Trent as a potential opportunity. The Powerful-Aggressive subtypes are particularly prone to human objectification due to their cynical worldview about people's positive intentions and the distortion that they must dominate and control others to avoid domination. Nonetheless, Joe was enamored by the potential for wealth and power and capitalized on Trent's affluence to build his spiritual empire.

Trent, also a narcissist, is the *Entitled Outcast* subtype. His belief in his innate specialness and elevated intellectual, spiritual, and material status creates a persona whereby he presents to others as snobbish and affected. Joe's initial disdain for Trent gives way to respect for his lack of intimidation. Like all Enneagram Type Eight personalities, Joe respects those who demonstrate courage despite their intimidating personas. However, what Joe really appreciates about Trent is his financial potential. Trent enjoys being associated with a sought-after spiritual figure, and the two begin what proves to be a messy but advantageous business and mentor–mentee relationship. Mutual exploitation underlies many contracts; when narcissism is the scaffolding, it only heightens the potential for abuse.

For many narcissistic people, particularly those with financial privilege, the world of business and finance comes easily due to their inherent confidence in their abilities, devaluation of emotional sensitivity, and desire for success and affluence. Trent can leverage his inherited wealth to ingratiate himself to others, a necessary tool since his personality is often off-putting and disagreeable. Despite his wealth and privilege, Trent sees himself as a victim who is hopelessly misunderstood by those around him. Joe, recognizing Trent's need to validate his flawed image, contends that his alienation stems from his spiritual giftedness, thus reinforcing Trent's ideal self-image. In return, Trent helps to build the spiritual mystique and exclusivity needed to draw in the savvy Silicon Valley elite who would become the bread and butter of his spiritual empire.

Joe's effectiveness as a spiritual teacher and mentor is double-edged, as we've already seen in Chapter 4; the interpersonal damage

CHAPTER FIVE

from his convoluted boundaries and psychological manipulation wreak havoc on the lives of others after they have worked with him for any length of time. Nonetheless, his reputation as an efficacious spiritual figure preceded him enough to draw the attention of those seeking further spiritual or material success. Perhaps the most apparent aspect of Joe's grift is the exorbitant prices of his services. However, as this subtype is often too aware, people will pay big bucks to be close to power. Branding his confronting spiritual style and coaching strategies as "spiritual technology" helped to put him at the forefront of a community obsessed with the latest and greatest advances. The promise of elevating one's consciousness at a modest $9,000 to $15,000 a class is a small price for spiritual and material enlightenment.

Not unlike Luke, Joe is a proponent of the NDA; however, in this instance, the agreement serves not only to protect Joe's proprietary "spiritual technologies" and curriculum but also to create a feeling of exclusivity. The presence of the NDA helps to solidify the Center for the Process as a cult because it discourages and even punishes the proliferation of ideas and practices by its members outside of the confines of the community.

As Joe builds his flock, he continues to foster relationships with his growing affluent clientele, further solidifying his financial success. By maintaining close one-on-one relationships with each student in the center, he also ensured a constant inflow of potentially personal information that could, if necessary, be weaponized against anyone he deemed disloyal, a tactic he employed liberally as the center devolved into disarray.

At the height of the center's success, Trent and Joe managed to create what appeared to be a vibrant spiritual community; however, under the surface lurked a restrictive feeling of secrecy and the flagrant juxtaposition of the high cost of services against a backdrop of spirituality. The students' fear of tarnishing their teacher helps to create an atmosphere of silence that, over time, lulls people into compliance. Trent's immature and superficial management of the center only helped to underscore the bubbling toxicity because his hatefulness and disdain for those around him were frequently directed at the staff.

In many toxic cults, a paradox exists between the spiritual ideologies espoused and the reality of the participants' experience in the group. Worse yet, when someone calls out those inconsistencies, people are gaslighted, punished, and rejected. The cardinal sin, of course, is criticizing the leader because to do so is often viewed as criticizing God.

The *Charismatic Bully*, much like the other Powerful-Aggressive subtypes, shares an inherent skepticism, cynicism, and mistrust of others with the Anxious-Skeptical types. Donna, a particularly cunning combination of the *Defensive Pessimist* and *Ambivalent Avoider* subtypes, helps underscore how even narcissists unconsciously attract others who reinforce their worldviews. In many ways, Donna's appearance at the center is a manifestation of the dysfunctional social dynamics that Trent and Joe instituted. As Joe's power increased, so did his paranoia. Thus, there was a need for a more reliable informant than Trent, whose emotionality and tempestuousness were challenging for Joe to manage. Donna proved loyal, competent, and willing to execute Joe's vision. However, her skepticism and tendency to hold others hostage to her various anxieties was a point of contention. The *Defensive Pessimist* enjoys gathering intelligence on others and often utilizes their superficial warmth and nonthreatening personas to ingratiate themselves with others. Her ability to infiltrate the larger group to please the boss also endows her with enormous power as the bridge between the commoners and the king himself. Donna's deeply held belief that no one can be trusted, along with taking up the mantle as the one who will uncover others' ulterior motives or poor moral character, is merely a projection of her own disowned unscrupulousness and duplicity.

Any charismatic narcissistic leader needs flying monkeys to help keep watch over the kingdom. Flying monkeys, whether narcissists themselves, enablers, or unassuming recruits, are an integral feature of any antagonistic social community. The leader's power is derived chiefly from those who, pledging their loyalty to the narcissist, help to

CHAPTER FIVE

keep the dysfunctional structures functioning smoothly and maintain the social order. Trent, Donna, Iona, and others help keep the center's orbit around Joe. This is particularly useful when things begin to devolve, as inevitably they do in inherently unstable systems. Smear campaigns are more easily executed when those who, under the illusion of the dysfunctional ideology, believe that dissenters, defectors, or criticizers are threatening one's own fundamental belief systems and community.

While the Vesuvian implosion of the center's operation was undoubtedly a massive blow to Joe's ego, it's an all-too-common phenomenon in organizations founded on the backs of antagonistic and exploitative social relationships. Like a cannibalistic viper pit, when fragile egos, resentments, and grievances bubble to the surface, a scorched earth strategy is often instituted by the *Charismatic Bully* (and many other narcissistic subtypes) as they attempt to regain power and control through intimidation and force. As Joe's mask drops (or is ripped away) and the glow of his conferred spiritual power dims, those who believe in his anointed status feel confused, betrayed, and enraged. In contrast, others remain intertwined, unable to sever spiritual or emotional ties with their perpetrator.

The aftermath of the dissolution of any close-knit group, particularly cults, can be catastrophic on many levels. For those who invested their time, psychic energy, money, relationships, and social and professional reputations rebuilding their lives when their idealized haven is sullied by the horror of narcissistic abuse, time and intense work with a narcissistic trauma-informed therapist is vital. Often, there are those who, despite the obvious dysfunction, can't sever their ideological or relational ties with the narcissist and will frequently remain loyal until the end. This phenomenon is seen in the clients who stayed with Joe. However, the quality of their relationship devolved as he expressed his disappointment and rage at those who abandoned him. As the narcissistic person's behavior is exposed, their self-superior worldview often shifts toward feelings of being victimized and subsequent martyrdom. They believe that they are being unjustly persecuted by those who are jealous of their power, success, and influence, and they spend considerable time convincing others that their attempts at retribution, revenge, and punishment are justified.

We'll further explore the ideological and systemic damage of narcissistic spiritual abuse in Chapter 6. However, it's worth noting that the relational damage of creating a community built on profound shared experiences (as in a spiritual or religious context) and the loss of community that results from the group's fracturing is often cited as the most challenging aspect of leaving a cultlike or narcissistic social environment. Ironically, the narcissist also feels profoundly aggrieved and betrayed by the group's implosion but remains unable to recognize their role in the dissolution because their psychological structures make it impossible for them to be the problem. To manage the trauma of the consequences of their actions, they globally employ the DARVO (deny, attack, reverse victim and offender) method for those who sever ties, seeing the world as against them and, in some cases, out to get them. However, because their relational attachments are relatively shallow compared to those who experience affective empathy, the *Charismatic Bully* (like many narcissistic subtypes) can quickly rebuild their social circle and replace old connections with new people who have not yet tired of their relational strategies.

The social effects of narcissism are broad and can, as we've seen, vary according to context. It's worth noting that those who grow up in narcissistic family systems tend to feel more at home in narcissistic social and work environments due to the sense of familiarity. That said, human beings are notoriously adaptive, and even those who came of age in the healthiest of environments quickly adapt to antagonistic or toxic environments to survive. Indeed, those with healthier modeling can typically recognize the adverse effects of such environments quicker and make changes or exit to prevent further psychological or emotional erosion. However, those relatively new to narcissistic group dynamics can quickly become apologists or enablers.

CHAPTER FIVE

Hopefully, by now, it's clear how the individual psychological defense strategies of our main characters (Luke, Sue, and Joe) have filtered from their close interpersonal relationships into their larger social and familial networks. While each of our exemplars, and their supporting castmates, has a unique method of performing their narcissism dependent on their subtype, they all employ the same basic relational tactics. Gaslighting, the DARVO method, the deployment of flying monkeys or smear campaigns, triangulation, minimizing, projection, flattery, guilt-tripping, silent treatment, and love bombing are in the greatest hits rotation of most narcissists.[8]

In the next chapter, we'll explore how narcissism affects thinking, cognition, and the values that underscore the political, relational, and social structures that scaffold our reality. We'll see how the defensive distortions and relational strategies of the narcissist have created social realities that contribute to dysfunctions, such as pollution, authoritarianism, exploitation, and worsening mental health crises.

CHAPTER SIX
THE CENTER CANNOT HOLD
Narcissistic Ideologies in Organizational, Political, and Familial Systems

Systems of a Down

Now that we've peeked behind the curtain of our three anti-heroes, Luke, Sue, and Joe, and the effects of their narcissistic defense strategies on their psychological functioning, interpersonal lives, families, and work relationships, we can now look at how the methods and ideologies adopted by narcissistic people become part of the cultural and institutional fabric. By now, it's likely clear that narcissism does not exist within a vacuum, affecting only those who come near the narcissistic person. Instead, it has broad implications far beyond their immediate reach. While most narcissistic people don't become powerful, rich, or famous, this doesn't mean that the systemic effect of their antagonistic relational strategies doesn't bear the same weight as those who do "make it." The narcissistic strategies of gaslighting, minimizing, blaming, excessive competition, hyper-individualism, exploitation, objectification, and other erosive interpersonal strategies are taught and passed down in a perverse intergenerational cascade and have found their way into our broader cultural values; they are now so commonplace within the wider social consciousness that they're rarely questioned and scarcely noticed.

In Chapter 2, we briefly discussed the concepts of holism and quantum interconnectedness and their role in the inextricable way

CHAPTER SIX

our psychological states affect our intimate and broader social circles. In this chapter, we'll see how the smaller relational damage of narcissistic defense strategies affects the macrocosmic machinations of our underlying systems through the proliferation of antagonistic, anti-empathic, and willfully individualistic ideologies that create social and cultural destabilization.

Since we've already covered some of the cultural effects of increasing narcissism in Chapter 2, namely, self-obsession, success, and personal exceptionalism narratives, and the rise of social media vanity, we can now focus on broader systemic ideological and institutional effects. All three characters' stories demonstrate interpersonal strategies that constellate around a few basic ideological suppositions: devaluation of empathy and vulnerability, authoritarianism, victim ideologies, hierarchical structures, disposability, exploitation and objectification, image and success preoccupation, and competition versus collaboration. Let us look at how these overarching themes are present within the fibers of our interobjective shared social, political, and economic realities.

Devaluation of Empathy and Vulnerability

The most obvious place to begin is the most fundamental psychological feature of the narcissistic personality structure: a lack of empathy. Because narcissistic people often experience significant deficits in affective, conceptual, and sometimes experiential empathy, they spend their lives either faking empathetic and compassionate resonance with others or devaluing, denigrating, or exploiting others' empathy. This is because, as we explored in Chapter 3, any perceived deficit (and most narcissists are somewhat aware that they lack these qualities) reveals a vulnerability and thus has the potential to render them inferior or inadequate in comparison to others. Whether or not they openly deride vulnerability and empathy (like we saw with Luke), overvalue their ability to care for and nurture others (like Sue) or mask their empathetic deficits through creating a persona that is extraordinarily empathetic to be superior (like Joe), their disowned envy of those who do experience empathetic resonance has an erosive effect on people around them.

As previously discussed, narcissistic people cannot be vulnerable because allowing their vulnerability into their conscious awareness would threaten the fragile, inflated superior ego they've built to compensate for their deep unconscious fears of being inadequate. Because they, like everyone else, often develop gifts and talents that balance specific weaknesses, their charisma, manipulation, and persuasive abilities or simply the strength of their egos usually make strong impressions on those around them. Vulnerable emotional expressions are avoided because such expression (particularly around others) implies weakness and weakness implies imperfection. Research demonstrates that humans are more comfortable (and even more attracted to) confident, self-assured people, viewing them as more desirable.[1] Narcissistic people, being more attuned to the realities of extrinsic success, are onto something important regarding their investment in communicating and maintaining a successful image. More broadly, the avoidance of vulnerability has become so ingrained in our cultural landscape that most proponents of traditional modern conceptions of masculinity have adopted vulnerability avoidance as a general dictum that says, "Man up." Nations, fearing that the expression of vulnerability would render them targets for war or exploitation, have adopted general behavioral ideology along the same lines with phrases such as the United Kingdom's "stiff upper lip" (to communicate the desirability of not showing emotion) or the United States', "Never let 'em see you sweat."

The philosophy of the stoics, while intended to teach the perennial notion of grace and balance under pressure, was perverted to scaffold the violent cultural ideologies of Ancient Rome (i.e., Spartans) and their brutal systemic conquests to rule the world. Since humans began to sort themselves into "civilized" communities, women have represented the nurturing, empathic, and compassionate duality to the masculine protective, justice-centered, and rational approach to life. Ancient Egyptians, Sumerians, Incans, and other civilizations recognized that for any culture to thrive, both dichotomies need equal

CHAPTER SIX

representation. However, the redemptive, restorative, and often profoundly mystical power of compassion and "feminine intuition" was eventually viewed with envy and suspicion and met with hatred and violence. Efforts to eliminate those who represented the "yang" principles can be seen throughout the histories of the world. When the Pharaohs of the late Egyptian dynasties began to see their priestesses and female kings as threats due to their immense power and respect among the people, a subsequent preference for stereotypical masculine principles was adopted. Ancient Greek philosophers, spurned by Aristotle with his focus on rationality, reason, and transcendence of human vulnerability, frailty, and emotion, hammered the final nail in the coffin of the Western world, giving birth to the proliferation of anti-empathic and subsequent anti-feminine ideologies that would underpin the history of the world. The ideological shift undoubtedly paved the way for immense economic, physical, and material expansion but gave birth to excessive value-laden binaries that still exist today. Disgust or avoidance of vulnerability and weakness is now so baked into most Western (and many non-Western) cultures that many don't question the underlying message of their humanity-denying suppositions.

Envy of empathy and avoidance of vulnerability, indeed, create impenetrable and formidable defenses, which is why as narcissistic people age their armor tends to become heavier and more challenging to pierce. On a systemic level, the avoidance and denigration of vulnerability and empathy have a variety of functions, including the proliferation of "grind" culture, excessive competitiveness, toxic masculinity, and the glorification of war and violence in media. Often, efforts to shift imbalanced strength and toughness narratives are met with derision and, throughout the 2010s, frequent lamenting and resistance to "the 'wussification' of America."

Luke's political campaign (as many before and after him) was built on the ideological avoidance of softness. Because we've been conditioned to believe that stentorian, impenetrable leaders are superior to those who can express malleability and vulnerability, his message resonated with an electorate sympathetic to the political externalization of his fears. Arguably, the primary animus behind authoritarianism is the desire for a proverbial strong man to whip others into shape and protect people from external threats from dangerous interlopers (typically positioned as "the other"). The fear of a vulnerable leader is a projection of our broader cultural fear and avoidance of individual vulnerability. So, while not everyone is narcissistic, the narcissistic notion that vulnerability or softness equals danger lives within the milieu. Indeed, some expressions of vulnerability can be dangerous and even life-threatening. For example, a limping, injured animal is undoubtedly vulnerable to predators. Still, as human egos often forget, most situations are not reducible to life or death, and the animalistic avoidance of showing weakness frequently becomes an obstacle to developing depth or cultivating deeper connections with others.

Alternately, vulnerability and empathy can become performative and even manipulative. Joe's use of selective compassion and performative empathy were tools to garner more power, influence, and loyalty from others. His career was built on modeling care and concern for others. Leveraging others' empathy for gain is an almost intuitive survival strategy for narcissistic people. On a broader level, it fuels objectification and commodification in the world at large (more on that later). Many predatory institutions count on others' empathy and vulnerability to function. We saw how Joe expertly capitalized on others' desire for connection and healing as the impetus for creating the Center for the Process. However, this merely demonstrated a near-universal phenomenon whereby empathy and compassion are constantly exploited by systems and structures that have dehumanized and objectified those within those structures. Proponents of low-vulnerability, high-strength perspectives will balk at the suggestion that there's anything wrong with the established structure, claiming that anyone who doesn't like it doesn't know how to win the game. They may be right. In this way, higher empathy can serve as a deficit in certain aspects of business or self-promotion. Some research also suggests that the more affluent someone becomes, the less empathy they typically exhibit.[2]

CHAPTER SIX

Proponents of "grind" culture or "playing the game" typically possess higher narcissistic traits and, as such, are seemingly less affected by its toxic assumptions. Terrance, a real estate investor I interviewed, echoed this sentiment:

> Yeah, I'd rather be strong than weak. Only weak people talk about how cool being weak is. There's no value to weakness in my world. I can smell weakness a mile away and won't hire someone who I think will cave under the slightest pressure. I learned that as a wrestler in school and use it in business. And I'm damn successful because of it. Sorry I'm winning, but don't be mad because I'm better at the game. (Terrance, 53, real estate investor)

Objectification, Commodification, and Disposability

Dehumanization occurs when we cease seeing others as individuals with emotional depth and variability and instead as extensions of ourselves or our personal aims, goals, or wishes. We've all been guilty of this at one point or another. Usually, when we're young, as we're learning autonomy and gaining more ego strength, getting our way sometimes takes precedence over honoring others' feelings, wishes, or plans (especially our parents'). Manipulating or deceiving your mom so you can stay at your friend's house an extra night is normal age-appropriate behavior for a 13-year-old. However, those who never grow out of that adolescent egocentric focus on their desires, wishes, wants, and needs are often called selfish. In fairness, anyone can revert to selfish egocentric behaviors in isolated instances, sometimes as a means of self-preservation. Narcissists, however, habitually view others as objects to be manipulated for their aims. This is a chronic and automatic relational strategy that often creates interpersonal strain. Their difficulties empathizing with others render other people two dimensional and disposable, except (and often in addition to) those to whom they're most attached (e.g., parents, partners, and children).

In Western culture, objectification of ourselves and others is built into our socioeconomic structure. By its very design, capitalism is a system built primarily on commodifying and objectifying goods and services (mainly created or conceptualized by human beings). This is not inherently problematic in and of itself, except that it's easy for someone's output to determine their overall worth as a human. At its worst, this economic ideology creates a world whereby the more you produce, the more valuable you are to society. Quantifying rewards, benefits, output, and value reduces human beings to cogs. This method of conceptualizing the world is inherent in the narcissistic worldview because to be the best, one must be able to suspend one's emotional experience to produce effectively. The suspension of emotion can help one be more efficient and has its advantages in the phenomenal world, and in some instances, it may be necessary (e.g., a heart surgeon suspending affective or somatic empathy to save a patient's life).

The reduction of humanity happens first within the narcissistic person's psyche. In all three of our characters' lives, we've seen how they equate their image and output in the external world with their intrinsic worth very early in their lives. This self-reduction, therefore, makes it much easier (and natural) to strip others of their intrinsic depth and worth and use them for their aims. For this reason, many narcissistic people thrive in systems where output determines value because it makes intuitive sense to them given that their psychological structure already supports this schema. The world increasingly values objectification to achieve success. Thinking of ourselves as machines and the notion of "doing what you gotta do" to make it points to the scrappy, rugged American (and increasingly non-Western) individualism that captures the spirit of empire-building entrepreneurship that made America a world superpower.

In our characters' lives, we repeatedly saw how the dissociation from their humanity led to dissociation from others. Luke views almost everyone as a tool for success and popularity or a pawn in his increasingly ambitious social aspirations. Sue views most of her relationships as a means to increase material wealth and security and believes others exist to ensure her satisfaction and happiness. Joe views others as objects to be manipulated to gain power, influence, and control. They all represent how success, power, and admiration have become the idols to which most in the Western world subjugate themselves. Even in interpersonal relationships, we are taught to view others as objects of our mental and emotional needs. If someone isn't giving you the attention you desire, leave them. If others don't validate your emotional reality, they're toxic. If others don't cosign our ideological perspectives, they're cancelable.

In some cases, we've become so intolerant of anyone who doesn't serve our emotional or physical objectives that we cut off, isolate, or cancel them to avoid the drain on our ideal aims, rendering us less able to deal with emotional or physical adversity should it arise. That human who stood in the way of our idealized physical or emotional experience then ceases to be a person and instead becomes something that can be ignored or discarded, all in the name of "protecting our peace." Therapeutic language is now weaponized in a way that supports objectification wrapped in self-care.

Some things (and people) are toxic and must be excised. However, our ability to discern true toxicity has been blunted due to excessive abuse of narcissistic ideologies that create hair-trigger responses to obstacles or discomfort, contributing to an increasingly less nuanced and emotionally deep life.

Social media and influencer culture, which we explored in Chapter 2, have helped to spawn new generations built on the altars of objectification and commodification. Every potential business venture is a talent (or pseudo-talent), interest, skill, opinion, or idea. Empires have been built on commodifying aspects of ourselves for human consumption, and social media platforms, such as Instagram, Facebook, X (formerly known as Twitter), and TikTok, help manifest real-world abundance by rendering ourselves as products. Moreover, delineating which products (people) are valuable and which aren't can only function inside an overarching climate of competition.

Competition over Collaboration

Viewing ourselves as commodities and objects for consumption increases the need to prove one's worth compared to other products' (people's) worth. Narcissists, because of their unconscious but agonizing fears of being inferior, are very often intensely competitive. This competitiveness is born out of a need to demonstrate their superiority to help bolster the nagging sense of their inadequacy. Some narcissistic subtypes, peripherally aware of their empathy or compassion deficits, will cultivate an identity as being more empathic, compassionate, and sympathetic than everyone around them.[3]

Americans are taught that competition is healthy. Athletes and sports lovers can attest to the thrill and temporary serotonin and dopamine boost accompanying winning (or winning vicariously through your team's or person's success). Winning provides us with feel-good hormones because it bolsters our egos. Temporarily, we know we (or our team) are better than the losers. We have concrete evidence that our training, skill, talent, investment, or hard work can be leveraged into something tangible that others can recognize as success. In moderation, demonstrating our superiority in a particular thing over someone else can be an excellent way to bolster our self-esteem and reinforce that our hard work or skill has "paid off." However, when our value stems solely from our superiority over others and winning (i.e., being the more valuable product or object) is the only way to generate positive self-regard, competition becomes a psychological necessity rather than a bonus.

Competition is built into our economic and educational structures. Most people are taught, whether overtly or through the socialization process, how to compete in early childhood and, ideally, learn that "winning isn't everything." However, anyone who's ever lost something and gotten a consolation prize or a "thanks for playing" medal knows that nothing quite measures up to the thrill of crushing the competition. Interestingly, but not surprisingly, people with greater empathy tend to score lower on competitive traits out of concern for the loser. Additionally, women, likely through some combination of socialized competitive inhibition and psychobiological predispositions, feel less aggressively competitive than their male counterparts.[4]

In Western culture, to counteract the overtly competitive ideologies that underlie our societal structure, we often teach children to

CHAPTER SIX

be humble and not "sore losers" since expressing our superiority too much is seen as distasteful and cruel to those who've lost. Nonetheless, children also learn that winners gain rewards (both emotional and physical) and losers don't. The result is a collective psyche that aims to be the best while carrying an associated shame in wanting to be exceptional.

Personality research demonstrates that competitiveness is a trait we all express to a greater or lesser degree. Some personality types are inherently more competitive than others, while others shun competition (usually out of fear of being disagreeable, disliked, or simply losing). In almost all instances, narcissistic people score high on competitiveness measures and, as such, typically thrive in environments where demonstrating their superiority over others is desirable or even required.[5] Luke, Sue, and Joe all exhibited high levels of competitiveness in various contexts. Luke was the most overtly competitive in the external world because he thrived in environments where he was tasked with demonstrating his superiority over others.

Competitiveness and a love of competition are undoubtedly advantageous in politics and business. Joe's competitiveness was linked to his need to be more powerful and influential than those around him, particularly those closest to him, to dominate his environment and everyone in it. In turn, those in the narcissist's spheres of influence compete for attention, admiration, affection, time, and positive regard. Their competitive orientation projects onto everyone around them, creating a competition feedback loop. People enjoy bolstering their ego and sense of importance by aligning themselves with winners. The human ego feels enhanced when it aligns itself with the best. And remember, the ego, like all entities, wants to survive and thrive.

Competition in families is considered developmentally natural, particularly among siblings who compete for superiority to gain admiration or attention from their parents or peers. Parental competitiveness with their children, however, creates a confusing and often damaging psychological landscape for the child. As we saw in Chapters 4 and 5, Sue's competitiveness and subsequent undermining and diminishing of her daughter was a heartbreaking example of the potentially necrotizing effects of "healthy competition" within a family system, particularly on the child who doesn't know whether to position the competing parent as friend or foe.

In unhealthy systems where competition is a vital structural component, amicable contests can quickly devolve into mudslinging or savage displays of domination. Although we're thousands of years removed from the brutal gladiator fights in the Coliseum, our tastes are slightly more refined, but our collective bloodlust remains intact. In politics, reality television entertainment, many contact sports, and even hip-hop lyrical battles, aggressive and unrelenting attacks on the competition demonstrate a sense of competence and fitness for leadership. In some industries, the more brutal one's attacks, the more respect is generated. Wars are only larger-scale expressions of this all-too-common relational version of competition and domination.

Although theoretically advantageous and less potentially acrimonious than competition, collaboration has become more desirable in professional settings. However, in most modern social structures where business or money is a factor, collaborative efforts often contain unavoidable psychological competitive elements. Indeed, some level of competitiveness might be advantageous and help push each entity to improve. Still, when competition is the dominating narrative in any system or ideology, it's difficult to tell how much of that fighting spirit is too much.

Research has shown that collaborative ideologies have some essential benefits over starkly competitive ones, such as higher job satisfaction, greater productivity, and a more pervasive sense of employee well-being and goodwill.[6] However, until humanity is relieved of its egocentrism and addiction to superiority, there will always be the potential for aggressive and toxic competitiveness to hijack even the most well-intentioned collaborative structures. The narcissistic potentiality in the human egoic structure will continually stoke feelings of self-doubt and inferiority and a subsequent need to prove our worth in the eyes of others.

CHAPTER SIX

Hierarchical Structures and Authoritarianism

"To the victor goes the spoils" is a phrase thought to be coined by New York Senator William L. Marcy after securing his victory over Andrew Jackson in 1828. Marcy understood that through victory, considerable power is conferred. Every structure, even the best attempts at egalitarianism or anarchy, produces leaders. In some structures, such as a democracy, a corporation or business, a sports team, or a board of directors, there is a straightforward method of winning dominion (however informal) over others to direct the progressive movement of the group's aims. Some structures (e.g., corporations, sports teams, and political structures) are more overtly competitive than others. In contrast, others assign leaders based on experience, knowledge, performance, or simply the recognition of a certain *je ne sais quoi* that imbues one person worthy of more power, respect, or attention over another.[7] Narcissists crave power because power ensures their needs, desires, and directives are more easily satiated. While some narcissistic people may superficially balk at the suggestion that they seek power, there is frequently an underlying need to control others out of a fear of being controlled and thus vulnerable.

Seeking leadership positions does not inherently imply that someone is narcissistic; prosocial traits, such as benevolence, empathy, and idealism, often drive leaders' decisions to pursue leadership roles. Groups frequently identify leaders because of their vision, fortitude, knowledge, or charisma. That said, being charismatic, knowledgeable, and strong doesn't guarantee that someone will make a good leader. Effective leaders are astute listeners as well as skillful communicators. They can leverage empathic qualities to understand the needs of those who follow them but often possess enough objectivity to step back and gain a broader picture of the goal and what is needed to achieve it. There are multiple leadership styles, such as democratic, pacifying, autocratic, affiliative, and coaching. Most people naturally utilize a combination of styles without realizing they are shifting to accommodate a particular situation or group. The best leaders can contextually assess which style is more effective.

Superficially, narcissistic systems can appear to embody diverse leadership structures, depending on the leaders, but invariably, authoritarian undertones lie beneath the surface. Consolidating and leveraging power and influence for the powerful people at the proverbial top of the food chain remains the bottom line in antagonistic systems. Maintaining superiority over others, whether, for example, in economic disparities, privileges, or exceptionalism, helps bolster the narcissistic psyche. On the surface, leaders may espouse collaboration, track the emotional needs of others, and coach and encourage others to strive to be better or even surpass the leaders themselves. In truth, surpassing the narcissistic leader or group of people representing "the powerful" is subtly undermined, and progress or ascent is roundly denied. There are those who, upon learning how to "play the game" in these systems, can differentiate themselves as the "cream of the crop," but often this requires sacrificing other more vulnerable (and thus undesirable) qualities and adopting an objectification or exploitative interpersonal style.

Meg described her work environment, a small boutique consulting agency run by CEO Jim, the *Ambivalent Underminer* subtype, as a confusing mixture of false encouragement, psychological undermining, and frustrating goalpost moving.

> Working for Jim was strange. It was magical at first because I so admired the work he did. When he poached me from the company I was working for, identifying my "talent" and "exceptional skills," I was flattered. He mentored me for a few years, promising to make me a business partner "in no time." But the goal kept moving, and on some level, I knew I would never get what he promised because somehow, I wasn't "quite ready yet." I stayed around thinking someday I would get the prize. I wasted 10 years of my life on the job because he dangled the carrot of power and autonomy in front of me to keep me around, all the while exploiting my skills. Once I got closer to him, I realized he didn't know all that much. He just used other people's talents. So I guess he had a talent for exploiting talent. His insecurity would never allow anyone to be on his level. However, it was a slow burn and never quite as overt as I might imagine workplace abuse. (Meg, 48, business consultant)

CHAPTER SIX

In narcissistic systems, advancement is possible only inasmuch as subordinates (or those deemed subordinate) don't seek too much influence, power, or control over their leaders. Only if the unspoken rule of "don't surpass me" is respected by the subordinate will there be incremental rewards for good behavior. However, any attempt to break away from or challenge the toxic leadership structure will be met with character assassination; financial or economic retribution; harassment (either direct or indirect via surrogates); or if you're lucky, being iced out by the angry king or queen.

To underscore the powerful narcissistic person's inherent value over subordinates is the deployment of surveillance, the proliferation of loyalty narratives, and structured punishment designed to minimize or prevent undermining the status quo. In all three exemplars, we saw various expectations (some spoken, others implicit) of obedience and loyalty and consequences for violating the terms of the social contract, whether in the implied familial silence Sue and Mark instituted to maintain their desired image as the ideal family, thus suppressing and even exacerbating their children's shame and psychological abuse, or with Luke and Joe, whose liberal use of NDAs and other threatening strategies was designed to maintain and consolidate their power and control and minimize the potential for being unmasked or exposed for any manipulative, coercive, or inappropriate behavior.

Globally, systems of inequality are built on the abject fear of inferiority that accompanies being surpassed by others they've deemed unworthy. The more insecure the power holder, the more fearful, autocratic, and overtly suppressive of subordinates' dissent or deviation. Scapegoating, blaming, intimidation, and coercion ensure the dominant stays dominant and the subordinates remain in their rightful (inferior) position.

Most political structures are hierarchical, and the health of a society can be gauged by how tolerant the electorate becomes of authoritarian or autocratic-leaning leaders. In times of uncertainty, change, or vulnerability, many seek strong, confident, and seemingly decisive leadership, often opening the door for narcissistic people with heavy doses of bravado to establish themselves as the answer to vulnerable people's problems.

At a microcosmic level, we saw this in our exemplars with Joe's cultlike following as he amassed a cadre of spiritual seekers searching to heal aspects of their psychospiritual lives or with Luke, who quite literally positioned himself as the charismatic tough guy savior who would swoop in to eliminate the excessive vulnerability and weakness he saw as undermining the fabric of society. However, Luke, Sue, and Joe are only examples of the holistic nature of human interaction. Modeling one's interpersonal and social relationships on authoritarian, hierarchical, or exceptionalist ideologies due to an increased need for power, influence, and admiration is a proverbial lab for larger-scale application in families, work environments, institutions, and governments.

Sensitivity, vulnerability, concern, and respect for others have been increasingly problematized first as "political correctness" and then as a full-scale referendum on compassionate respect for others labeled as a war on "woke" or other catchy monikers that point to the intolerance of nuanced humanity and its sensitivity. Across the world, the rise of narcissistic relational leadership styles in the public square has steadily increased since 2016, intensifying ideological divides and fueling the fires of division, anger, and intolerance for difference.[8]

Authoritarianism and toxic leadership styles rely heavily on simplified narratives, such as "us versus them," "good versus bad," "all billionaires are evil," "blue pill versus red pill" and reduce the complexities of human relationships and structures to suspiciously simple dichotomies. This allows people to align themselves with a position viewed as superior while others are considered inferior. This often reflects the narcissistic or toxic leaders' psychological reductionism that fails to see others (or themselves in many respects) as complex three- or four-dimensional beings and leads to alienation, objectification, and devaluation of one's humanity.

As we saw with Sue and Joe in particular, narcissistic people often position themselves curiously as both victor and victim—the benevolent, well-intended friend, mother, boss, employee, or

CHAPTER SIX

coach; the person who was blessed (or cursed) with unique talents and skills; *and* the undervalued victim, who is unappreciated, overlooked, and mistreated by those who don't recognize their genius or contributions.

Victim Ideologies

Actions taken under the claim of oppression can, if left unmitigated by an empathetic and humane perspective, become extreme and easily destructive. Authentic oppression occurs when one with less social, cultural, economic, or physical power is suppressed, silenced, disempowered, censored, or otherwise diminished by those with more significant power capital. While this is a grossly reductive definition of systemic oppression, a nuanced discussion of oppressive power dynamics is obviously beyond the scope of this book. Nonetheless, everyone, on some level, could undoubtedly find instances of varying degrees of oppression in their lives due to some aspect of their identity within various social or cultural contexts. For example, a white American male being tried for theft in an Angolan court has less cultural, social, and political power because of the contextual realities of that experience. We've all dealt with feelings of being silenced for our racial, cultural, ethnic, religious, sexual, or gender experiences or because we don't share a dominant viewpoint or we've broken some spoken or unspoken code of conduct that reveals something unpopular about our position.

Systemic oppression, however, must incorporate the complexities of economic, social, cultural, and political experiences. Over time, these experiences carry a history that reproduces or upholds inequitable, corrosive, or inhibiting systems of power. As such, they have systematically disenfranchised others through various methods of overt, covert, or implicit control. These systems, whether on an institutional or smaller social scale, create, at least on the level of physical reality, a victim–abuser relational archetype. Much could be said about this paradigm since, in recent years, it has been thwarted and subverted due to, in some instances, misunderstanding the victim–abuser's archetypal social roles and, in other cases, to bolster others' ill-treatment, retaliation, anger, or moral indignation. As with any role in human affairs, the victim–abuser dichotomy represents a complex mixture of extrinsic and intrinsic variables. Typically, the one with greater power in a particular dynamic is more likely to misuse or abuse the other. Power is, of course, a shifting variable that is also contextual and nuanced.

We've discussed how narcissists crave and seek power as a means of maintaining their superiority and ensuring their needs and desires are satiated. However, narcissistic people, as we've observed with all three exemplars, often position themselves, at least in their subjective assessment, as the victim. While the inner landscape of the narcissist frequently gives rise to feeling grandiose, powerful, superior, talented, successful, beautiful, and intelligent, the contrasting "vulnerable" self-talk gives rise to feelings of being small, weak, inferior, unremarkable, unattractive, and stupid.

Self-aware narcissists speak openly about the self-worth roller coaster that lies underneath the surface of their arrogant or haughty behavior. For many, the slightest failure, embarrassment, or thwarted desire can swing them into the horrific potential that they are nothing, an unfortunate representation of their self-simplification, objectification, and polarization turned inward. However, rather than acknowledge the realities of their own inherently flawed and vulnerable existence, they often develop a psychological schism whereby they believe the world is out to get them because of their brilliance, talent, beauty, success, or skill and thus project their own subconscious or unconscious flagellation onto others.

The result is the often aggrieved, mistreated, and unappreciated narrative that gave rise to the notion of the "vulnerable narcissist." In both my research and a survey of modern narcissistic personality research over the past decade, it's become increasingly clear that most narcissistic people swing between the vulnerable and grandiose poles. However, because some subtypes are more externally and linguistically positive, it was believed that there was a contrast between the grandiose and the vulnerable narcissist.

CHAPTER SIX

The DARVO method appears to be an inevitability in most narcissistic interpersonal relationships. Because the narcissist cannot accept or integrate criticism from others without overly personalizing it, they must deny any suggestion that they have transgressed another. That denial invariably follows an attack on the other person (a referendum on the initial criticism). It is justified only because they have been unfairly judged, condemned, criticized, corrected, or even told they've hurt someone else. The sheer inability of the narcissistic person to be wrong (which for them often translates as "bad") must thereby create a victim ideology that allows them to feel entitled to punish, attack, or reprimand others. Indeed, some narcissists are more adept at hiding their victim ideologies and may superficially allow for "constructive criticism" or "feedback," seeming gracious in the face of others' assessments of their transgressive or selfish behavior or attitudes. However, the victim self often waits patiently for an opportunity to rebalance the scales and correct the power imbalance.

Without feedback, it's often difficult to parse one's psychological feeling of being victimized from the reality of victimization. Humans can easily feel victimized by all manner of perceived transgressions. The incredibly gray area surrounding victimization has created a bit of a cultural quagmire, which then requires that credence be given to any feeling of victimization, bullying, or mistreatment. Everyone at some point in their lives, particularly if one makes it into adulthood, has been both the victimizer and the victim. However, as we develop and begin to detach from the weight of our personal histories and narratives, having experienced a more comprehensive range of interpersonal, social, and cultural scenarios, we ideally place less of our identity in either role. For some, this often requires acknowledgment of their victimization through education, therapy and counseling, or other forms of prosocial measures that both validate and help to dis-identify them from their victimized positions. A pervasive victim mentality carries with it a deep sense of resentment, anger, sadness, and depression and a pervasive sense of powerlessness and loss of agency. In healthy psychological and social systems, feelings of pervasive victimization channel anger and feelings of being transgressed into a desire to correct injustices, potentially with wide-reaching effects. In unhealthy, narcissistic, or otherwise toxic systems, victimization narratives are often predicated on more precarious grounds, such as viewing equity, fairness, criticism, emotional honesty, or simply not getting one's way as egregious and worthy of attack and condemnation. In unhealthy systems, the reality of power dynamics is no longer relevant, and only the subjective, aggrieved perception of unfairness or attack remains. In South Africa, the reality of the racial indignities of apartheid was roundly disregarded or ignored when those opposing broader equality saw equity efforts as unfair and unjust and thus worthy of aggressive revolt. In toxic egoic systems, equity accountability feels like punishment and criticism. The fragility of the insecure human ego can subvert and, by proxy, minimize actual injustice, relegating it to precariously subjective realms designed only to maintain the ego's need to be superior.

For the narcissistic, sociopathic, or psychopathic person, viewing oneself as a victim can have chilling effects on those believed to be perpetrators. A 2024 documentary directed by Chris Smith and titled *The Hollywood Con Queen* is a compelling true crime documentary about a mysterious impersonator who allegedly scammed and remotely abused hundreds of hopeful Hollywood industry actors, photographers, art directors, and others by posing successfully as male and female film executives, producers, and directors with enticing but fake projects via the phone. The documentary builds to a fever pitch as *Hollywood Reporter* investigative journalist Scott Johnson tracks down the elusive Indonesian con man, Hargobind Tahilramani, who was behind the attacks that affected an estimated 500 people and created damages of $2 million.

Tahilramani finally agrees to be interviewed by Johnson for an opportunity to tell his side of the story in which he spins an emotional, albeit indulgent narrative with legitimate indignities, such as being sent to a gay conversion camp, and other questionable transgressions, such as not being "appreciated" for his talent by his college debate team (an offense he punished by calling in bomb threats to debate competitions and writing fake suicide letters blaming his

CHAPTER SIX

peers). The maudlin and at times confusing autobiography amounts to what he considers a justification for his crimes, believing that the world's mistreatment of him warranted his deception, entrapment, and financial and sexual abuse. Tahilramani's aggrieved narrative is a relatively small-scale example of how a narcissistic victim ideology can lead to astounding justifications for unethical, unsavory, or downright violent behavior.

Larger-scale victimization narratives include some of the most atrocious crimes committed against humanity by people such as Adolph Hitler, whose anger and disgust at the greedy Jews whom he blamed for his economic and cultural failures early in his life, arguably fueled his militant and spectacularly violent attempt to erase them from the planet. The Emperor Nero, Pol Pot, Lenin, Joseph Stalin, Benito Mussolini, Joseph McCarthy, Saddam Hussein, the Ku Klux Klan, the inquisitors of the Spanish Inquisition, and the list, unfortunately, goes on and on, all utilized some measure of scapegoating and victimization ideology to justify their transgressive, violent ideologies and actions against their fellow human beings.

So what do we do now? Even though we've seen how the psychological, relational, social, ideological, and philosophical assumptions of the narcissistic structure can affect virtually every sphere of human life, don't throw up your arms in exasperated defeat because it seems impossible to free ourselves from its potentially decaying effects. In attempting to offer a relatively concise and digestible place to begin to work with narcissism as a general feature of the human psyche, I couldn't help but look to the transpersonal since the way out, in my estimation, cannot be solved through the mechanisms of the ego and its various creations.

CHAPTER SEVEN

OUT OF DARKNESS

Breaking Free of Narcissistic Dysfunction

Meeting Our Shadows

Throughout this book, I have provided snapshots of the human ego in various stages and states of dysfunction. This has been an exploration of narcissism from the psychological to the systemic. When I wrote in *The Narcissist in You and Everyone Else* that "everyone is a little bit narcissistic," many people had a visceral and sometimes angry reaction. Some of this is because, as we've already discussed, narcissism has been correlated with a deeply pathological psychological disorder that carries with it a heavy clinical bias. Some of this is because there is something innate that triggers recognition (however slight) in one or more of the 27 narcissistic subtypes. When I made the audacious and intentionally provocative observation, I was attempting to provoke thoughtful consideration of our collective narcissistic tendencies because I know from personal and professional experiences the potential lies within everyone to flirt with callous, self-interested behaviors, thoughts, or emotional expressions. I also know that the narcissistic people I've met, interviewed, been in relationships with, and studied are, in fact, just people. When delving into the shadowy recesses of human psychology, it's easy to caricaturize human beings because of some disturbance or variation in their psychological structures into the supervillains in the story of our lives. This tendency is understandable given their heightened ability to harm with little to no consideration for their destructive effect. However, our characterization of the human tendency to disown uncomfortable realities reflects our innate capabilities to harm.

To restate a gem of perennial wisdom, we can recognize only what is a part of us. Narcissists and narcissistic adjacent people (i.e., sociopaths and psychopaths) appear to express more of the human collective shadow externally, and their increasing prevalence serves, at least in part, as a signpost to wake up the rest of us to the collective increase in grandiosity, selfishness, and loss of compassion.

Narcissism will continue to proliferate until each person does their part to recognize, confront, and ultimately accept the more uncomfortable features of the human experience. Even the most conscientious, diligent, empathetic, and compassionate person has intentionally or unintentionally made an entirely self-interested decision and consequently upset or disturbed someone else. There's nothing inherently wrong with this, as unfortunate as it is. The dysfunctional aspect of human behavior, and ultimately narcissism, is not necessarily that people hurt people. That is an inevitability in human affairs. However, the denial or refusal to see our effect and the abdication of responsibility for the damage we have caused ultimately perpetuate cycles of pain and trauma and impede healing.

Carl Jung, the prolific (and less sex-obsessed) student of the father of modern psychology, Sigmund Freud, wrote elegantly about the human shadow.

> The shadow is that hidden, repressed, for the most part inferior and guilt-laden personality whose ultimate ramifications reach back into the realm of our animal ancestors and so comprise the whole historical aspect of the unconscious. . . . If it has been believed hitherto that the human shadow was the source of evil, it can now be ascertained on closer investigation that the unconscious man, that is, his shadow, does not consist only of morally reprehensible tendencies, but also displays a number of good qualities, such as normal instincts, appropriate reactions, realistic insights, creative impulses, etc.[1]

Jung understood that the shadow is a remnant of the supposedly transcendent id impulses and holds within it the most beautiful and reprehensible potentialities of human expression.[2] The psychological shadow is threatening only because it looms, often undetected, behind us as we focus on content acceptable to our idealized self-conception. Many, ignoring it at their own peril, are unaware of its potentially mischievous effects on their contentedness and potential to sabotage, damage, or even destroy.

The shadow is not inherently good or bad, yet it exists as an inextricable aspect of the human experience. Like the ego, it waits (sometimes impatiently) to be engaged, prodded, and ultimately accepted as part of our psychic totality, aiding our growth and development. Like a child begging to be acknowledged through temper tantrums, whining, or aggressive behavior, the shadow calms down once it is seen. Its menacing threats and uncomfortable truths become nothing more than passing clouds in the totality of human awareness.

Much of what we've explored through this book's exemplars and subsequent analysis are various expressions of the collective human shadow brought to light through relationships. The people in the case studies in this book are no more inherently villainous than the most benevolent of saints. However, what sets them apart is that their awareness and concern for their negative effects is blunted and, at times, nonexistent, creating discord and havoc and laying waste to relationships. Their shadows have grown darker under the cover of unconsciousness.

Ignoring the personal shadow gives birth to heavier and more oppressive expressions of the collective shadow. I challenge you to think of one aspect of human suffering that doesn't have its roots in some selfish, uncompassionate, or narcissistic idea or defense. And what's worse, ignoring the underlying root of suffering and dealing topically with the results only perpetuates their inevitable reincarnation in human history. We have created a world in our collective shadows, and the phenomena, events, and experiences we've created reflect humanity's consciousness at any given point in history. The periods of extreme darkness, such as the Salem witch trials, slavery throughout history, the horrors of World Wars I and II, genocide, the Dark Ages, the Inquisition, and apartheid, are all manifestations of people's egoic fear and defensiveness, disowned and allowed to mutate and attack their traumatized human hosts under the cover of darkness. Scapegoating, violence, greed, deception, betrayal, coercion, subjugation, domination, and cruelty can exist only within a spectrum of their correlated positive states. Ignoring that these states, behaviors, and emotions exist as potentials in all humans allows them to take root deep within the psyche, shape our futures, reframe our pasts, and be born again and again, age after age.

Owning the Shadow of Narcissism

We all play a role in enabling narcissistic behaviors by not acknowledging our narcissistic potential. Many people have a visceral, defensive reaction to the notion that everyone should confront their narcissism, which, in my estimation, is just a visceral response to the fear inherent in the exploration of the shadow. As human beings, darkness holds a primitive, visceral repulsion. We have evolved to fear what lurks in the darkness because it could quite literally kill us. Fearing the darkness in an unknown, wild forest is rational, and hypervigilance or avoidance could save our lives. In most cases, the darkness and shadows of our psyches are not fatal but create ample ground for various dysfunctional thought patterns, emotional reactions, and behaviors that having been unexplored, become insidious and silent saboteurs of our peace and healthy relationships. Like the collective shadow, avoiding psychological darkness only strengthens its power.

During an interview for my first book, I was asked several times if I thought people use the term *narcissism* too liberally. As discussed in Chapter 2, I agree that the term, now a popular social media buzzword thrown around for clicks and views, has lost its gravity and is becoming increasingly meaningless. In retrospect, avoiding the word and, as a result, the concept as a human reality is a by-product of our desire not to deal with its existence, if not in our psyches, then in our families, communities, or economic and political systems. However, relegating the term *narcissism* to only the most extreme cases lulls us into a false sense of security, believing that, like Beetlejuice, if we don't say his name, he can't get us. But Beetlejuice lives in our heads, sleeps beside us in bed, leads our Bible study classes, performs our knee surgeries, and writes our legislation. A little fame, fortune, or recognition, and we could all awaken the little narcissistic beast inside and be a hop, skip, and jump away from acquired narcissism.

Some clinical psychologists caution others not to overgeneralize or even use the term *narcissism* in everyday life, which is appropriately gatekeeping a psychological condition that according to their academic conditioning, is relatively rare. However, the result of excessive gatekeeping of the terminology and relegating it to the deepest recesses of human psychopathology supports denial and increased unconsciousness.

Stress, trauma, and prolonged adversity can force even the most well adjusted among us into a defensive pattern that could easily come across to others as insensitive, selfish, or self-involved. These defense mechanisms evolved to help shelter us from psychological ruin and temporarily blunt or shut down whatever empathic capabilities we may have so we can survive. A developmental or environmental perspective of narcissism suggests that narcissists have become trapped in a defensive state and perceive themselves as perpetually under threat of psychological ruin, necessitating inflation or overexaggeration of their importance. Feeling as though the world owes us something either because of our exaggerated positive or negative self-importance is a natural response to a world in which we have, in reality, scarcely little control. Justifying our thoughts and emotions and their corresponding behaviors, if not acknowledged through honest self-reflection and radical accountability, helps us fuse with our unacknowledged shadow material. Over time, without radical acceptance of the shadow, we harden, turn brittle, and treat others as objects that support or prevent our distorted self-important image.

Many people believe narcissists don't suffer from their shadow tendencies because of their apparent bravado and relatively blunted sensitivity. However, living in a codified defensive state most of the time is not only exhausting but also incredibly painful and ultimately destructive. If life is a constant battle to prove to your fragile ego that you are important and worthy of love, admiration, and attention, and most of your conscious attention goes toward supporting that aim, you have little room to enjoy life authentically. This manner of living also leaves scant room to foster deep connection through expressing genuine vulnerability or experiencing self-acceptance that is not contingent on your external accomplishments or superiority in relationship to another.

> I understand that people don't like me very much because I'm constantly seeking attention and validation. I compete unnecessarily with everyone. I undercut others' success. I talk badly about other people who make me feel inferior. I feel like I need to be seen constantly, or I don't exist because I cannot feel myself. I don't know if I'm here if someone isn't paying attention. It's exhausting, but I can't tell anyone how exhausted I am because I don't want them to know I'm not always feeling amazing. The few times in my life I've let my guard down and allowed myself some vulnerability, I had to cut off the relationship shortly after because they've peeked behind the curtain. Everything I do feels like I'm about to fail and be humiliated. I'm just so tired. (Shep, 36, attorney, a Disingenuous Opportunist)

NOT SELF WORKSHEET

On your own piece of paper, respond to the following prompts.

1. I am NOT
   (List five negative or positive adjectives that do NOT represent your character or personality characteristics.)
2. I'm annoyed with or avoid or dislike people who
3. People who know me well would NEVER describe me as
4. Think of the most selfish, arrogant, insensitive, or narcissistic person you know and describe their behavior, attitudes, or emotions.

5. Reflect on a time when you've been hurt by someone else and describe what they did and how they did it that made the experience or treatment painful.
6. Now that you've recorded your responses, complete the following worksheet and cultivate a kind of clinical detachment. Try looking at yourself from a third-person perspective and observing the reactions as they arise as though you were observing or judging someone else, just as you did above.

SHADOW REALIZATION WORKSHEET

On your own piece of paper, respond to the following prompts.

1. I AM
   (Re-list the adjectives you've written in the above exercise and give an example of when YOU have demonstrated the quality.)
2. I try to avoid being seen as
   (Using your narrative from the NOT SELF WORKSHEET, think about how your behavior, attitudes, and thoughts prevent you from being seen in whatever way you deem to be negative, objectionable, unacceptable, or simply not you. Example: I am not a selfish person. I try hard to avoid being selfish by being helpful to others and trying to be supportive of my friends and family.)
3. If someone met me, they would describe me as
   (Use your narrative from the previous exercise to complete this response.)
4. Think of ways you can identify or see yourself reflected in the most selfish, arrogant, unaware, or narcissistic person you described in the NOT SELF WORKSHEET and reflect on your behavior, attitudes, or emotions.
5. Think of a time when you've hurt someone else and describe what you did and how you hurt the other that might've made the experience or treatment so painful.

CHAPTER SEVEN

Congratulations! Filling out the worksheets may have been uncomfortable if you've never done shadow work. However, take heart. The deepest part of you that desires to know itself beyond its mind-made story thanks you for participating, and you may notice a deeper sense of self-awareness flowering. Now that you've completed this exercise notice if you're inclined to make the content of either worksheet a part of your self-definition. Upon completing the second exercise, many people have egos that launch into feelings of guilt, shame, self-flagellation, or embarrassment. Add that to a story of who you are and what you've done, which is another way the ego tries to make itself important. This exercise is intended to illuminate aspects of our disowned ego identification and does not encompass the entirety of who you are.

Some people have an exceedingly difficult time filling out the NOT SELF WORKSHEET because they feel judgmental, negative, or mean, which in and of itself reveals an ego whose self-conception is one of being nonjudgmental, positive, and pleasant, which is still a story. Many people have trouble turning the negative adjectives around to themselves. If you are this person, I encourage you to think of examples where you have exhibited the quality, even if it's not pervasive or consistent. The exercise aims to illuminate how our indictments and negative judgments of others (even if our judgment of their negative behavior seems justified) are more appropriate indictments of ourselves. Furthermore, our behavior, particularly how we uphold our social image, is often guided by our desire not to be seen in the objectionable ways we pointed out in others.

Finally, if the final question revealed behavior where you owe someone an apology and feel comfortable reaching out to that person, please do so. If the person is unavailable or you don't feel comfortable contacting them, write your apology down, read it to yourself, and release yourself from any guilt or shame you've harbored. What's most important in this exercise is self-forgiveness for being a human and the ability to take accountability for pain (whether intentional or unintentional) you may have caused and then let it go.

It's ubiquitous for shadow work to bring up an incredible amount of shame for our shortcomings and make that shame part of our ego. Many people derive an immense part of their self-image from laboring over their faults, failures, and mistakes. They make themselves as important as the most arrogant and inflated among us, imagining themselves as the worst person in the world, undeserving of forgiveness or repentance. Both are distorted self-conceptions, and neither is closer to the truth of who someone is beyond the mental–emotional noise that clutters our inner landscape.

A Word to Narcissistic Abuse Survivors

If you have suffered from narcissistic abuse, suggesting forgiveness for someone who has irrevocably changed your life and diminished your sense of safety and trust in the world feels insulting. The good news is that forgiveness can be a perk to healing but isn't necessary. However, acceptance is. Accepting that the person and the relationship are as they were helps release the understandable resentment accumulated from the abuse dynamic. Acceptance doesn't mean that the old emotions, thoughts, and memories won't, at times, bubble to the surface. Those must also be accepted because the alternative, not accepting the other person, yourself, or your experience, will result in a sure-to-lose war against reality. If the person could behave differently, they likely would have. Remember that when narcissism becomes the primary modus operandi of the ego structure, it increases one's unconsciousness of oneself and one's impact can help free you from excessive blame or anger. The unfortunate reality of narcissistic abuse is that the unprocessed, unacknowledged, and denied vulnerability, pain, and trauma of the person creates unnecessary suffering for them and those in their lives. While suffering is an inevitable part of the human experience, primarily because of the ego, suffering is enhanced and prolonged with increased unconsciousness. Narcissists, like everyone else, experience the grief of a loved one dying, fall ill, lose relationships, and eventually face death. All efforts to avoid the inevitable existential, temporal experience of being human will punctuate and eventually conclude everyone's life.

Those of us who have suffered from narcissistic abuse or have, at some point in our lives, found ourselves in an interpersonal, social, or institutional dynamic with a narcissist tend to give an incredible amount of power to the narcissist. It can rapidly become the proverbial invisible monster under our bed, threatening our peace and equilibrium, and we often haunt ourselves by forgetting that narcissism and the person are separate entities. People are just people, and seeing beyond their defense strategies (however extreme, damaging, or insidious) can be difficult, particularly when they seem to have entirely relinquished themselves to their codified ego armoring. However, we cannot demand or expect anyone else to have empathy or compassion if we cannot practice it with ourselves. Many blame themselves for not "seeing the red flags" or feel like they "should've known better" in retrospect when reflecting on a damaging antagonistic relationship. This self-condemnation perpetuates the cycle of abuse.

Working with a narcissistic-informed trauma therapist or coach is incredibly important since recognizing the nuances of narcissism can be difficult without proper training. Narcissistic abuse can create increased feelings of anxiety, relationship avoidance, depression, nightmares, excessive restlessness, and paranoia.[3] However, it's vital that you do not make victimhood a central part of your identity because this only strengthens egoic feelings of righteousness and judgment and tends to blunt the ability to empathize or sympathize with others if they don't validate your experience. Validation should be sought from a professional therapist, psychologist, social worker, coach, or mentor who understands narcissism. Others will likely, albeit unintentionally, deny or minimize your abuse, which only serves to reproduce the gaslighting and minimization that you experienced during the relationship. Their minimization isn't personal but instead reflects their lack of education or awareness of narcissism and other antagonistic personality styles as well as their discomfort with their shadows.

Center of the Universe

This book's title is double-sided and encompasses various levels of meaning. We have followed characters who see themselves as the center of the universe, believing that the world and everyone in it should orbit around their desires and wishes out of a deep need to be significant. Narcissists and other highly egocentric people (whether positively or negatively identified) overestimate their importance in the grand scheme of life.

Another interpretation of being the center of the universe is the recognition that we often create our realities through our emotions, thoughts, ideas, and actions. Physics and popular self-help wisdom tell us we attract what we want. If we are to capitulate to this universal law, we must also be willing to accept the immense responsibility of being a creator and destroyer of the world. Narcissistic people quite often create a world where people capitulate to their desires. Due to their relational strategies, they create situations that help others view them as more important, unique, talented, intelligent, or valuable than others and thus justify their treatment of others under this supposition. How could they not believe that the world of self-importance they've constructed isn't the truth? Their realities (however skewed or distorted) are proving them right. However, life and the will of the universe inevitably exert their ultimate power, and the futile struggle for dominance and control often becomes a way of life, creating many of the negative, unhealthy, or toxic dynamics demonstrated in this book. They are no different than anyone else because we all play a high-stakes game of reality creation and grow frustrated when the world or other people don't play it the way we want.

Externally shifting narcissistic systems take various forms in the phenomenal world, challenging unfair, unjust, and inequitable systems. Refusing to accept egocentric, selfish, violent, or power-focused ideologies or speaking truth to power, particularly when people's humanity, rights, or decency is threatened, is not only empathetic but essential to ensuring our survival as a species. As the world increasingly grows egocentric, image obsessed, power hungry, and exclusionary,

CHAPTER SEVEN

it will take self-aware and courageous pioneers to challenge self-delusion with radical honesty. The human body is a microcosmic universe consisting of trillions of cells that work unimaginably to create a functioning, conscious organism.

The mind, an atemporal, non-thing that seems to govern our conscious experience of reality, is an expression of the universe and contains the power to expand, heal, or destroy depending on its level of consciousness at any given moment. Healing our familial trauma and refusing to reproduce toxic systems of relating and acknowledging and accepting the fallibility and humanity of those we may have trusted to care for us is not for the faint of heart. Being the center of the universe means that you have the immeasurable power of compassion, empathy, and acceptance of what is and that through that awareness, you are quite literally changing the world.

NOTES

INTRODUCTION

1. This narcissistic subtype is charming, superficial, and duplicitous and strives to gain success and influence through appearances and associations with those who mirror their grand self-image. Being the most status conscious of all the 27 subtypes, they need fame and popularity to feel worthy, and they can be disingenuous, opportunistic, and focused on style over substance.

2. For a comprehensive exploration of narcissism at the psychological level, I encourage you to read *The Narcissist in You and Everyone Else: Recognizing the 27 Types of Narcissism*.

CHAPTER ONE

1. The DSM-5, or *Diagnostic and Statistical Manual of Mental Disorders, Fifth Edition*, is the latest version of the standard reference for the clinical diagnosis of mental health conditions.

2. Sterlin L. Mosley, *The Narcissist in You and Everyone Else: Recognizing the 27 Types of Narcissism* (Lanham, MD: Rowman & Littlefield, 2022).

3. Igor Nenadić, Carsten Lorenz, and Christian Gaser, "Narcissistic Personality Traits and Prefrontal Brain Structure," *Scientific Reports* 11, no. 1 (2021): 15707, https://doi.org/10.1038/s41598-021-94920-z.

4. Oxidative stress is an imbalance of free radicals and antioxidants in the body that leads to cell damage. Royce J. Lee, David Gozal, Emil F. Coccaro, and Jennifer Fanning, "Narcissistic and Borderline Personality Disorders: Relationship with Oxidative Stress," *Journal of Personality Disorders* 34, Supplement (March 2020): 6–24, https://doi.org/10.1521/pedi.2020.34.supp.6.

5. Gregor Zvelc, "Object and Subject Relations in Adulthood: Towards an Integrative Model of Interpersonal Relationships," *Psychiatria Danubina* 22, no. 4 (December 2010): 498–508.

6. Trauma bonding is a relational process whereby two individuals bond through shared traumatic experiences. In the case of narcissistic relationships, the narcissist may utilize their own infliction of relational trauma by suggesting that the trauma created in the relationship is healthy or somehow strengthens the interpersonal connection.

7. Delroy L. Paulhus and Kevin M. Williams, "The Dark Triad of Personality: Narcissism, Machiavellianism, and Psychopathy," *Journal of Research in Personality* 36, no. 6 (December 2002): 556–63, https://doi.org/10.1016/s0092-6566(02)00505-6.

8. Niccolo Machiavelli, *The Prince* (Reader's Library Classics, 2021).

CHAPTER TWO

1. Dean Radin, *Supernormal: Science, Yoga, and the Evidence for Extraordinary Psychic Abilities*, read by Tom Perkins (New York: Crown/Deepak Chopra, 2013), audiobook, 2:44:30–2:45:00.

2. Jonah Engel Bromwich, "Paris Hilton Said She Invented the Selfie. We Set Out to Find the Truth," *New York Times*, November 20, 2017, sec. Style, https://www.nytimes.com/2017/11/20/style/paris-hilton-selfie.html.

3. Stephane Mouchabac, Redwan Maatoug, Ismael Conejero, Vladimir Adrien, Olivier Bonnot, Bruno Millet, Florian Ferreri, and Alexis Bourla, "In Search of Digital Dopamine: How Apps Can Motivate Depressed Patients, a Review and Conceptual Analysis," *Brain Sciences* 11, no. 11 (2021): 1454, https://doi.org/10.3390/brainsci11111454.

4. Allied Market Research, "Influencer Marketing Market Statistics, 2032," accessed October 1, 2023, https://www.alliedmarketresearch.com/influencer-market-A07914.

5. B. A. Primack, J. B. Colditz, K. C. Pang, K. M. Jackson, and A. M. Porter, "Promoting Public Health in the Digital Age: A Public Health Approach to Evaluating the Risks and Benefits of Online Social Networking," *Media and Communication* 6, no. 1 (2018): 13–14.

6. Monica Anderson and Jingjing Jiang, "Teens, Social Media and Technology 2018," Pew Research Center, published May 31, 2018,

https://www.pewresearch.org/internet/2018/05/31/teens-social-media-technology-2018/.

7. Scott J. Fatt and Jasmine Fardouly, "Digital Social Evaluation: Relationships between Receiving Likes, Comments, and Follows on Social Media and Adolescents' Body Image Concerns," *Body Image* 47 (2023): 101621, https://doi.org/10.1016/j.bodyim.2023.101621; and Jasmine Fardouly, Phillippa C. Diedrichs, Lenny R. Vartanian, and Emma Halliwell, "Social Comparisons on Social Media: The Impact of Facebook on Young Women's Body Image Concerns and Mood," *Body Image* 13 (2015): 38–45, https://doi.org/10.1016/j.bodyim.2014.12.002.

8. Tom Nichols, "The Narcissism of the Angry Young Men," *The Atlantic*, January 29, 2023, https://www.theatlantic.com/ideas/archive/2023/01/lost-boys-violent-narcissism-angry-young-men/672886/?fbclid=IwAR0QDMqiC526cgM55XFUnX5JBiSjI6eSFo23mRRGO1TkY1TBl7LPjjICdQ8.

9. Nichols, "The Narcissism of the Angry Young Men."

10. Jesse Emspak and Kimberly Hickok, "Quantum Entanglement: Unlocking the Mysteries of Particle Connections," Space.com, last modified October 29, 2024, https://www.space.com/31933-quantum-entanglement-action-at-a-distance.html.

CHAPTER THREE

1. Narcissistic rage is an intense, exploitive, and often overreactive emotional outburst by people with narcissistic personality traits or narcissistic personality disorder. Typically, narcissistic rage erupts when they perceive threats to their self-esteem, value, innate gifts, talents, accomplishments, or self-worth. Narcissistic rage is often displayed when others question the narcissist's motivations.

2. Sterlin L. Mosley, "The Excited Enthusiast," in *The Narcissist in You and Everyone Else: Recognizing the 27 Types of Narcissism* (Lanham, MD: Rowman & Littlefield, 2022), 289.

3. Linda L. Carpenter et al. "Effect of Childhood Physical Abuse on Cortisol Stress Response," *Psychopharmacology* 214, no. 1 (September 14, 2010): 367–75, https://doi.org/10.1007/s00213-010-2007-4.

NOTES

CHAPTER FOUR

1. Faith Hill, "The Mystery of Partner 'Convergence,'" *The Atlantic*, February 2, 2024, https://www.theatlantic.com/family/archive/2024/02/relationship-convergence-similar-personality/677534/.

2. Eleesha Lockett, "How to Help Children of Narcissistic Parents," Healthline, published February 21, 2024, https://www.healthline.com/health/mental-health/children-of-narcissistic-parents#:~:text=A%202012%20study%20suggested%20that,traumatic%20stress%20disorder%20(PSTD).

3. Psychopathy must be differentiated from being a psychopath, which, although not a formal diagnosis, implies a cluster of antisocial personality disorder traits characterized by lawlessness and a propensity toward violence, exploitation, and subjugation of the weak. We must also delineate this from the popular use of the word *psychopath* to denote a serial criminal.

4. Sterlin L. Mosley, *The Narcissist in You and Everyone Else: Recognizing the 27 Types of Narcissism* (Lanham, MD: Rowman & Littlefield, 2023), 109.

5. *Narcissistic supply* is a colloquial psychological term used to describe the energy, validation, and psychological scaffolding narcissistic people derive from feeding from others' attention, admiration, and engagement, whether positively or negatively.

CHAPTER FIVE

1. The nondisclosure agreement (NDA) is a *binding contract between two or more parties that prevents sensitive information from being shared with others.*

2. Peter M. Vernig, "Family Roles in Homes with Alcohol-Dependent Parents: An Evidence-Based Review," *Substance Use & Misuse* 46, no. 4 (August 24, 2010): 535–42, https://doi.org/10.3109/10826084.2010.501676.

3. Minna Lyons et al., "'Never Learned to Love Properly': A Qualitative Study Exploring Romantic Relationship Experiences in Adult Children of Narcissistic Parents," *Social Sciences* 12, no. 3 (March 7, 2023): 159, https://doi.org/10.3390/socsci12030159.

4. The more obviously vulnerable subtypes include all three of the Moody-Entitled types, *The Defensive Pessimist*, *The Overreactive Rebel*, and *The Unassuming Manipulator*.

5. Bessel van der Kolk, *The Body Keeps the Score: Brain, Mind, and Body in the Transformation of Trauma* (New York: Viking, 2014).

6. Thomas Hyphantis et al., "Narcissistic Rage: The Achilles' Heel of the Patient with Chronic Physical Illness," *Patient Preference and Adherence* 3 (2009): 239–50, https://doi.org/10.2147/PPA.S5499.

7. The internet has given rise to the proliferation of an online cult where no specific leader exists, called the QAnon conspiracy; rather, its members are enlisted through the dissemination of exclusive knowledge and information from the enigmatic Q (refer to Chapter 6 for a more detailed discussion of this phenomenon).

8. Refer to the glossary for a definition of these strategies.

CHAPTER SIX

1. Sean Murphy, "The Attractiveness of Confidence," SPSP, published September 15, 2016, accessed January 29, 2024, https://spsp.org/news-center/character-context-blog/attractiveness-confidence#:~:text=Confidence%2C%20in%20turn%2C%20was%20a,means%20we%20weren't%20measuring.

2. Daisy Grewal, "How Wealth Reduces Compassion," *Scientific American*, April 10, 2012, accessed February 20, 2024, https://www.scientificamerican.com/article/how-wealth-reduces-compassion/.

3. The Dark Empath narcissistic variants and, more specifically, the Prideful-Flattering and Moody-Entitled types are prone to overestimating their empathetic capacities.

4. Nicholas Stanger et al., "Empathy Inhibits Aggression in Competition: The Role of Provocation, Emotion, and Gender," *Journal of Sport and Exercise Psychology* 38, no. 1 (February 2016): 4–14, https://doi.org/10.1123/jsep.2014-0332.

5. Andrew F. Luchner et al., "Exploring the Relationship between Two Forms of Narcissism and Competitiveness," *Personality and Individual Differences* 51, no. 6 (October 2011): 779–82, https://doi.org/10.1016/j.paid.2011.06.033.

6. Rekha Krishnan et al., "An Interaction Ritual Theory of Social Resource Exchange: Evidence from a Silicon Valley Accelerator," *Administrative Science Quarterly* 66, no. 3 (November 27, 2020), https://doi.org/10.1177/0001839220970936.

NOTES

7. *Je ne sais quoi* is a French euphemism that translates to "I don't know what" in English. This phrase often describes an ephemeral quality in something or someone that is attractive or compelling.

8. International Institute for Democracy and Electoral Assistance, "Global State of Democracy Report 2021," accessed May 28, 2024, https://www.idea.int/gsod-2021/global-report#:~:text=2.1%20CHALLENGES&text=Since%202016%2C%20and%20for%20the,negative%20trend%20(Figure%202).

CHAPTER SEVEN

1. C. G Jung, *The Collected Works of C. G. Jung*, Vol. 9, Part 1, *Archetypes and the Collective Unconscious* (Princeton, NJ: Princeton University Press, 1981).

2. From the American Psychological Association: "*n.* in psychoanalytic theory, the component of the personality that contains the instinctual, biological drives that supply the psyche with its basic energy or libido. Sigmund Freud conceived of the id as the most primitive component of the personality, located in the deepest level of the unconscious; it has no inner organization and operates in obedience to the pleasure principle. Thus, the infant's life is dominated by the desire for immediate gratification of instincts, such as hunger and sex, until the ego begins to develop and operate in accordance with reality."

3. Crystal Raypole, "12 Signs of Narcissistic Abuse Syndrome (and How to Get Help)," Healthline, last modified September 20, 2024, https://www.healthline.com/health/narcissistic-victim-syndrome#overview.

GLOSSARY

Narcissistic Relational Strategies

In the following pages, you'll find expanded definitions of some common relational strategies utilized by narcissistic people. It's important to note that anyone can utilize one or more strategies in varying contexts. The use of one or more of these strategies does not necessarily mean the person is narcissistic. However, narcissistic people invariably use many, and in some cases, all these strategies regularly in their interpersonal relationships.

Badgering: A relational strategy whereby a person persistently hammers a particular point, often to emotional exhaustion. This tactic is sometimes used to manipulate a desired response or outcome. In conflicts, it's a tool to provoke a reaction. Narcissists employ badgering to wear down others, aiming to fulfill their own needs, force agreement, or demean those who have crossed them.

Blame Shifting: An interpersonal strategy intended to abdicate or evade responsibility for a mistake, error, or misstep. Many people utilize blaming due to a fear of being wrong, bad, or at fault. However, narcissists cannot accept responsibility for their harmful actions and thus shift blame to others to avoid being wrong.

DARVO Method: The DARVO (deny, attack, reverse victim and offender) method is a critical narcissistic interpersonal strategy whereby the narcissist (or perpetrator) of a particular offense against another is unable to accept responsibility for their effect (deny) and when confronted or called to account for their behavior, words or actions proceed to make the person who highlighted the perpetration wrong through admonishment, judgment, or overt anger (attack). By making the other person the offender, the perpetrator then becomes the aggrieved, misunderstood, or victimized party, and the original complainant becomes the aggressor (reverse victim and offender).

Flattery: Excessive or insincere praise or compliments given to another to elicit positive regard, reciprocal praise, or a particular outcome. Narcissistic people often utilize flattery as a means to an end to get their practical, emotional, or financial needs, desires, or wishes met.

Flying Monkeys: A term originating from the Frank Baum story, *The Wizard of Oz*, describing the Wicked Witch of the East's grotesque army of winged monkeys deployed to attack Dorothy and her friends. Flying monkeys deployed by narcissists are typically friends; surrogates; family members; colleagues; or in the case of political or public figures, fans and constituents who are expected to defend the narcissist's character, deny or diminish the negative detractor, and attack the narcissist's perceived enemies. Flying monkeys may also be instructed or feel obligated to ignore, cut off, or exclude targets. Quite often, flying monkeys are both complicit in and victims of narcissistic abuse because they are unaware of the extent of the narcissist's behavior against the designated enemy and have believed the narcissistic person's aggrieved story. At other times, flying monkeys must defend the antagonistic person's narrative to stay in their good graces and avoid becoming targets.

Gaslighting: A psychological manipulation tactic whereby a person attempts to convince another that the other's perceptions of behavior, events, emotional experiences, or even reality are inaccurate, distorted, or imaginary (usually over time). Gaslighting differs from lying in that there is a coercive and active component of attempting to persuade the other from their perceptions to suit the gaslighter's agenda. Gaslighting is not simply lying, nor is it a perceptual disagreement. Over time, gaslighting erodes the victim's confidence and can, in extreme cases, contribute to derealization or dissociation from reality, leaving the victim in a state of psychological distress and confusion.

Goalpost Moving: A process where conditions for reward, completion, progress, or success are continually adjusted, making it difficult to reap benefits. Goalpost moving can be used in interpersonal relationships (e.g., if you're nicer to me, I'll finally propose) or professional relationships (e.g., one more project, and you'll finally be eligible for that promotion) if the proposed reward remains fleeting. Narcissists utilize this tactic to keep expectations and conditions nebulous, to keep the other party seeking approval, and to avoid delivering promised rewards or benefits as a means of control.

Going Nuclear: A conflict strategy where a person becomes excessively angry, cruel, or reactive to retaliate against someone for a perceived transgression or insult. Narcissists "go nuclear" to intimidate or control others into submission and often demean their perceived transgressors through verbal insults; criticisms; and in some cases, physical, financial, or emotional violence, sometimes publicly, to maximize the effect.

Guilt-Tripping: An interpersonal strategy where one person continues to belabor a misstep, wrongdoing, mistake, or perceived transgression, usually to induce the other to do something. Narcissists use this tactic to keep others indebted to them and may hold onto grievances, annoyances, or anger to control or manipulate the other person's emotions or behavior.

Infantilizing: To treat another adult or intellectually or emotionally capable person as a child. Infantilizing is common in adult child–parent dynamics or similar power dynamic relationships. Narcissistic people infantilize others both as a means of maintaining

GLOSSARY

the psychological upper hand as superior and because they believe they possess superior decision-making skills, intelligence, or judgment. In narcissistic relational dynamics, infantilizing is typically prolonged, engendering physical, emotional, or financial dependency, and strengthens the narcissistic person's control and influence over the other.

Love Bombing: A manipulative and often deliberate relational tactic that involves showering another person with attention, praise, affection, admiration, or promises of an idyllic future. Love bombing differs from the "romantic phase" of interpersonal relational dynamics, where both parties express excessive positive, optimistic regard for each other and their future; love bombing is employed by one party to manipulate or coerce the other into a relationship or to fast-track a relationship by creating a falsely deep bond. Narcissists employ love bombing as both an unconscious and conscious relational strategy. People with narcissistic traits typically experience shallower emotions; thus, they may be excessively (and genuinely) excited or naively idealistic about the potential of a new relationship or situation, only to succumb to shifting disappointment and eventual abandonment or denigration of the love object after their superficial idealization wanes. Some narcissistic people utilize love bombing consciously to charm or coerce others into intense connection, creating a dependency and emotional need that only they can fill. The effect on victims is destabilizing because it creates a chemical and psychological dependency on the love bomber's praise and attention, producing feelings of hopelessness, anxiety, and depression when the attention is removed. Love bombing keeps victims enmeshed in abusive or adversarial relationships.

Minimizing: Reducing the importance or effect of something. In healthy human relationships, minimizing can help reduce the negative perceptions or effects of a perceived harmful event, emotion, or situation and help others gain perspective. In narcissistic or antagonistic relationship dynamics, minimizing is utilized to reduce and diminish the other person's emotional, physical, or mental experiences; history; complaints; concerns; or anxieties. Narcissists utilize minimization partially as a feature of their empathy deficits because they often experience other people's concerns, emotions, or problems as less important than their own. In many cases, minimization serves the narcissist's agenda. Minimization allows continued adverse treatment, selfishness, or other objectionable behaviors to persist because other people's concerns are reduced and made secondary to the narcissist's ultimate aims.

Projection: A psychological defense strategy most people utilize whereby behavior, emotions, or motives are externalized and displaced onto another person, object, animal, or situation. In narcissistic or antagonistic relational dynamics, projection allows the perpetrator to evade or avoid responsibility by placing their conscious or unconscious motives, emotions, or thoughts onto others. Projection makes disowned psychological content more acceptable to scrutinize, attack, or judge.

Shaming: Causing shame and embarrassment in another for a perceived infraction. In narcissistic dynamics, shaming is utilized to control and coerce others into adhering to the narcissist's prescriptions of appropriate conduct and to bolster their feelings of moral, ethical, or emotional superiority.

Silent Treatment: An interpersonal conflict strategy in which the perpetrator actively ignores the object of their anger or disappointment. Silent treatment is particularly erosive because it denies the humanity of the victim by effectively erasing their existence. Narcissistic people utilize this strategy to communicate their disapproval or to control the other person, who they hope will find the withdrawal of their attention distressing.

Smear Campaign: An active effort by an aggrieved person to defame, delegitimize, or diminish the perceived perpetrator. In narcissistic relational dynamics, smear campaigns are embarked upon by the narcissists themselves when they believe they have been betrayed or disrespected. These campaigns may be covert and engaged in private interactions or overt and public. Smear campaigns can also be enacted through flying monkeys, through the implicit or direct suggestion from the narcissist. The effect is an erosion of the victim's public image and emotional, physical, or financial security and increased feelings of isolation as well as helps elicit fears of increased or more significant retaliation.

Triangulation: A relational strategy whereby one person uses implied or overt threats of exclusion, attack, or manipulation against another. Triangulation often involves talking about another person behind their back and attempting to influence or coerce the target into a desired outcome or response. Triangulation creates interpersonal disharmony and is often used to "divide and conquer," whereby the perpetrator maintains control over all parties. Triangulation is used frequently in interpersonal conflicts and contributes to miscommunication because one party attempts to engender support or validation from another and control outcomes or responses.

BIBLIOGRAPHY

Allied Market Research. "Influencer Marketing Market Statistics, 2032." Accessed October 1, 2023. https://www.alliedmarketresearch.com/influencer-market-A07914.
Anderson, Monica, and Jingjing Jiang. "Teens, Social Media and Technology 2018." Pew Research Center. Published May 31, 2018. https://www.pewresearch.org/internet/2018/05/31/teens-social-media-technology-2018/.
"APA Dictionary of Psychology." Accessed May 28, 2024. https://dictionary.apa.org/id.
Bromwich, Jonah Engel. "Paris Hilton Said She Invented the Selfie. We Set Out to Find the Truth." *New York Times*, November 20, 2017, sec. Style. https://www.nytimes.com/2017/11/20/style/paris-hilton-selfie.html.
Carpenter, Linda L., Thaddeus T. Shattuck, Audrey R. Tyrka, Thomas D. Geracioti, and Lawrence H. Price. "Effect of Childhood Physical Abuse on Cortisol Stress Response." *Psychopharmacology* 214, no. 1 (September 14, 2010): 367–75. https://doi.org/10.1007/s00213-010-2007-4.
Emspak, Jesse, and Kimberly Hickok. "Quantum Entanglement: Unlocking the Mysteries of Particle Connections." Space.com. Last modified October 29, 2024. https://www.space.com/31933-quantum-entanglement-action-at-a-distance.html.
Fardouly, Jasmine, Phillippa C. Diedrichs, Lenny R. Vartanian, and Emma Halliwell. "Social Comparisons on Social Media: The Impact of Facebook on Young Women's Body Image Concerns and Mood." *Body Image* 13 (2015): 38–45. https://doi.org/10.1016/j.bodyim.2014.12.002.

BIBLIOGRAPHY

Fatt, Scott J., and Jasmine Fardouly. "Digital Social Evaluation: Relationships between Receiving Likes, Comments, and Follows on Social Media and Adolescents' Body Image Concerns." *Body Image* 47 (2023): 101621. https://doi.org/10.1016/j.bodyim.2023.101621.

Grewal, Daisy. "How Wealth Reduces Compassion." *Scientific American*, April 10, 2012. Accessed February 20, 2024. https://www.scientificamerican.com/article/how-wealth-reduces-compassion/.

Hill, Faith. "The Mystery of Partner 'Convergence.'" *The Atlantic*, February 22, 2024. https://www.theatlantic.com/family/archive/2024/02/relationship-convergence-similar-personality/677534/.

Hyphantis, Thomas, Augustina Almyroudi, Vassiliki Paika, Panagiota Goulia, and Konstantinos Arvanitakis. "Narcissistic Rage: The Achilles' Heel of the Patient with Chronic Physical Illness." *Patient Preference and Adherence* 3 (2009): 239–50. https://doi.org/10.2147/PPA.S5499.

International Institute for Democracy and Electoral Assistance. "Global State of Democracy Report 2021." Accessed May 28, 2024. https://www.idea.int/gsod-2021/global-report#:~:text=2.1%20CHALLENGES&text=Since%202016%2C%20and%20for%20the,negative%20trend%20(Figure%202).

Jung, C. G. *The Collected Works of C. G. Jung*. Vol. 9, Part 1, *Archetypes and the Collective Unconscious*. Princeton, NJ: Princeton University Press, 1981.

Katie, Byron. "Judge-Your-Neighbor Worksheet." The Work.com. Accessed May 28, 2024. http://thework.com/wp-content/uploads/2019/02/jyn_en_mod_6feb2019_r4_form1.pdf.

Krishnan, Rekha, Karen S. Cook, Rajiv Krishnan Kozhikode, and Oliver Schilke. "An Interaction Ritual Theory of Social Resource Exchange: Evidence from a Silicon Valley Accelerator." *Administrative Science Quarterly* 66, no. 3 (November 27, 2020). https://doi.org/10.1177/0001839220970936.

Lee, Royce J., David Gozal, Emil F. Coccaro, and Jennifer Fanning. "Narcissistic and Borderline Personality Disorders: Relationship with Oxidative Stress." *Journal of Personality Disorders* 34, Supplement (March 2020): 6–24. https://doi.org/10.1521/pedi.2020.34.supp.6.

Lockett, Eleesha. "How to Help Children of Narcissistic Parents." Healthline. Published February 21, 2024. https://www.healthline.com/health/mental-health/children-of-narcissistic-parents#:~:text=A%202012%20study%20suggested%20that,traumatic%20stress%20disorder%20(PSTD).

BIBLIOGRAPHY

Luchner, Andrew F., John M. Houston, Christina Walker, and M. Alex Houston. "Exploring the Relationship between Two Forms of Narcissism and Competitiveness." *Personality and Individual Differences* 51, no. 6 (October 2011): 779–82. https://doi.org/10.1016/j.paid.2011.06.033.

Lyons, Minna, Gayle Brewer, Anna-Maria Hartley, and Victoria Blinkhorn. "'Never Learned to Love Properly': A Qualitative Study Exploring Romantic Relationship Experiences in Adult Children of Narcissistic Parents." *Social Sciences* 12, no. 3 (March 7, 2023): 159. https://doi.org/10.3390/socsci12030159.

Mosley, Sterlin L. "The Excited Enthusiast." In *The Narcissist in You and Everyone Else: Recognizing the 27 Types of Narcissism*, 208–225. Lanham, MD: Rowman & Littlefield, 2022.

Mosley, Sterlin L. *The Narcissist in You and Everyone Else: Recognizing the 27 Types of Narcissism*. Lanham, MD: Rowman & Littlefield, 2022.

Mouchabac, Stephane, Redwan Maatoug, Ismael Conejero, Vladimir Adrien, Olivier Bonnot, Bruno Millet, Florian Ferreri, and Alexis Bourla. "In Search of Digital Dopamine: How Apps Can Motivate Depressed Patients, a Review and Conceptual Analysis." *Brain Sciences* 11, no. 11 (2021): 1454, https://doi.org/10.3390/brainsci11111454.

Murphy, Sean. "The Attractiveness of Confidence." SPSP. Published September 15, 2016. Accessed January 29, 2024. https://spsp.org/news-center/character-context-blog/attractiveness-confidence#:~:text=Confidence%2C%20in%20turn%2C%20was%20a,means%20we%20weren't%20measuring.

Nenadić, Igor, Carsten Lorenz, and Christian Gaser. "Narcissistic Personality Traits and Prefrontal Brain Structure." *Scientific Reports* 11, no. 1 (2021): 15707. https://doi.org/10.1038/s41598-021-94920-z.

Nichols, Tom. "The Narcissism of the Angry Young Men." *The Atlantic*, January 29, 2023. https://www.theatlantic.com/ideas/archive/2023/01/lost-boys-violent-narcissism-angry-young-men/672886/?fbclid=IwAR0QDMqiC526cgM55XFUnX5JBiSjI6eSFo23mRRGO1TkYlTBl7LPjjICdQ8.

Primack, B. A., J. B. Colditz, K. C. Pang, K. M. Jackson, and A. M. Porter. "Promoting Public Health in the Digital Age: A Public Health Approach to Evaluating the Risks and Benefits of Online Social Networking." *Media and Communication* 6, no. 1 (2018): 13–14.

Radin, Dean. "Chapter Seven: Seeing Through the Illusion." In *Supernormal: Science, Yoga, and the Evidence for Extraordinary Psychic Abilities* [audiobook], 2:44:30–2:45:00. New York: Crown/Deepak Chopra, 2013.

Raypole, Crystal. "12 Signs of Narcissistic Abuse Syndrome (and How to Get Help)." Healthline. Last modified September 20, 2024. https://www.healthline.com/health/narcissistic-victim-syndrome#overview.

Stanger, Nicholas, Maria Kavussanu, David McIntyre, and Christopher Ring. "Empathy Inhibits Aggression in Competition: The Role of Provocation, Emotion, and Gender." *Journal of Sport and Exercise Psychology* 38, no. 1 (February 2016): 4–14. https://doi.org/10.1123/jsep.2014-0332.

Van der Kolk, Bessel. *The Body Keeps the Score: Brain, Mind, and Body in the Transformation of Trauma*. New York: Viking, 2014.

Vernig, Peter M. "Family Roles in Homes with Alcohol-Dependent Parents: An Evidence-Based Review." *Substance Use & Misuse* 46, no. 4 (August 24, 2010): 535–42. https://doi.org/10.3109/10826084.2010.501676.

Zvelc, Gregor. "Object and Subject Relations in Adulthood: Towards an Integrative Model of Interpersonal Relationships." *Psychiatria Danubina* 22, no. 4 (December 2010): 498–508.

INDEX

abandonment, 78, 95, 124, 126, 222
ableism, 12, 13–14
abuse, 69, 77, 85, 110
addiction, 148, 156–57, 161. *See also* alcohol; substance abuse
addictive response to narcissistic behavior, 99, 107, 114, 126–27
affluence, 160–61, 175, 185. *See also* wealth
aggression: narcissistic subtypes and, 18, 21, 22; psychopathy and, 9
aggressive behavior (in case studies), 48, 69–70, 72, 77, 96, 171–72
alcohol, 147, 148, 153, 156. *See also* addiction; substance abuse
Ambitious-Deceptive (narcissistic subtypes), 18–19, 67, 145
Ambivalent Avoider (narcissistic subtype), 23, 143, 177. *See also* James (case study: Luke); Donna (case study: Joe)
Ambivalent-Neglectful (narcissistic subtypes), 22–23, 145
Ambivalent Underminer (narcissistic subtype), 20, 193
anger, 77, 78, 79–80

antagonism, 103–4, 144–45, 150, 159, 181
antagonistic personality traits, 3, 4, 13, 110
anti-empathic ideologies, 182, 184
anxiety, 36, 46–47, 110, 146
Anxious-Skeptical (narcissistic subtypes), 20–21, 177
appearance, 18, 35, 167–68, 213n1
attention: avoidance of, 160; narcissism and, 2, 15, 18, 33, 53; need for, 47–48, 50, 51, 61, 64, 66–67
authoritarianism, 40, 185, 192–96
authority, 74, 77–78, 112, 123. *See also* oppositional defiant disorder

badgering, 219
biology, narcissism and, 6
blame, 67, 113, 165
blame shifting, 219
body image, 35, 36
The Body Keeps the Score, 162
boundaries: lack of, 49, 96, 115, 124, 142; need for, 53, 55, 56, 80, 163
brain, 6, 31, 107, 126–27

229

INDEX

Bruce (case study: Luke), 130–36, 142. *See also* Intellectual Elitist
bullying, 34–36, 55, 142, 144, 159

Callie (case study: Sue), 151–53, 159, 160. *See also* Moralistic Inquisitor
cancel culture, 37–38, 188
capitalism, 186–87
caregivers, 6, 7
case studies: Bruce (Intellectual Elitist), 130–36, 142; Callie (Moralistic Inquisitor), 151–53, 159, 160; Donna (Defensive Pessimist and Ambivalent Avoider), 168–70, 171, 172, 177; Dylan (Ruthless Workaholic), 101, 103, 146, 149–51, 155–56, 159; James (Ambivalent Avoider), 134, 137–39, 143, 144; Joe (Charismatic Bully), 68–81, 111–27, 163–78; Luke (Gleeful Charlatan), 46–56, 83–97, 130–45; Sue (Entitled Caregiver), 56–68, 97–111, 145–63; Trent (Entitled Outcast), 164–66, 167–68, 169, 171–72, 175, 176–77
charisma, 50, 122, 124, 192
Charismatic Bully (narcissistic subtype), 22, 68, 78, 124, 173–74, 177, 178, 179. *See also* Joe (case study)
child development, 6
children and childhood, 52–53, 76–77, 108, 110–11
chronic illness, 162. *See also* illness
coercion, 123, 124, 194, 224
collaboration, 191
commodification, 186–87, 188–89

compassion, 14, 183–84. *See also* empathy
compassion fatigue, xiii
competition, 48, 65, 103–4, 108, 157–58, 188–91
conflict avoidance, 85, 87, 95, 96, 144
control over others, 114–15, 121, 123, 127, 166, 192
coping strategies, 161, 163
couples counseling, 118, 126
creative outlets, 67
criticism, 51–52, 103–4, 109, 152
cults, 174–75, 176, 177, 178, 179, 217n7
Cynical Tyrant (narcissistic subtype), 22

Dark Empath (narcissistic type), 122, 124, 173–74, 217n3
dark triad traits, 10–11, 121
Dark Voyeur (narcissistic subtype), 20
DARVO (deny, attack, reverse victim and offender), 179, 198, 219–20
defense, psychological, 14, 25–26, 180, 223
defense mechanisms, 10, 205
Defensive Pessimist (narcissistic subtype), 20, 177, 216n4. *See also* Donna (case study: Joe)
defensive state, 205–6
democratic civilizations, decline of, xiv. *See also* authoritarianism
depression: narcissistic abuse and, 110, 126, 162, 210; substance abuse and, 136, 140, 144, 147, 148. *See also* mental health
depression, postpartum, 91, 93, 97
diplomacy, 80

INDEX

discrimination, 13, 14
Disingenuous Opportunist (narcissistic subtype), xii, 18, 206, 213n1. *See also* Santos, George
disloyalty, fear of, 168, 176
disorders, psychological, 3–4, 13, 110
dissociation, 187, 221
divorce, 120, 154–55
Donna (case study: Joe), 168–70, 171, 172, 177. *See also* Ambivalent Avoider; Defensive Pessimist
DSM-5, 2, 3, 9, 213n1
Dylan (case study: Sue), 101, 103, 146, 149–51, 155–56, 159. *See also* Ruthless Workaholic

ego, 6, 38–39, 186, 190
emotion, avoidance of, 47, 55, 96. *See also* vulnerability
emotional intelligence, 46–47, 52, 55
emotional sensitivity, 159–60
empathy, 151, 160, 187, 189, 192; devaluation of, 182–83, 184; narcissism and, 2, 6, 7
empathy, affective/experiential, 123, 187
empathy, cognitive, 123
empathy, performative, 185
empathy, quantum, 8
empathy, somatic, 8, 187
empathy burnout, xiii
enabling, 52–53, 97, 157, 158, 161
Enneagram personality system, 5, 16, 20, 64, 77, 124, 144, 175
Entitled Caregiver (narcissistic subtype), 17, 56, 65–66, 106, 107, 157, 161. *See also* Sue (case study)

Entitled Outcast (narcissistic subtype), 19, 175. *See also* Trent (case study)
entitlement, 39, 62, 67, 99, 100, 102, 103, 106
environment, development of narcissism and, 6–7
exceptionalism, 27–28, 39, 195
excusing behavior, 88, 138–39
expectations, social, 36–37
external validation, 2, 6, 32, 64

family, narcissism and, 7, 110–11, 156–63
favoritism, 101, 103, 108, 146
feelings wheel, 55
feminine/masculine duality, 183–84
Flattering Networker (narcissistic subtype), 18
flattery, 17–18, 50, 59, 220
Flippant Rake (narcissistic subtype), 21
flying monkeys, 177, 220
Fussy Masochist (narcissistic subtype), 19

gaslighting, 25, 137, 162, 220–21
gender, 39–40
gender dysphoria, 77–78
gender transition, 75–76, 113
Gleeful Charlatan (narcissistic subtype), 21, 46, 54, 96. *See also* Luke (case study)
goalpost moving, 193, 221
going nuclear, 221
Google search statistics, 12, 25
grandiosity, xi, 2, 8, 197
grind culture, 184, 186
guilt-tripping, 101, 221

INDEX

Hedonistic-Exuberant (narcissistic subtypes), 21, 145
Helpful Supporter (narcissistic subtype), 64
The Hollywood Con Queen, 199–200

id, 203, 218n2
illness, 151, 155–56, 162. *See also* depression; mental health
image management, 91, 131, 132, 134, 135, 140
immigrant communities, 63–64
impulse control, 110
individualism, 26, 187
infantilizing, 221–22
inferiority, feelings of, 60, 61, 65, 91, 94. *See also* superiority
influencers, 31–33, 188. *See also* social media
Intellectual Elitist (narcissistic subtype), 20, 142. *See also* Bruce (case study: Luke)
intergenerational trauma, 110–11, 156–63
internalization of narcissist strategies, 163
interpersonal relationships, narcissism and, 39
intervention strategies, 54–56, 66–68, 79–81
intimacy, 2, 8
intimate/sexual (narcissistic subtypes), 16, 17, 18–19, 20, 21, 22, 23
intrinsic value, 187
isolation, 91, 92, 94–95

James (case study: Luke), 134, 137–39, 143, 144. *See also* Ambivalent Avoider

jealousy, 17, 107, 110, 113
Joe (case study), 68–81, 111–27, 163–78. *See also* Charismatic Bully
Johnson, Scott, 199
Jung, Carl, xiv–xv, 202–3. *See also* shadow

leadership, 54, 191, 192–93, 194, 195
love bombing, 18, 84, 94, 125, 222
Lowen, Alexander, 121
loyalty, expectations of, 171, 172, 177
Luke (case study), 46–56, 83–97, 130–45, 184. *See also* Gleeful Charlatan

Machiavellism, 10
Mafia Don (narcissistic subtype), 22
main character syndrome, 32–33
maligning others, 120
manipulation, 49, 53, 124. See also coercion
Manipulative Seducer (narcissistic subtype), 18
marketing/advertising, 31–32
masculinity, 39–40, 78, 118, 183, 184
mediation, familial, 151, 160
mental health, 3–4, 13, 52, 90, 136, 140, 147, 148; narcissism and, 97, 126, 127, 162; social media and, 34–36
merging (of personalities), 95–96
millennials, 28
minimizing, 144, 210, 222–23
Miserly Misanthrope (narcissistic subtype), 19
moodiness/unpredictability, 98–99
Moody-Entitled (narcissistic subtypes), 19, 216n4, 217n3

Moralistic Inquisitor (narcissistic subtype), 17, 160. *See also* Callie (case study: Sue)
moralizing, 17, 151, 160

narcissism, 15, 190, 201–2; factors in formation of, 5–7, 158–59; incidence of, xi, xiv, 4, 25; larger impacts of, 129–30, 163, 179, 181–82; use of term, 1–2, 11–12, 204–5
Narcissistic Personality Disorder (diagnosis), 2–4, 12, 215n1
narcissistic rage, 53, 215n1
narcissistic relational styles, 195
narcissistic supply, 66, 127, 216n5
narcissistic subtypes, 5, 15–23, 45, 145; Ambitious-Deceptive, 18–19, 67, 145; Ambivalent Avoider (James, Donna), 23, 143, 177; Ambivalent-Neglectful, 22–23, 145; Ambivalent Underminer, 20, 193; Anxious-Skeptical, 20–21, 177; Charismatic Bully, 22, 68, 78, 124, 173–74, 177, 178, 179; Cynical Tyrant, 22; Dark Empath, 122, 124, 173–74, 217n3; Dark Voyeur, 20; Defensive Pessimist (Donna), 20, 177, 216n4; Disingenuous Opportunist, xii, 18, 206, 213n1; Entitled Caregiver (Sue), 17, 56, 65–66, 106, 107, 157, 161; Entitled Outcast (Trent), 19, 175; Flattering Networker, 18; Flippant Rake, 21; Fussy Masochist, 19; Gleeful Charlatan (Luke), 21, 45, 46, 54, 96; Hedonistic-Exuberant, 21, 145; Helpful Supporter, 64; Intellectual Elitist (Bruce), 20, 142; intimate/sexual, 16, 17, 18–19, 20, 21, 22, 23; Mafia Don, 22; Manipulative Seducer, 18; Miserly Misanthrope, 19; Moody-Entitled, 19, 216n4, 217n3; Moralistic Inquisitor (Callie), 17, 160; Neglectful Grouch, 22; Overreactive Rebel, 21, 216n4; Powerful-Aggressive, 22, 54, 121, 124, 175, 177; Powerful Protector, 77; Prideful-Flattering, 17–18, 66, 67, 107, 217n3; Puritanical Fussbudget, 17; Remote-Intellectual, 19–20; Rigid-Moralistic, 17; Ruthless Workaholic (Dylan), 18, 159; Selfish Hedonist, 21; self-preservation, 16, 17, 18, 19, 20, 21, 22; sexual/intimate, 16, 17, 18–19, 20, 21, 22, 23; social, 16, 17, 18, 19, 20, 21, 22, 23; Tempestuous Diva, 19; Unassuming Manipulator, 23, 216n4; Untouchable Star, 18–19; Zealous Crusader, 17
narcissist relationships with other narcissists, 143
NDAs (non-disclosure agreements), 143–44, 176, 216n1
neglect, 160, 161
Neglectful Grouch (narcissistic subtype), 22
neurodivergence, 3, 57
Nichols, Tom, 39–40
nurture, formation of narcissism and, 5–6

objectification, 186–87, 188
open relationship, 113, 116–17, 119

INDEX

oppositional defiant disorder, 70, 72, 77. *See also* authority
oppression, 196
Overreactive Rebel (narcissistic subtype), 21, 216n4

paranoia/trust issues, 168, 171, 173, 177. *See also* suspiciousness
parenting styles, 47, 49, 57, 89, 90, 150
perfectionism, 151, 152, 160
political rhetoric, 40, 140
political structures, 194, 195
politics, 40, 90, 141
popularity, 35, 49, 50, 51, 59, 61–62, 187
possessiveness, 114–15, 124
power, 141–42, 168, 194; narcissism and, 145, 192, 197
Powerful-Aggressive (narcissistic subtypes), 22, 54, 121, 124, 175, 177
Powerful Protector (narcissistic subtype), 77
pragmatism, 80
Prideful-Flattering (narcissistic subtypes), 17–18, 66, 67, 107, 217n3
projection, 96, 109, 159, 160, 223
promiscuity, validation from, 65
psychological defense, narcissism as, 14
psychological disorders, 2–4, 110
psychopathy, 9–10, 121, 199, 216n3
public figures, 40–41, 43–44, 91, 140, 141, 143
public vs. private behaviors, 101, 110, 160–61

Puritanical Fussbudget (narcissistic subtype), 17
purpose, sense of, 27

quantum social behavior/entanglement, 41–44, 181–82

Radin, Dean, 27
rage, 77, 78, 79–80
reality television, 29–30, 31, 32, 33
reasonable accommodation, 14
rejection, familial, 109, 157–58
rejection, fear of, 124
relational strategies, narcissistic, 39, 161, 163, 181, 195, 211, 219–24
relationship dynamics, 116–17, 125–26
religion, 174
Remote-Intellectual (narcissistic subtypes), 19–20
resentment, 39, 66, 67, 101
Rigid-Moralistic (narcissistic subtypes), 17
Ruthless Workaholic (narcissistic subtype), 18, 159. *See also* Dylan (case study: Sue)

Santos, George, xi–xii
scandal management, 135–37
seduction, 93–94. *See also* love bombing
self-awareness, 8, 125, 164, 197
self-esteem, 50, 53, 109, 189; social media and, 35, 36
self-importance, 2, 32–33, 205
Selfish Hedonist (narcissistic subtype), 21
self-preservation (narcissistic types), 16, 17, 18, 19, 20, 21, 22

sexual favors, 61–62, 98
sexual harassment, 92, 135
sexual or intimate (narcissistic subtypes), 16, 17, 18–19, 20, 21, 22, 23
sexual relationships, 74, 75, 76
shadow (Jungian philosophical concept), xiv–xv, 201, 202–3, 204, 205
shadow work, xviii, 207–9
shame, 50, 52, 55–56, 65, 67, 161, 208–9
shaming, 5, 150–51, 223
shaming, public, 38
sibling relationships, 150, 151, 153. *See also* favoritism
silent treatment, 101, 104, 105, 223
smear campaigns/defamation, 136–37, 178, 223–24
social (narcissistic subtypes), 16, 17, 18, 19, 20, 21, 22, 23
social media, 25, 28, 30–32, 33–37, 188
sociopathy, 10, 199, 202
somatic defense strategy, 121
spending money, 99–100, 101–2, 103
spirituality, narcissism and, 114, 121–22, 124, 164, 168. *See also* cults
stress, 76–77, 162, 205
stress, oxidative, 6, 213n4
substance abuse, 155, 156, 158, 162. *See also* addiction; alcohol
success, ideas of, 36–37, 57, 59, 60
Sue (case study), 56–68, 97–111, 145–63. *See also* Entitled Caregiver
superiority: conflicting messages about, 190, 191; examples of, 60, 62, 110, 141, 142, 160; narcissism and, 39, 123, 178, 189, 195, 197; psychopathy and, 9
survivors of narcissistic abuse, 1, 127, 162, 209–10. *See also* therapy
suspiciousness, 80, 169, 171. *See also* paranoia

Tahilramani, Hargobind, 199–200
tantrums, 57–58, 105
Tempestuous Diva (narcissistic subtype), 19
therapy, 54, 127, 178, 198, 210
toxic masculinity, 39–40
toxic positivity, 37
transactional relationships, 65
transgender identity/gender identity, 70, 71–72
trauma, familial roots of, 162
trauma bonding, 9, 81, 214n6
Trent (case study: Joe), 164–68, 169, 171–72, 175, 176–77. *See also* Entitled Outcast
triangulation, 125, 126, 224
Trump, Donald, xiii
trust issues, 169, 170

Unassuming Manipulator (narcissistic subtype), 23, 216n4
undermining, 104, 158, 169
Untouchable Star (narcissistic subtype), 18–19

validation, external, 2, 30
van der Kolk, Bessel, 162
victim–abuser archetype, 196–97
victim ideologies, 196–200
victimization, 121, 200
violence, 9–10, 37–40, 183, 184, 200

INDEX

vulnerability, avoidance of, 2, 46, 55, 74, 79, 80, 142, 182–85
vulnerable narcissists, 8–9, 161, 197

wealth, 150, 168. *See also* affluence
Wegscheider-Cruse, Sharon, 156
Western culture, 12–13, 25–28, 159, 184–90
work environments, toxic, 135, 137–38, 144, 171, 193–94

worksheet for self-evaluation ("not self worksheet"), 206–27
worksheet for shadow realization, 207

young adults, narcissism in, xi

Zealous Crusader (narcissistic subtype), 17

ABOUT THE AUTHOR

Sterlin Mosley, Ph.D., is an assistant professor of human relations at the University of Oklahoma. He teaches classes on personality psychology, social change, cultural awareness, and women's and gender studies. He holds a master's degree in human relations counseling, specializing in personality typologies and personality pathology, and a Ph.D. in intercultural communication. Dr. Mosley has researched the Enneagram personality typology for over 10 years and is a certified Enneagram coach and teacher.

Dr. Mosley has developed and facilitated numerous undergraduate and graduate courses; professional workshops; trainings; and lectures on personality, empathy, culture, gender, sexuality, spirituality, and communication. Dr. Mosley is the cofounder and CEO of Empathy Architects. He provides personal and professional coaching and develops and facilitates workshops on the Enneagram personality system, consciousness, empathy, narcissism, and other systems to help foster greater awareness and positive change. Dr. Mosley is also a ballet dancer and founded a dance company for which he is a resident choreographer and artistic director. He currently resides in Norman, Oklahoma.